THE CURRENCY
OF EROS

Women of Letters

Sandra M. Gilbert and Susan Gubar
General Editors

The Currency of Eros

WOMEN'S LOVE LYRIC
IN EUROPE, 1540-1620

Ann Rosalind Jones

INDIANA UNIVERSITY PRESS ● *Bloomington and Indianapolis*

The paper used in this publication meets the minimum requirements of American
National Standard for Information Sciences—Permanence of Paper for Printed
Library Materials, ANSI Z39.48-1984.

Manufactured in the United States of America

Library of Congress Cataloging-in-Publication Data

Jones, Ann Rosalind.
The currency of Eros : women's love lyric in Europe, 1540–1620 /
Ann Rosalind Jones.
p.   cm. — (Women of letters)
Includes bibliographical references.
ISBN 0-253-33149-8 (alk. paper)
1. Love poetry, European—Women authors—History and criticism.
2. European literature—Renaissance, 1450–1600—History and
criticism. 3. Women in literature. 4. Sex role in literature.
I. Title. II. Series.
PN1181.J66 1990
809.1'4099287—dc20   89-45412
                                                                        CIP

1 2 3 4 5 94 93 92 91 90

For Peter,
amant, amico, and soul brother

Contents

Foreword

"On the Field of Letters"

> Then Lady Reason . . . said, "Get up, daughter! Without waiting any longer,
> let us go to the Field of Letters. There the City of Ladies will be founded on a flat
> and fertile plain, where all fruits and freshwater rivers are found and where the
> earth abounds in all good things. Take the pick of your understanding and dig
> and clear out a great ditch wherever you see the marks of my ruler, and I will
> help you carry away the earth on my own shoulders."
>
> I immediately stood up to obey her commands and . . . I felt stronger and
> lighter than before. She went ahead, and I followed behind, and after we had
> arrived at this field I began to excavate and dig, following her marks with the
> pick of cross-examination.

So wrote Christine de Pizan at the beginning of the fifteenth century in *The
Book of the City of Ladies*, the first feminist utopia. She was imagining a
"strongly constructed and well founded" community which would be inhabited by "ladies of fame and women worthy of praise," and one of her
speakers prophesied, "as a true sybil, that this City . . . will never be destroyed, nor will it ever fall, but will remain prosperous forever, regardless of
all its jealous enemies. Although it will be stormed by numerous assaults, it
will never be taken or conquered."

Founded on the "Field of Letters," the female literary tradition *is*, at least
metaphorically speaking, the City of which Christine dreamed. Yet despite
the optimism of this Renaissance woman's vision, most of its walls and tow-
ers disappeared from view for centuries. Even when its individual inhabitants gained recognition as "ladies of fame and women worthy of praise,"
the avenues they strolled and the cafes where they conversed were largely
forgotten. Louise Labé, Aphra Behn, Jane Austen, Charlotte Bronte, George
Eliot, Emily Dickinson, Gertrude Stein, Virginia Woolf—all these figures
were duly recorded in literary histories, but their membership in a "strongly
constructed and well founded" community—a *female* literary community—
went, until recently, unremarked. Only in the last two decades, in fact, have
feminist critics established thematic and stylistic links between women from
very different places and periods. Moreover, only in recent years have scholars begun "to excavate and dig" in a general effort to recover the lives and
works of forgotten or neglected "women worthy of praise." Mary Wroth,
Mary Astell, Charlotte Smith, Kate Chopin, Charlotte Perkins Gilman, Mary
Elizabeth Coleridge, H.D., Zora Neale Hurston—all these figures had been
relegated to the margins of literary history despite the fact that they too deserved places on the "fertile plain" where Christine's utopia was founded.

Our "Women of Letters" series is designed to introduce general as well as
academic readers to the historical situations and aesthetic achievements of

many of the citizens of Christine's City. The national, chronological, racial, ethnic, economic, and social circumstances of these women vary widely: the contours of the female literary community are complex, its highways and byways labyrinthine and often unfamiliar. Thus each volume in this series will pay close attention to what is in effect a single neighborhood. At the same time, precisely because the subject matter is complex, no volume in the series is intended as an encyclopedic guide to women writers in a particular place or period. Rather, each book will have a distinctive argument of its own, framed independently by its author; we should stress that we have not provided blueprints or even construction codes to the surveyors of our City, all of whom have used their own methodologies and developed their own critical perspectives. We do, however, expect that every volume will explore the individual situations of literary women in their specific cultural contexts.

Finally, we should emphasize that we see this series as part of an ongoing project in which a range of feminist critics, scholars, essayists, novelists, and poets have increasingly participated in recent years, one that seeks to understand the strictures and structures that may have affected (or will affect) the lives and works of, in Christine's words, "ladies from the past as well as from the present and future." Such a project can by its nature come to no definitive conclusion, offer no single last word, because the City of Ladies, along with our vision of the Field of Letters, is growing and changing all the time. Furthermore, the heightened awareness on the part of current feminist theorists that such a City has always existed, and that it is ever evolving, has itself transformed our general sense of history, putting in question received modes of periodization, traditional genre hierarchies, and what once seemed to be universal evaluative criteria. Yet, diverse as may be the solutions posed by different thinkers to theoretical problems presented by contemporary literary study, we hope that in their various ways the volumes in this series will confirm Christine's faith that the City she helped found might be a "refuge" as well as a "defense and guard" against enemies and that it would be "so resplendent that you may see yourselves mirrored in it."

Composed c. 1405, Christine's utopia went unpublished and virtually untranslated for more than five centuries, a fact that gives special urgency to the admonitions with which she concluded her text. Indeed, her advice should still be taken to heart by those who study the field of women's letters: ". . . my dear ladies," Christine counseled, "do not misuse this new inheritance" but instead "increase and multiply our City." And as she herself knew, such a resettlement of the old grounds can best be accomplished by following "the marks" of Reason with "the pick of cross-examination."

Sandra M. Gilbert and Susan Gubar

Acknowledgments

I began to think about women, history, and poetry in an unofficial seminar on feminist theory at Cornell University in 1976. Among its rule-breaking poets and irreverent critics, thanks especially to Julia Epstein, Beth Goldsmith, Kate Kazin, Tobe Levin, Leah Tregebov and Sharon Willis. In the early days of research on women writers, many scholars were extremely generous with information about poets entirely new to me; I'm grateful to Carole Armbruster, Fiora Bassanese, Elaine Beilin, Mary Ellen Lamb, Tita Rosenthal, and Betty Travitsky.

Thanks, also, to three more than Renaissance men for stimulating friendship and encouragement when it mattered: Alan Sinfield, Len Tennenhouse, and Frank Whigham. Peter Stallybrass knows how much I owe him (and, like me, never forgets it). Thanks, as well, to the members of the Five-College Renaissance Seminar and to Harvard's New England Seminar on Women in the Renaissance for lively and critical discussions.

If I were as fluent in improvisation as the poets I study, I would compose on the spot a dedicatory sonnet to three women who, after graduate school training in the Renaissance much like mine, entered the 1980s by renegotiating their academic formation and opening up new audiences for new work on gender and representation: Margie Ferguson, Maureen Quilligan, and Nancy Vickers.

Finally, thanks to four very modern feminists whom I count on for decades more of dialogue: Michèle Barrett, Cora Kaplan, Jacqueline Rose, and Mary Russo.

I also record my gratitude to Smith College for generous sabbatical support and leave time during the eight years I worked on this book, especially for a Mellon Humanities Fellowship, which allowed me to begin research at the British Library in 1983. To the staff there and at Houghton Library, I am grateful for many services, especially the red-tape breaking of younger workers. I am also grateful to Thalia Pandiri and Alfonso Procaccini for help in translating Latin mottos and Petrarchan formulas.

For permission to reprint material that appeared in early articles, I thank *Yale French Studies* (62: "Assimilation with a Difference: Renaissance Women Poets and Literary Influence"); University of Chicago Press ("City Women and Their Audiences: Louise Labé and Veronica Franco," in *Rewriting the Renaissance*, ed. Margaret Ferguson, Maureen Quilligan, and Nancy Vickers); Methuen, U.K. and U.S.A. ("Nets and Bridles: Early Modern Conduct Books and Sixteenth-century Women's Lyric," in *The Ideology of Conduct*, ed. Nancy Armstrong and Len Tennenhouse); and Columbia University Press ("Surprising Fame: Renaissance Gender Ideologies and Women's Lyric," in *The Poetics of Gender*, ed. Nancy Miller). For permission to reproduce illustrations, thanks to the Folger, Houghton, and Huntington Libraries.

Introduction

Imitation, Negotiation, Appropriation

This study of women's love lyric during the Renaissance argues that female poets were able to write and to publish because they drew upon certain potentially productive contradictions in early modern culture. The eight poets I analyze occupied different cultural and class situations, but they shared the problem of writing in social and literary circuits dominated by men as models, mentors, readers, and critics. A first contradiction these women confronted was a mixed message about writing itself. Ideological pressures worked against their entry into the public world of print: female silence was equated with chastity, female eloquence with promiscuity. Yet at the same time humanist culture celebrated eloquence in general as the distinguishing skill of male scholars, politicians, courtiers, and poets. A second contradiction was that the history of love lyric provided only male models to women poets. Readers and writers of both sexes in the Renaissance shared the expectation that the poet enters the literary realm through imitation, that is, by participating in some recognizable way in preestablished literary modes— most directly, by invoking the texts of a magisterial predecessor. But women love poets faced a problematically gendered set of traditions. The amorous discourses available to them (Roman elegy, pastoral, Neoplatonism, Petrarchism) had been constructed by male writers, who represented women as the silent objects of love rather than its active, articulate pursuers. This doubly constrained relation to high literary culture, which silenced women while praising copious speech in men and which provided insistently masculine perspectives as the only legitimate frameworks for composition, imposed particular rhetorical demands on a woman love poet. How was she to justify her self-publication to a suspicious public? How was she to make herself intelligible as a desiring subject through lyric conventions that assigned her the position of mysterious or inaccessible other?

The situation of women poets in the sixteenth century—difficult but not impossible for those rare few who had access not only to literacy but to publishing—makes particular theoretical demands on a feminist critic in the twentieth. As I began working on this love poetry, I, too, came up against persistent contradictions. On one hand, as feminist critics have done since the 1960s, I take gender ideologies seriously: I assume that they work, that they shape subjectivities and determine behavior. As I continued my research into prohibitions against women's self-display in public, I saw how

1

variously and forcefully male writers attempted to drive women off the stage of literary performance, through gentle persuasion as well as threat and insult. If the hundreds of early modern texts urging that women be confined to the private sphere privileged by rising classes were even partly effective (and their numbers and ingenuity, as well as much recent historical scholarship, suggest that they must have been), I should logically have expected to find that women were successfully shaped into obediently silent, publicity-shunning daughters, wives, and widows—that is, that they never considered writing at all, or that their writing somehow still affirmed the silence enjoined upon them. But as feminist archeology continued to unearth women widely read in their day and as women's texts were reassessed, no longer assumed to be private confessions but recognized as maneuvers within the shared textuality of their time, it became clear to me that some sixteenth-century women effectively resisted injunctions to shamefast modesty. The more I read of their lyrics, the more I recognized that they had found ways to maneuver within the chastity-silence equation, men's ownership of education and publishing, and the masculine perspective built into erotic conventions named after founding fathers and sons (Plato, Ovid, Petrarch). Women were interpellated by the Nom/Non du Père, but they were not interpellated into a tragic female speechlessness. Women poets made themselves heard *through* the gridwork of gender rules and lyric tradition.

I develop my analysis of these poets starting from a central concept in Marxist cultural studies: *negotiation*, in the sense of a range of interpretative positions through which subordinated groups respond to the assumptions encoded into dominant cultural forms and systems of representation. The systems studied by writers at the Center for Contemporary Cultural Studies at the University of Birmingham are modern media such as film and television, but their theorization of audience response has great explanatory power for the mixed process of acceptance and resistance through which women poets responded to the gender ideologies and poetic norms of early modern Europe. The feminist film critic Christine Gledhill, building on Stuart Hall's theorization of audience response to mainstream media in the twentieth century, emphasizes that reigning discourses are neither seamless wholes nor swallowed whole:

> The term 'negotiation' implies the holding together of opposite sides in an ongoing process of give-and-take. As a model of meaning production, negotiation conceives cultural exchange as the intersection of processes of production and reception, in which overlapping but non-matching determinations operate. Meaning is neither imposed, nor passively imbibed, but arises out of a struggle or negotiation between competing frames of reference, motivation and experience. This [process] can be analysed at three different levels: institutions, texts and audiences.[1]

This focus on contestatory responses to signifying practices shapes my study in several ways. The give-and-take formulation, which follows from the Gramscian concept of "hegemony" as a series of compromises by which dominant groups must continually work to win consent from less powerful groups,[2] opens up the possibility that women poets were drawn into, even cultivated in, their particular urban or national cultures, rather than uniformly censored by a monolithic, male-dominated literary establishment. In addition, Gledhill's emphasis on production and reception as a two-way circuit is highly relevant to the Renaissance because of its adherence to imitation as a principle of composition. All writers in this period presented themselves as readers; and their readers understood that the poet was alluding to, commenting on, or reworking other poems. Group improvisation, the circulation of manuscripts before they were printed, and coterie collaboration in publishing also positioned writers as audiences and producers simultaneously.

Above all, Gledhill's definition points to the contradictory determinations that make negotiated responses to a dominant ideological system possible. In early modern Europe different definitions of proper feminine behavior were emerging in different centers of cultures in transition (the court, the city and its bourgeois household); at the same time, contrasting decorums of idealization and erotic frankness were circulating in a mixed lyric tradition. In my first chapter I trace out different models of the ideal woman in order to show that actual women faced conflicting gender ideologies, varying according to class, nation, and religion. One or more of these non-matching, competing frames of reference could be appropriated and emphasized by women poets pursuing their own interests—interests not necessarily the same as those of the classes to which such women belonged but shaped by the conventions of eloquence and the institutions that regulated those conventions.

This book, then, studies negotiations between two complex institutions: the mixed gender ideologies produced by political and social transformations in early modern Europe, and the network of classical, early Renaissance and contemporary texts composing the discursive territory of sixteenth-century love poetry. I approach women poets as participants in those social changes and, in the literary realm, as both readers and producers, audiences as well as performers of erotic rhetoric—typically, in fact, co-performers with the male poets they cite, revise, and challenge.

Stuart Hall's definition of three possible "viewer" positions toward contemporary media messages offers an entry into the range of women poets' responses to the conventions of male-authored love poetry in this early period.[3] The "dominant/hegemonic" viewer position receives and reproduces a public text obediently. What is officially communicated is clearly understood; the viewer/reader accepts the conventional connotations, the implied values and assumptions, encoded into the message. Hall's example is a television viewer acceding to the political bias built into a network news program, which he or she then reproduces in discussing the issues presented on the screen. An analogous position for a Renaissance reader of poetry would be the response that Thomas Greene calls reproductive or "sacramental" imitation, the close repetition of a model "as though no other form of celebration could be worthy of its dignity."[4] An example: women writers often repeated the terms of Neoplatonism in a "liturgical" way in the Renaissance because, as a theory and vocabulary dignified by scholars and courtly figures such as Ficino and Castiglione's hero Bembo, it authorized its followers as philosopher-poets—regardless of their sex. But a transgression of gender rules occurs when a woman adopts the authority encoded into this philosophical discourse. Strict adherence to Neoplatonic ideals on the part of a woman poet, then, cannot be read simply as adulatory imitation (even if this is the reading she aspires to). It is, rather, the strategic adoption of a prestigious discourse that legitimates her writing. When a member of the sex systematically excluded from literary performance takes a dominant/hegemonic position toward an approved discourse, she is, in fact, destabilizing the gender system that prohibits her claim to public language—although with limited disturbance to that system.

Most significantly for my study, a "negotiated" viewer position is one that accepts the dominant ideology encoded into a text but particularizes and transforms it in the service of a different group. The negotiated position "acknowledges the legitimacy of . . . hegemonic definition while, at a more restricted, situational level, it makes its own ground rules—it operates with exceptions to the rule." To read and imitate a poetic convention in this way would be to accord a "privileged position" to its perspective and tropes "while reserving the right to make a more negotiated application to 'local conditions' "—for example, to the fact that a woman is producing the text: "This negotiated version of the dominant ideology is thus shot through with contradictions, though these are only on certain occasions brought to full visibility. Negotiated codes operate through what we might call particular or situated logics; and these logics are sustained by their differential and unequal relation to the discourses and logics of power" (Hall, 137). What makes this formulation so apposite for women's lyric is that men poets' love conventions were indeed discourses and logics of power. Like Roman elegy, Neoplatonism and Petrarchism were systems of metaphor and rhetoric organized around a male gaze, constituting and affirming male erotic fantasy as the governing frame of reference.[5] However critically or ironically such discourses were reproduced, they continued to provide models for apprentice poets—that is, for young men. In Renaissance culture women's uses of such conventions were bound to be situated, local events, a minority's interventions into a masculine symbolic system. To think in terms of negotiation rather than coerced repetition or romantic rejection of literary models opens up a whole spectrum of women's responses to the logics of power.[6]

Several stages of a negotiated response come clearly into view in a poem such as Pernette du Guillet's Epigram 28. The poem was published among others written in a Neoplatonic dialogue with the older male poet Maurice Scève, toward whom Pernette took the position of philosophic and poetic disciple. Like Scève in his lyric collection *Délie*, Pernette celebrates the chaste though erotic relationship labeled in Neoplatonic vocabulary as "saincte amytié," and she represents herself as humble imitator of the master poet. But the dominant position attributed to Scève in most of Pernette's epigrams is abruptly challenged in this one, in which she rejects her "Master's" sway over her with the claim that he has tried to treat her too literally as a master would. To announce her resistance both to the man and to the elevated linguistic register he establishes as a norm in *Délie*, the woman poet adopts a new vocabulary. Against the idealized terms in which Neoplatonism theorized the lovers' spiritual equality, she opposes a direct, colloquial language of power:

> Si je ne suis telle que soulois estre,
> Prenez vous en au temps, qui m'a appris
> Qu'en me traictant rudement, comme maistre,
> Jamais sur moy ne gaignerez le prys.

> If I am no longer as I used to be,
> Blame time for it, which has taught me
> That by treating me harshly, as a master,
> Never will you gain supremacy over me.

If this is negotiation, one of the parties seems to be stalking away from the bargaining table. The drama of rebellion modulates into a compromise, however; Pernette proposes a treaty based on both new and old terms. She promises conditional loyalty to the man and to the poetic tradition with which he is identified by accepting his loyalty as a guarantee that she can safely return to his code of behavior and language—to which, she reminds him, he is equally accountable. Her promise of faithfulness is posited on evidence of equal fidelity from him, as initiator of the Neoplatonic relationship to which she recommits herself:

> Et toutesfois, vous voyant tousjours pris
> En mon endroit, vostre ardeur me convye
> Par ce hault bien, que de vous j'ay compris,
> A demeurer vostre toute ma vie.

> And yet, seeing you still eager
> For my company, your ardor persuades me
> In the name of that high good I discovered through you,
> To remain yours all my life long.

Throughout the epigram Neoplatonism remains the frame of reference, but Pernette takes different positions toward it. Negotiations are broken off, then reopened, in the course of a give-and-take in which a "politics of signification" is clearly being enacted.

A third reader/viewer position is also possible: an oppositional position from which the ideological message and force of the reigning code is rearticulated, that is, pulled out of its dominant frame of reference and subver-

sively inserted into an "alternative frame of reference." The code is
maintained but its benefits are reassigned to a nonhegemonic group. The
need for such appropriation was lucidly pointed out by a French critic, Claudine Hermann, in her 1976 study of how masculine tradition places women
writers as "thieves of language," as trespassers on men's intellectual and
linguistic territories.[7] Louise Labé, for example, in the dedicatory preface to
her *Euvres*, encourages other women to study and to write in order to prove
the injustice of men's denying access to education to an equally capable sex;
she goes on, in her poems, to invoke her own eloquence as the object of
admiration by discerning readers throughout Europe. In this way, she
detotalizes the humanist program and its restriction of learning and eloquence exclusively to men. In effect, she is kidnapping literary training and
rhetoric and claiming them for an alternative community of female poets.
More locally, when Veronica Franco adopts the vocabulary of dueling, a
code elaborated to legitimate contests between men, in order to defend herself against attacks on her honor as woman and courtesan, she is *resituating*
a language of patrician culture, "misunderstanding" the etiquette that limits
its use to men defending their honor. Openly oppositional uses of lyric convention are rare among the poets I study here, but they are clearly visible in
Labé and Franco. Their texts demonstrate a protofeminist identification with
women as a group and the desire to construct an alternative frame of reference centered on the sex traditionally excluded from the languages of the
public world.

This exclusion limits the usefulness of the gynocritical focus that has illuminated connections among women writers and readers in later periods, in
Victorian England, for example, or the antebellum United States. Elaine
Showalter's woman-centered interpretative method, like her mapping of the
relations between dominant and muted cultures, draws on anthropological
theory that applies only in a limited way to a sex-gender system as highly
controlled and class-differentiated as that of Renaissance Europe.[8] During the
sixteenth century, earlier women's communities such as nunneries, and
women's labor networks such as the silk-weaving Béguines, were being closed
down or taken over by men.[9] The construction of female class identities also
minimized bonds among women. It is striking how often writers on family
discipline for the rising bourgeoisie warn young women against either model-
ing themselves on women of higher rank (moral, not economic status, is invoked as the basis of feminine virtue) or gossiping with women of their own
social station. And women's low rate of literacy prevented them from forming
the influential reading public to which publishers in later centuries responded.

A more useful approach for this period is the recognition that women
need to be read in relation to the male writers and male-defined discourses
of their time, as Myra Jehlen argues.[10] I have found, as she suggests, that
reading women with and against their sixteenth-century male contemporaries brings new aspects of the writing of both sexes into view. A new category
of half-private, half-public physical sites made upward mobility available to

men and women: the humanist academies and urban salons in which social advancement was possible for the polished self-presenter of either sex, as long as he or she belonged to the relatively privileged class that held and attended such open houses. But the narcissism and calculating rhetoric encouraged in the self-display and improvisatory wit expected of men in such groups stand out in contrast to the humility and idealizing seriousness adopted by women such as Pernette du Guillet and Gaspara Stampa, addressing older or more highly placed men. The power play involved in exposing a female beloved to the view of male connoisseurs in the descriptive enumeration of the *blason* is exposed by women poets' much less frequent and less visually fixated uses of the genre. And the consolidating processes through which male poets shore up their insecure social status (honored advisor or mere entertainer to courtly patrons?) by identifying with heroes of classical mythology such as Zeus, Apollo, and Orpheus are illuminated by women poets' more apologetic or pathetic invocations of figures such as Echo and Philomel. The extreme codification of Neoplatonism and Petrarchism establishes a common linguistic ground against which gender-differentiated writing practices come into high relief.

In fact, love poetry centralizes sociosexual differences as no other literary mode does. The narrator of epic or prose romance is not necessarily marked by gender; the speaker in erotic poetry always is. If women are disempowered by their placement in a visual and symbolic order structured around men's fantasies, and if worldly as well as verbal power is always at stake in reigning love discourses,[11] then a woman love poet is certain to disarticulate and remobilize the sexual economy of her culture. Renaissance gender decorum closed women off from the literary genres most privileged because most publicly oriented: epic, tragedy, political and philosophical theory. But love lyric, as an ostensibly private discourse, an art of the inhouse miniature, could conceivably be allowed them.[12] In practice, however, the ideological matrix that associated open speech with open sexuality in women made love poetry an especially transgressive genre for them, the genre of a semiprivate sphere that broke down secure categories. The woman love poet, exposing desire for a man who was not her husband to the gaze of a mass readership, was a public woman—a term that in the sixteenth century meant a whore.

The intense opposition women had to negotiate in their use of erotic convention is evident in the variety of ways male readers attacked such poets or reconstructed them to make them fit for general consumption. Male contemporaries accused Louise Labé of selling her body to all comers, in analogy with her presentation of her sonnets to any and all of her printer's customers; they accused Gaspara Stampa of plagiarizing her lyrics, stealing poetic language from the sex to which it belonged by precedent and propriety; they accused Mary Wroth of sexual abnormality, of a hermaphroditic in-mixing of inappropriate ambition. Later literary criticism took a sanitizing approach, shifting such poets into a purely private realm by treating their texts as diaries or letter collections, confessions intended only for the eyes of the beloved.[13] Yet these responses also reveal that some negotiations of Renaissance gender expectations were more successful than others. Pernette du Guillet and Tullia d'Aragona found effective male protectors, and Labé and Franco had the confidence to provoke their critics openly. Even so, the most daring among these poets recognized the necessity of propitiating their audiences, and the most cautious challenged the assumptions encoded into the conventions they adopted.

I have paired poets according to parallels between their social situations and the forms of negotiation they invent to win over their publics. Circumstances of geography and national culture vary in each chapter, but the poets in each pair use similar methods to make a place for themselves among the social and literary conventions of their milieux. The four pairs are ordered along a continuum that moves from most adaptive to most oppositional positions, from less to more overtly contestatory responses. I begin with a technique of accumulative recombination of dominant discourses. Isabella Whitney and Catherine des Roches graft previously distinct vocabularies into a new hybrid that legitimates them as poets. Through a process of self-justificatory *contaminatio* (citation from multiple sources, in this case, from diverse genres), they link learned and popular languages into a set of permissions to write. Whitney combines the familiar letter, moral maxims, the female-voiced lament of Ovid's *Heroides*, and the conventionally masculine role of the conduct-book writer in order to reproach an unfaithful man for his moral failings. Des Roches, too, draws on conduct-book models; she combines them with Neoplatonic terminology, aligning definitions of the proper housewife and daughter with a representation of the ideal couple, also for the purpose of criticizing an unfaithful man. Both women invoke accepted forms of women's work—domestic labor, whether paid or unpaid—to compensate for their own unconventional employment as professional writers. In spite of certain differences in origin and class (Whitney was the daughter of country gentry, Catherine des Roches of urban lawyers), they shared a similar relation to publishing in their respective cities. Both wrote to live, so they constructed personae that earned them the right to publish and the expectation of a respectful reading.

The strategy studied in chapter 3 is the construction of a public self through group identification: the woman poet dramatizes her participation in a prestigious literary circle. Pernette du Guillet and Tullia d'Aragona were coterie poets who took advantage of mixed social circuits available in their cities (the urban salon, the humanist and courtly academy) to establish links with well-known male intellectuals. Through mutually profitable exchanges of praise, the women drew on the reputations of famous men to build poetic reputations for themselves. Pernette, a young noblewoman, and Tullia, a courtesan who claimed royal descent and cultivated the Medicis of Florence, both compose poetic dialogues, that is, texts addressed to recognized interlocutors, in order to define themselves as public figures engaged in intimate conversations with cultural heroes.

A third strategy is less explicitly appropriative but finally more oppositional: the poet negotiates class displacement and emotional frustration by proving her competence in pastoral, a genre that traditionally legitimated complaint and satire. Gaspara Stampa, a *virtuosa* (self-employed musical performer) who came from what had been a rich merchant family and aspired to the patrician circles of Venice, and Mary Wroth, a noblewoman fallen from favor at the court of James I, both adopt Arcadian conventions as a vehicle for protest. They demonstrate their skill in an elevated mode of literary performance but use its idealistic perspective as a lens through which to call public criticism down upon the most privileged performers of the genre: men belonging to the feudal nobility or the Jacobean court circle from which the woman poet is excluded.

Finally, in openly oppositional strategies, Louise Labé and Veronica Franco take possession of masculine discourses on behalf of their sex as a whole. Firmly established in upwardly mobile social groups (Labé as daughter and wife of the prosperous artisanal/mercantile bourgeoisie, Franco as elite courtesan with links to the Venetian patriciate) and living in open cities, they regender vocabularies of male rivalry and sexual pursuit. They steal the humanist and popular discourses of Lyon and Venice in order to launch counterattacks on men whom they represent as enemies to all women. At the same time, they desublimate amorous conventions. Labé's secure social position allowed her to adopt the outspoken eroticism of Roman elegy, and Franco's profession as courtesan required that she address explicitly sexual language to her reader-clients.

By arranging chapters in this order, I do not mean to imply a progression in poetic value. Each set of negotiations requires different but equally complex and interesting maneuvers. The contrast between the poets of chapter 5 and the six previous writers does suggest, however, that conditions permitting or demanding an openly contestatory and erotic discourse for women included a clearly marked economic and social position, the support of powerful men, and a framework of political and class flexibility more available in international merchant cities such as Lyon and Venice than on the margins of local courts or the estates of landed nobility. It was not queens and duchesses, but *bourgeoises*, the daughters of emergent merchant and professional classes, who negotiated sixteenth-century love lyric most adventurously— that is, in the most oppositional and group-identified ways.

I share with materialist feminists such as Judith Newton the conviction that women's history should be read as a process of struggle and creative accommodation to social realities and cultural forms, rather than "a tragic and timeless story of individual suffering"[14]—or of group suffering under immutable patriarchal and symbolic orders. I want to resist interpretative frameworks that doom women of the past—or the present—to a relentlessly disempowered relation to political and cultural practices. These poets demonstrate that a relatively privileged feminine subject, although always already caught up in the politics of gender ideology and the grip of dominant signifying systems, could nonetheless be mobile within those systems. To read women writers—the rare few who prevailed among the violent gender hierarchies of early modern Europe—is to recognize how variously they negotiated their subordination to men's social power and masculine orders of language. These powers and orders put women into circulation as agents as well as objects of exchange. In Neoplatonic gatherings, they quickly learned to use the reigning language to their own advantage. In the humanist circuits that celebrated eloquence, they became seekers of fame rather than mere guarantors of it to men (in the role of Petrarch's Laura/lauro); they were active in acquiring and dispensing poetic reputation. In the commerce of sex, the courtesan's body was for sale, but she spoke as well as being spoken for; her texts provided the symbolic capital that set the terms for any cash transaction. Working within and transforming the lyric discourses and systems of literary exchange in early modern Europe, women poets exploited the fluidity of eros as a "currency":

Currency
1. The fact or condition of flowing, flow; course.
2. 'Fluency': readiness of utterance; easiness of pronunciation.
3. Of money: The fact or quality of being current or passing from man to man as a medium of exchange; circulation.
1699 Locke . . . : 'Tis the receiving of them by others, their very passing, that gives them authority and currency.
4. That which is current as a medium of exchange; the circulating medium (whether coins or notes).
5. The fact or quality of being current, prevalent, or generally reported and accepted among mankind; prevalence, vogue; esp. of ideas, reports, etc. (*Oxford English Dictionary*)

A note on names: Social and literary-critical convention has it that women whose last names end in "de" plus a place name or noble family name are called by their first names, on the model of the medieval aristocracy: Christine de Pisan is "Christine," Anne de Beaujeu is "Anne." In the Renaissance, the status of such names was not as clear; women had considerable choice about calling themselves after their fathers, their husbands, their mothers, or their possessions. The Dames des Roches, as they are formally called on their title pages, actually had the last name Fradonnet, from Madeleine's first husband and Catherine's father. But they adopted "des Roches" from the name of a piece of country property they owned, perhaps because it suggested the status of landed nobility. I have followed the convention of using first names for Tullia d'Aragona, Pernette du Guillet, and Catherine des Roches; I hope my readers will not take this usage as patronizing. (I do not, at least, call Gaspara Stampa, the possessor of a forthright bourgeois surname, "Gasparina"—little Gaspara—as her early twentieth-century editor did.) It is cheering, to my mind, as well as convenient that the less problematic last names of the bourgeoisie are in the majority in this study.

ONE

The Mirror, the Distaff, the Pen

The Ideological Climate of Women's Love Poetry

The early modern period in Europe was one of rapid and contested social change, stimulated by centralized courts, increased nationalism, and the rise of merchant and professional classes in the cities. As new class identities were constructed, ideals of feminine virtue proliferated and women became the objects of constant scrutiny. Ruth Kelso suggested in her survey of Renaissance conduct books that as humanist men began to justify their involvement in growing city-states by appealing to classical defenses of engagement in the *polis*, they displaced the Christian duties they were abandoning onto women. That is, male intellectuals leaving the monasteries to become tutors, advisors, and ambassadors to noble families, rising clans, and new political bureaucracies compensated for their engagement in the emergent secular world by immuring women more firmly in the household, a conceptual sphere in which residual virtues such as piety, chastity, silence, and withdrawal from the world were rewritten as specifically feminine qualities.[1]

Kelso's explanation for the intense surveillance of women during the sixteenth century provides one particular historical location for Virginia Woolf's observation in *A Room of One's Own* that masculine identity has always depended on women's collaboration: "Women have served all these centuries as looking-glasses possessing the magic and delicious power of reflecting the figure of man at twice its natural size."[2] Defenses of the new man in early modern Europe, whether he was a city merchant, a courtier, a member of the gentry, or a Protestant paterfamilias, required a female partner to affirm the self-representation of the rising group. Luce Guillerm, introducing a set of French texts on women's conduct, points out that such models were invented not to free women but to enlist them in support of men's class identities, a process reinforced by condemnations of "bad" women as the inverse of the ideal: "In this image system (which is . . . quite distinct from actual social practice) the symbolic position of woman is essential: the model that turns her into a 'subject' assigns her this positive role only insofar as she reflects the rightful power [of men]. Outside this mirror-existence, she can only represent what is repressed by the constraints she internalizes."³ Guillerm raises a further issue in this passage: the gap between theoretical declarations of how women should behave and the ways they actually did behave. One impetus for the increase in theoretical demands formulated in conduct books was certainly that women were flouting them in practice. One consequence was that conservative humanists drew ammunition from classical pronouncements on proper womanhood and from residual literary modes, material drawn on in turn by writers constructing male and female characters positioned in the gender debates of the era. Shakespeare assigns his tamed shrew, for example, lines drawn from a variety of conservative definitions of the proper wife to affirm a long-standing ideal of female obedience.

Because the depiction of the ideal woman was a central aspect of social practice in the Renaissance, I will analyze its ideological supports in detail. Gender debates established a horizon of expectations that had to be confronted by any woman who wanted to write. Definitions of proper feminine conduct were inserted into a gamut of oral and printed forms whose diversity suggests how persistently and in how many media these messages proliferated: sermons, stage plays, popular ballads; advice and letters from parents; treatises in Latin, intended for fathers, religious advisors, and magistrates; practical household handbooks and moralists' pamphlets addressed to female audiences; best-selling satires pillorying rebellious women. Illustrations such as those in Richard Brathwaite's *The English Gentlewoman* (1631), in which the ideal woman is shown in attitudes emblematic of such virtues as proper "Apparell" and "Honour," reinforced the message (fig. 1). To imagine a woman as a carrier of class values and to *produce* her through family training, educational practices, and social rituals was to demonstrate to society at large the control the men of a particular social group had over their daughters and wives, a control often contrasted to the negligence or impotence attributed to fathers and husbands elsewhere in the social hierarchy. Counterimages of corrupt daughters of the aristocracy, venal merchants' wives, hypocritically rigid Puritan maidens, and Irish wild women could be invoked to confirm the merit of the bourgeois householder, the liberal gentleman, the Anglican conformist, or the "righteous" colonizer.⁴

More positively, the ideal woman was represented as a complement to the kind of man she affirmed. The Florentine patriciate, for example, justified the mercantile energy of its men by updating the figure of the thrifty housewife who conserved what her husband acquired, balancing profit-making in the world with order at home. Idealized depictions of life in the ducal palace required the presence of the court lady, trained in the witty repartee through which she elicited polished speech from the male courtier. A site and an audience for self-elevating performances by men on the rise was provided by the hostess who presided over a city salon. Although such a woman might be the wife merely of a middle-rank professional or a wealthy artisan, intellectuals including humanists, poets, publishers, and

Fig. 1. Richard Brathwaite, *The English Gentlewoman* (1631). (Henry E. Huntington Library and Art Gallery.)

their admirers took on shared luster from being seen in such gatherings. As each of these new centers of power—the merchant patriciate, the court, the urban coterie—claimed legitimacy for itself, each was intent on elaborating a new ideal of femininity.

Feminist historians have reached a consensus that such changes did not, as Burkhardt and his followers claimed, bring the same kinds of freedom to women as they did to men.[5] The Protestant emphasis on marriage freed men from monastic constraints, but reformed religion rigorously defined the duties of the wife, particularly her obedience to her husband, as part of a system in which the household was seen as a private model of the hierarchy that structured the public world.[6] As household work (baking, spinning and weaving, dairying) gave way to guild and mercantile production, the economic usefulness of middle-class women diminished, sometimes to be replaced, at least in public judgment, with a decorative idleness for which they were envied and reproached.[7] And the early humanist belief in the value of educating women, limited from the start to expanding the private accomplishments of women of high rank, succumbed to a bourgeois emphasis on modest piety and family-centered usefulness, intensified by an anti-aristocratic backlash.[8] If women had a Renaissance, it was a problematic one, fraught with prohibitions arising from the conflicting interests of emergent social groups.

A complex set of interdictions faced the few women who sought and won visibility as writers during the sixteenth and early seventeenth centuries. They were only rarely queens and princesses, whose exalted rank and exceptional tutors gave them atypical access to literary fame. The eight love poets studied in this book belonged to lower milieux. Most acquired unofficial training and stimulating audiences in the mixed-rank, mixed-sex coteries of commercially and culturally vital cities such as Lyon, Poitiers, and Venice. Others, such as Tullia d'Aragona and Mary Wroth, occupied positions on the fringe of court circles: the Medici's Florence and James I's Whitehall. Only two, Louise Labé and Pernette du Guillet, had financial support from a husband. The others wrote to earn a living, not through publishers' fees (which were minimal) but through contacts that could lead to paying clients for musician-singers such as Gaspara Stampa and courtesans such as Veronica Franco, to royal patronage, courted by Catherine des Roches and Mary Wroth, or, at the least, to further publication, achieved by Isabella Whitney in London.

These women were driven by economic necessity and the ambition for fame to transgress social dictates that forbade public self-display to women. In order to produce collections of poems, convince publishers to print them, and win critical acclaim, all had to write their way through limits on women's speech, their education, and their access to masculine literary traditions. What were the constraints upon women's participation in literary production? What contradictions in the system of early modern gender ideologies left room to move? Were there any positive arguments or models for women poets' activity? My view is that these poets' texts are strategies for maneuvering within restrictions and turning the contradictions among different discourses of femininity to their òwn advantage. I read their poems as processes of negotiation with the social and literary conventions of a period during which women were constantly looked at but rarely encouraged to make themselves heard.

THE *DONNA DI PALAZZO*: CONDUCT BOOKS, WOMEN AT COURT, AND URBAN COTERIES

Late medieval conduct books written by women for queens or members of the high nobility posit a role for women that was totally rejected in later Renaissance tracts. Christine de Pisan, for example, in the long section of her *Livre des trois vertus* (1405) devoted to the behavior of a queen or baroness, imagines a woman who listens to the petitions of her husband's subjects, intercedes with him by means of informed and carefully rehearsed arguments, and listens to male advisors to prepare herself to reply to demands and debates. This is an active ideal, based on polished public speech and the responsibility of representing power to a crowd of subjects. A hundred years later, the queen of France, Anne de Beaujeu, wrote similar advice to her daughter in *Les Enseignements d'Anne de France à sa fille Susanne de Bourbon* (composed in 1504). Anne, too, foresaw a life of public visibility for her daughter, whether she became a lady-in-waiting to a queen or married into a royal position. She recommends that Suzanne read not only the lives of saints but the sayings of "philosophers and ancient sages";[9] she reminds her of the importance of dressing and moving well, a duty especially important for noblewomen, who "in all things . . . are and ought to be the mirror, model and example for others" (65). Married noblewomen should be easily accessible to guests and servants, and they should speak firmly and loudly: "wives . . . rightly must have more of an audience and therefore more freedom in all matters than other women, both in speech and otherwise." Although Anne is aware of the eagerness for scandal at court and the dangers women face there, she expects that her daughter will find wit and pleasure in "good company" and that her virtue will be strengthened by being exposed to risk: "for however beautifully and well guarded a castle may be, if it has never been assaulted, what reason is there to praise it?" (130).

This confidence in women's ability to withstand the temptations of court life is completely lacking in courtesy books written by men, which proliferated in the early sixteenth century in response to the needs of men at court.[10] The feminine equivalent of the courtier, the *donna di palazzo* or *dama*, was officially employed as lady-in-waiting to a queen or princess. A revealing set of instructions for the profession was composed by Annibal Guasco for his daughter, whom he sent to Catherine, the Duchess of Savoy, in Turin: *Ragionamento . . . a D. Lavinia sua figliuola della maniera del governarsi ella in corte* (1586). Guasco expected Lavinia to serve her duchess at table, to entertain her by singing and playing instruments, and to act as her secretary (for this purpose he had her taught chancellery script). He believed that his daughter's advancement was closely bound up with her chastity; he warns her that she must protect her "honestà" and her reputation at every moment and recommends "modest taciturnity" as a sign of purity of heart. He also recognizes that engaging in the light, teasing conversation of courtiers is no simple matter. He advises Lavinia to proceed cautiously in such exchanges, watching what the women around her do, and he reminds her that "there is no cure for the loss of chastity; it besmirches a woman even after her death."[11]

Guasco's worry about his daughter's chastity makes explicit a deep anxiety in courtly advice-books, typified in Castiglione's *Courtier* (1528). The reason for this anxiety was that the lady was also at court to serve courtiers as stimulus and audience. Castiglione represents life at the Gonzagas' court at Urbino as a carefully choreographed dialogue between appreciative women and the men whose accomplishments they mirror back to them. In Book III, on the court lady, he makes her role as erotic catalyst explicit in a speech by Cesare Gonzaga:

> for like as no Court, how great soever it be, can have any sightlinesse or brightnesse in it, or mirth without women, nor any Courtier can bee gracious, pleasant or hardie, nor at any time undertake any galant enterprise of Chivalrie, unlesse he be stirred with the conversation and with the love and contentation of women, . . . the Courtiers talke is most imperfect evermore, if the entercourse of women give them not a part of the grace wherwithall they make perfect and decke out their playing the Courtier. (188; 340)[12]

The court lady, that is, is a training partner for the courtier as he rehearses the refined speaking and graceful manners central to his role. But this paradise of mutually civilizing gender relations is threatened by the tension presumed to exist between women's talk and their chastity. Castiglione at first depicts a world of innocent intimacy: "There was never agreement of will or hartie love greater between brethren than there was between us all. The like was betweene the women, with whom we had such free and honest conversation, that everye man might commune, sitte, dallye and laugh with whom he lusted." Yet he immediately adds a revealing qualification: "But such was the respect which we bore to the Dutchesse will, that the selfe same libertie was a very great bridle. Neither was there any that thought it not . . . the greatest griefe to offend her" (20; 86). Oxymoron here ("libertie" as a "bridle") signals a conflict deeply embedded in the ideological complex that shapes *The Courtier*. In the gender theory Castiglione inherited from a less courtly world, "free and honest conversation" with a woman is a contradiction in terms: to be open to men's speeches is the same as being open to their embraces. Citing the Old Testament description of the prostitute as "full of words, loud and babbling," in contrast to the good housewife whose useful virtue is linked to her closed doors and few words, popular wisdom aligned silence with chastity in opposition to frank speech and promiscuity.[13] However carefully this link between access to women's talk and access to their bodies is repressed in courtly discourse, it remains under the surface to trouble Castiglione's idealizing group portrait.

For one thing, it is significant that Castiglione uses the term *donna di palazzo* rather than *cortegiana*, a word that had meant "courtesan," in the sense of highly placed prostitute, since the late fifteenth century.[14] The language of the urban street exposed assumptions being disguised in the interest of men's self-fashioning in ducal settings. Pietro Aretino, a satirist who moved in both milieux, spelled out a connection Castiglione suppressed. In his *Ragionamenti*, a set of dialogues on prostitution, he equates men at court with women in the streets: "Today's whores are like today's courtiers, who, if they wish to live in pomp and plenty, are forced to cheat and swindle. . . . For one courtier who has bread in his coffers, there are hordes that scrounge for crusts."[15] In a higher register, Castiglione treads the fine line between the erotic appeal and the sexual purity required of the court lady in remarks attributed to Giuliano de' Medici, whose qualifications demonstrate syntactically how difficult it is to balance the contradictory elements of courtly femininity. Because the court lady must be beautiful, Giuliano says, she must also be very careful of her reputation, "and so behave her selfe, that she be not onely not spotted with any fault, but not so much as with suspicion." Accordingly, a complex system of checks and balances is required in her speech:

> there belongeth to her above all thinges, a certaine sweetness in language . . . wherby she may gently entertaine all kinde of men with talke worthie the hearing and honest. . . . Accompanying with sober and quiet manners, and with the honestie that must alwaies be a stay to her deeds, a readie liveliness of wit, wherby she may declare her selfe far wide from all dulnesse: but with such a kind of goodness, that she may be esteemed no less chaste, wise and courteous than pleasant, neate conceited and sober, and therefore must she keepe a certaine meane verie hard, and (in a manner) derived of contrary matters, and come just to certaine limittes, but not to passe them. (190–91; 343)

Castiglione was not alone in registering the difficulty of promoting the generalized erotic function of women at court while preventing their transgression of norms of chastity. His nervously contradictory definition of feminine virtue is restated in other courtesy books, including Stefano Guazzo's *La civil conversatione* (1574). In the dialogue of Book II, Guglielmo, the speaker obviously in need of refinement, blurts out the assumption concealed in the portrait of the court lady: talking to women is equivalent to having sex with them. When Annibal, the enlightened tutor, says that he is now going to discuss "la conversatione delle donne," Guglielmo expects to hear about relationships with prostitutes, that is, women "with whom men try their manhood withall in amorous encounters" ("con le quali si giuoca alle braccia").[16] Like the English word "intercourse," Guazzo's "conversatione" has two gender-differentiated meanings: with men it is social, with women it is sexual. Annibal corrects this mentality by invoking the conventional argument that women at court refine men's spirits and polish their language. But the exchange exposes the difficulty of assigning women a positive role in the public sphere when the concept of "a public woman" had an entirely sexual and therefore negative connotation in the culture at large.

The court lady's function did in fact include a sexual dimension, however etherealized. As Castiglione's Giuliano says, she was expected to join in the "wantonest talke" without succumbing to actual wantonness. To paraphrase Foucault, erotic conversation was not prohibited but elicited from her.[17] In order to defuse the strains built into this role, literary codes were inscribed as a model for social practice. The Neoplatonism of Cardinal Bembo at the end of Book IV of *The Courtier* is one attempt to transform gender relations at court into a process of mutual spiritual ascent: Bembo rewrites Plato to include marriage as a goal. Coming later and lower on the class scale, Guazzo adopts the Petrarchan mix of desire and awe to praise a royal patroness at Casale. Guazzo's metaphors of enticing restraint make it clear that he is giving a difficult assignment to women. His ideal lady's conversation is so wonderful for its sweetness, the loftiness of her words, and the chastity of her ideas that "the mindes of the hearers intangled in those three nets, feele themselves at one instant to be both mooved with her amiableness and bridled by her honesty" (241; 300).

Fraught with ambivalence as such assignments were, they nonetheless provided an opening for women, both socially and verbally. Considerable social mobility seems to have been possible for women at court. Anne Boleyn, for example, the granddaughter of a tenant farmer who had her trained in French, music, riding, and other graces and sent her to the court of France in 1519 as a lady-in-waiting, finally married a king. Guazzo reports similar class crossovers in the second book of *La civil conversatione*: "about the French Queene, certayn meane Gentlewomen enter into such credit that they are come to be maryed to the cheefe Gentlemen in Fraunce, without any peny given to them in dowrye by their father" (II:78; 418). At the end of his advice book Guasco alludes to possible benefices from the Piedmontese noblewomen whom Lavinia will meet at court. The position of lady-in-waiting had less direct political influence attached to it than did the career of courtier, but it allowed women room to maneuver in their own interest—and, outside the court, to imagine themselves as poets.

In fact, a series of satirical attacks on women at court suggest that their self-advancement was attracting hostility. One instance was Alessandro Piccolomini's dialogue, *La Raffaella*, written as a Carnival joke for fellow humanists in the Accademia degli Intonati in Siena in 1538. His heroine is advised by an old woman who echoes many of the liberal recommendations in *The Courtier*: she reveals her secrets for painting and dressing, and she argues that there is no harm in keeping a secret lover as long as one's husband remains in the dark about it. The dialogue links its attack on courtly flirtation with a warning to husbands about wives' inconstancy.[18] Bertrand de La Borderie's satire of a venal, self-promoting woman, "L'Amie de court" (1541), suggests that women courtiers' ambitions were taken as targets for satire by the middle sixteenth century in France, as well.[19] In England, Ben Jonson's epigram on "The Court Pucell" (from *The Under-wood*, published in 1640 but written earlier) depicts the court lady as a manipulator of male rivalry and, almost hysterically, treats her literary ambition as a form of grotesque lesbian aggression:

> Do's the Court-Pucell then so censure me,
> And thinkes I dare not her? let the world see.
> What though her Chamber be the very pit
> Where fight the prime Cocks of the Game, for wit? . . .
> What though with Tribade lust she force a Muse,
> And in an Epicoene fury can write newes
> Equall with that, which for the best newes goes,
> As aerie light, and as like wit as those?[20]

An important similarity among these attacks is that they interpret courtly ideals from a new class perspective. The greed for power and profit attributed to all three antiheroines demonstrates how threatened men produced representations of "bad" women to criticize the world of privilege from which they were excluded and to displace their own search for gain in that world onto female villainy.[21]

La Borderie's critical portrait stirred up a flurry of reaction, including Antoine Héroët's "La Parfaicte Amye" and Charles Fontaine's "La Contr'amye de Court," Neoplatonic texts that defend a re-etherealized heroine against La Borderie's self-interested speaker. But Fontaine's poem does not appear to have been aimed primarily at a courtly audience. He was a professional writer, the son of a doctor, entering a debate that promised to appeal to a wide variety of readers, not only in Paris, the court city, but in Lyon, where his pamphlet was published. His heroine identifies herself as the daughter of "an honest merchant" who taught his daughters the love theory of *The Symposium* himself because he admired well-educated people more than the proud and immoral rich.[22] In this *querelle*, as in its Italian and English parallels, urban humanists and professionals were appropriating the high vocabulary of Neoplatonism as a medium for social criticism and literary rivalry with court poets.

This downward movement of courtly discourse is significant for women poets because they, too, participated in the bourgeois adoption of Neoplatonism, although they were more likely to be performers than critics of its vocabulary. When Pernette du Guillet's *Rymes* were published in Lyon in 1545, they included a poem written in direct response to the La

Borderie debate. In her second Elégie, entitled "Parfaicte Amytie," she, like Héroët's "Amye," defended herself against charges of triviality and promiscuity. Pernette and Catherine des Roches, in Poitiers, typify the ways women poets could put courtly formulas for feminine behavior into practice outside the court, in the urban salons where Castiglione's dialogues were imitated by a mixed-rank city population. As women had been expected to speak at court, so they were allowed to speak at these upwardly aspiring gatherings. As the *donna di palazzo* balanced erotic chat with unfailing chastity, *la dame du salon* appropriated the Neoplatonic code to establish relationships with men in city coteries and to affirm the purity of those bonds. The difference is that while Castiglione and the poets of the *querelle des amies* wrote to propose masculine models for womanly behavior, a woman such as Pernette wrote to win admiration for herself as a poet. The conflict assumed to exist between women's volubility and their virtue not only complicated the practical value of courtly conduct books; their portraits of women engaging in dialogue with men offered a model for women's poetry in other settings. In the urban coteries where courtly etiquette was imitated, bourgeois women took the encouragement of noblewomen's speech in the interest of the courtier as permission to write on their own account.

MARRIAGE MANUALS:
PATRICIAN AND BOURGEOIS
FAMILY THEORY

A totally different attitude toward women's speech and visibility in the public world governs conduct books addressed to male heads of households in the merchant and professional classes. These texts insist obsessively that women must be restrained to the private sphere. An early example, Leon Battista Alberti's *Della famiglia*, written in the 1430s, records a merchant clan's view of the extended family as an economic unit requiring particular contributions from its women. In the second book, *De re uxoria*, Lionardo, the elder spokesman for the family, says that wives are useful above all for producing sons. Therefore they should be chosen on the basis of good health and a chaste reputation and married young, because girls at this age are pure, modest, and malleable to their husbands' wishes.[23] Most of this second book is dedicated not to marriage, in fact, but to a defense of trade as an honorable activity. Writing to legitimate the occupation of his kinsmen and strengthen the clan, Alberti defines women's role in the family as multiplying its sons and preserving their wealth. In his third book, *Economicus*, he expands on a classical source, Xenophon's *Oeconomicus*, to lay out a specific program for training a wife. The hero of the dialogue, Giannozzo, holds up his wife, whom he has taught to busy herself only with domestic affairs, as a paragon of domestic virtue: "I often spoke against those bold, impudent women who try so hard to find out their husbands' or other men's affairs outside the home" (217). He insists that she forgo public self-display ("a wife and mother must be proper and above reproach if she wants the rest of the family to learn to be proper and modest," 224) and forbids her to gossip: "To speak with moderation has always been a sign of seriousness and dignity in a woman. . . . You should, therefore, prefer to listen in silence rather than talk." He also promises her that she will benefit from overseeing all the household servants and possessions: "being busy will be very good for you. At night you will eat with more appetite, you will be healthier, you will have more color in your cheeks, and will look fresh and beautiful" (230–31). The model here is industry, obedience, and a natural, earned beauty. Artifice of any kind, like preoccupation with the public world, is dismissed as unprofitable.

Alberti's injunction to silence as a sign of feminine virtue is repeated throughout early Italian treatises. Francesco Barbaro, in his *De re uxoria* (1416, dedicated to Lorenzo de' Medici), sternly banishes even noble wives from public speech. In this attitude, he resembled many of his humanist contemporaries, who encouraged women to study but insisted that those studies be used only in private, familial contexts. Lionardo Bruni, for example, wrote in *De studiis et literis*, a 1405 treatise dedicated to a noblewoman, Baptista di Montefeltro, "Rhetoric in all its forms—public discussion, forensic argument, logical fenc[ing], and the like—lies absolutely outside the province of woman."[24] Barbaro is even more emphatic in his prohibition of public speech to women, especially married women. He writes, "Loquacity cannot be sufficiently reproached in women . . . nor can silence be sufficiently applauded. . . . we require that wives be perpetually silent whenever there is an opportunity for frivolity, dishonesty and impudence."[25]

Why is such danger presumed to haunt women's presence and conversation in public places? Like Guazzo's Guglielmo, Barbaro's governing fear is that men's access to women's speech makes access to their bodies possible as well. He tells the story of a Roman matron who withdrew her arm from view when a young man praised its beauty, telling him, "it is not a public one." Barbaro's comment on the anecdote makes his assumptions explicit: "the speech of a noblewoman can be no less dangerous than the nakedness of her limbs" (205). He contrasts the political duties of the free Venetian citizen, assumed to be a man, to the chaste silence of the Venetian woman, twice invoking the paradox of silent eloquence to exclude women from the rhetorical skill that male humanists celebrated as the basis for their own careers: "women should believe that they have achieved the glory of eloquence if they honor themselves with the outstanding ornament of silence. Neither the applause of a declamatory play nor the glory and adoration of an assembly is required of them, but all that is desired of them is eloquent, well-considered and dignified silence" (206).

Limits on a woman's use of her education were also proposed in the Thomas More circle in England. Several recent commentators have argued that More, the Spanish humanist Juan Luis Vives, and Richard Hyrde, the tutor of More's children and translator of Vives, have been overestimated for their enlightened attitude toward feminine learning.[26] Vives certainly matches Barbaro. He forbids the reading of Roman love poets and their imitators in a diatribe against counterfeit and corruption in his *De Institutione Foeminae Christianae* (1523), arguing that shamefastness, opposed to the desire for fame and to the lust associated with it in Barbaro's scheme, should control the well-taught girl. He defines shamefastness through a series of negations that would make imagining a writer's career impossible: "Of shamefastness cometh demureness and measurableness, that whether she think aught, or say or do, nothing shall be outrageous . . . nor presumptuous . . . nor wanton . . . nor ambitious; and as for honours, she will neither think herself worthy of nor desire them, but rather flee them; and if they chance to her, she will be ashamed of them as of a thing not deserved."[27] In his later *De Officio Mariti* (1529) Vives fulminates against exactly the open, mixed-sex conversation that Castiglione was praising at the court of Urbino: "Eloquence is not fit or convenient for women. . . . But nowadays they call her eloquent, that with long and vain confabulation, can entertain one, and what should a man think that she, being unlearned, should talk with a man little wiser than herself, but that, that is either foolish or filthy? And this they call the gentle entertainment of the court, that is to say, of the school, where they learn other like arts of their master the devil" (206). And in the same text Vives warns husbands that their wives' reading will lead them to contrariness, poetry-writing, and long-windedness: "Let not thy wife be overmuch eloquent, nor full of her short and quick arguments, nor have the knowledge of all histories, nor understand many things, which are written. She pleaseth not me that giveth herself to poetry, and observing the art and manner of the old eloquence, doth desire to speak facundiously" (207).

Other members of the More circle shared Vives's caution toward women's education. They concede that women's reason is as amenable to teaching as men's and that learning improves their moral character, but they insist that the family is as far as a woman's training should take her. More, in a letter to his daughter Margaret, praises her for putting her "knowledge of most excellent sciences" to purely private use: "But you, sweet Meg, are rather to be praised for this, that seeing you cannot hope for condign praise of your labours; yet for all this you go forward . . . and contenting yourself with your own pleasure in learning, you never hunt after vulgar praises, nor receive them willingly. . . . And for your singular piety and love towards me, you esteem me and your husband a sufficient and ample theatre for you to contend with" (189). Richard Hyrde, the translator of Vives and celebrator of More, stresses Margaret's modesty rather than her linguistic skill in his preface to her translation of Erasmus's treatise on the Paternoster (1524), where he defends women's reading of Greek and Latin on the basis of a double standard. Uplifting texts from the past are useful to women because their educational needs are different from their husbands': "he liveth more forth abroad among companie daily, where he shall be moved to utter such craft as he hath gotten by his learning. And women abide most at home, occupied ever with some good or necessary business" (165). Hyrde, too, praises Margaret for putting the improving effects of education to work in her marriage rather than in the world at large: "with her virtuous, worshipful, wise and well learned husband, she hath by the occasion of her learning and his delight therein, such especial comfort, pleasure and pastime, as were not well possible for one unlearned couple to take together, or to conceive in their minds, what pleasure is therein" (168). Margaret More's "privacy," as it is invoked in this group text, could never have been a model for the independent entry into the public sphere required of a woman who published her own poems.

Giovanni Bruto, in *La institutione di una fanciulla nata nobilmente* (published in Italian and French in Anvers in 1555, translated into English by Thomas Salter in 1579), rejected even the intellectual pursuits Hyrde praised in Margaret More. Though a humanist himself, he forbade humanist and belleletristic accomplishments to women. He wrote the book not for a nobly born maiden, as the title suggests, but for Marietta Cattaneo, the daughter of a Genoese shipping magnate. He links the education of noblewomen to elitism and corruption and advises Marietta to imitate them not for their social status but for their virtue. Her models should be "not onely those that be more noble than her self, and more mightie or more riche, but . . . those that be the moste vertuous and wise, . . . knowing that in the worlde there bee manie noble ladies and rich Dames inferior to her."[28] She should sew and spin, he says, not learn philosophy, classical or foreign languages, or music; she should read the Scriptures, not "ballades, Songes, sonettes and Ditties of dalliance." Ignorance is safer than erudition in a wife: "And sure I suppose there is no Manne of reason and understanding but had rather love a Mayden unlearned, and chast, than one suspected of dishonest life, though never so famous and well learned in Philosophie" (B8v). The treatise as a whole argues for the *dis*-education of women. Bruto concludes by denigrating heroines of Greek philosophy and poetry. Instead he celebrates the distaff and the spindle, emblems of housewifery tirelessly invoked throughout early modern Europe (perhaps because they were decreasingly necessary in the wealthy private household as a result of the expansion of the cloth-making trades). Nostalgically, Bruto prescribes the distaff, not the pen. No literary ambitions are to be harbored by the merchant's daughters:

> let them be restrained to the care and governement of a familie, and teache them to be envious in following those, that by true vertue have made little accoumpte of those, that to the prejudice of their good names, have beene desirous to bee reputed Diotimes, Aspaties, Sapphoes and Corinnes. For such as compare the small profit of learnyng with the great hurt and domage that commeth to them by the same shall soon perceive . . . how far more convenient the Distaffe, and Spindle, Nedle and Thimble were for them with a good and honest reputation

than the skill of well using a penne or wrighting a loftie verse with diffame dishonour, if in the same there be more erudition than vertue. (C2r)

Frenchmen were less dismissive of women writers than was Bruto, but they too limited literary practice to queens and noblewomen. The poet Agrippa d'Aubigné, for example, writing to his daughters around the turn of the sixteenth century, acknowledges the writing of Marguerite de Navarre, a queen, and also of bourgeois poets such as Louise Labé and Madeleine and Catherine des Roches. But then, invoking class hierarchy to reinforce gender constraints, he tells his daughters that only royal women should write. He strengthens the prohibition by reminding them that their future as wives and mothers makes such accomplishments inappropriate for them:

> I have seen that such knowledge is almost always useless to Demoiselles of your middling rank, for the least fortunate have abused it rather than used it, and the others have experienced the truth of the saying that when the nightingale has little ones, she no longer sings. I would say further that too much mental training makes the heart haughty, and from this I have seen two evils arise: contempt for housework and for . . . a less capable husband, and dissension. So I conclude that I absolutely do not want to encourage the practice of literature for anyone except princesses.[29]

In England, writers attacked the presumed idleness of aristocratic women and the folly of parents and suitors who tried to imitate their social superiors. Protestant preachers saw such class-climbing as spiritually dangerous and economically foolish. Thomas Becon, named as the author of *The Christian State of Matrimony* (1543), advises men against seeking wives from families higher placed than their own. Such women will be "froward and scolding" and "so ladylyke and high in the insteppe . . . that they think that theyre husbands ought of very duty to give them place."[30] The humbly trained women of lower classes are better prospects for domestic peace, which, he stresses three times, depends on female silence: "Get unto thee such a wyfe, as fereth God, loveth hys word, is gentle, quiet, honest, silent, of few words" (B5r). Edward Hake, in a sermon published in 1574, *A Touchestone for this time present*, denounces the misuse to which ambitious parents of the lower gentry and urban professions put their daughters' education, at the expense of their sons': "the substaunce whiche is consumed in two Yeares space uppon the apparaill of one meane Gentleman's Daughter, or uppon the Daughter or Wife of one Citizen, would be sufficient to finde a poor Student in the universitye, by the space of fowre or five Yeeres at the least."[31] Hake does not limit daughters to household tasks but recommends practical labor outside the home: "I would to God that maydes at the least wise might be brought up, if not in learning, yet in honest trades and occupations." He blames upwardly aspiring parents for educating their daughters in coquetry instead: "it is to be lamented (as a case too grievous) such parents as do bring up their daughters in learning, do it to none other ende, but to make them companions of carpet knightes, & giglots, for amorous lovers" (C5r).

The opposition between profitable effort and miseducated vanity is still evident in Thomas Powell's advice to a London father, *The Art of Thriving, or the plaine path-way to preferment* (1635). Powell rejects dancing and French lessons in favor of cooking and needlework, and he concludes that literary interests, both reading and writing, lead middle-class girls only to flirtation and self-aggrandizement. Less tolerant than D'Aubigné, Powell mocks the airs of aristocratic women as well as forbidding them to daughters of his patron's class:

> Instead of *Song* and *Musick*, let them learne Cookery & Laundry, and in steade of reading Sir Philip Sidney's Arcadia, let them read the grounds of good Huswifery. I like not a female poëtesse at any hand: let greater personages glory their skill in Musicke, the posture of their bodies, their knowledge in languages, the greatnesse and freedome of their Spirits and their arts in araigning of men's affections, at their flattering Faces: this is not the way to breede a private Gentlemans daughter.[32]

Suspicion of women too eager to be seen and heard in public was not limited to conduct-book writers for the citizen class. Richard Brathwaite exploited contemporary attacks on the theater in order to recommend pious privacy, silence, and self-restraint to *The English Gentlewoman* (1631): "Make then your Chamber your private Theatre, wherein you may act some devout Scene to Gods honour. . . . It is *Occasion* that depraves us; Company that corrupts us."[33] Like his Italian predecessors, Brathwaite links free speech and sexual scandal, opposing the courtly view that witty speech is a woman's best protection against seduction. He recommends that "our wanton Curtezans . . . teach their tongues to be Orators of modesty. . . . Their tongues are held their defensive armour; but in no way detract they more from their honour, than by giving too much free scope to that glibbery member" (78). Brathwaite concludes with a fiercely elaborate metaphor, rewriting a Homeric formula (men's teeth as fences against angry speech) by invoking women's teeth as a constraint on their natural garrulity: "What restraint is required in respect of the tongue may appeare by that ivory guard or garrison with which it is impaled. See, how it is double warded, that it may with better reservancy and better security be restrained!" (88).

The rise of Protestantism in England intensified controls on women's speech. Rather than privatizing the family as a haven from political hierarchy in the outer world, Protestant commentators defined it as the basic unit of that hierarchy. William Perkins in his *Christian Oeconomie: or a short survey of the right manner of erecting and ordering a Familie, according to the Scriptures* (written in Latin, translated into English in 1609) links women's obedience in the family to other forms of social subordination necessary to maintain order: "The Holie Ghost in the booke of the Scriptures, hath in

great wisedom commended both Rules for direction, and examples for imitation, to Husbands and Wives, to Parents and Children, to Masters and Servants." Family training comes first; hence its importance: "For in this first
Societie, is as it were the Schoole, wherein are taught and learned the princi-
ples of authoritie and subjection."[34] William Gouge, an influential London
minister, likewise defined the husband as the master in a series of inter-
related hierarchies in his sermons, published with the title *Of Domesticall
Duties* (1622). The husband "is as a Priest unto his wife. . . . He is the highest in the family, and hath both authority over all; . . . hee is as a king in his
owne house."[35]

A major difference between the relations of subject to king and of wife
to husband, however, is that in Gouge's scheme, subjection was more than
a matter of external political structure; it was to be deeply internalized by
women as a psychological and spiritual condition. He ends a series of remarks on obedience by specifying what the motive behind the wife's humility toward her husband should be: "Here lyeth a maine difference
betwixt true, Christian, religious wives and meere naturall women: *these*
may be subject on by-respects, as namely, that their Husbands may the
more love them . . . or that they may the more readily obtaine what they
desire at their Husbands hands. . . . But the *other* have respect to Christ's
ordinance, whereby their Husbands are made their head, and to Christ's
Word and Will, whereby they are commanded subjection" (317). Gouge
comes to this conclusion after a series of specific directions about how
wives should address their husbands. He forbids the wife to use her husband's first name or endearments such as "Sweet, Sweeting, Heart, Sweet-
heart, Love, Joy" (and, more fancifully, "Ducke, Chicke, Pigsnie"); he allows only terms that stress the greater power of the husband, such as
"Master" followed by his last name. This attention to language is a vivid
instance of an early recognition that language *constructs* subjectivity, that
the installation of a certain discourse, an institutionalized style of speech,
produces the attitudes written into that particular speech. Gouge recommends a regime of deferential address from wife to husband because the
daily practice of that deference will force her simultaneously to demonstrate and to internalize the subservience demanded of her by seventeenth-century Protestantism.

A central emblem appears in many directives for women, whatever
country they were written in: the wife as a mirror to her husband. Robert
Greene identifies the source of the metaphor in a long passage in *Penelope's
Web* (1587):

> *Plato* in his *Androgina* doth say that a wise woman ought to thinke her husbands
> manners the lawes of her life, which if they be good, she must take as a forme of
> her actions, if they be bad, she must brooke with patience. His reason is thus. As
> a looking glasse or Christal though most curiously set in Ebonie, serveth to small
> purpose if it doth not lively represent the proportion and lineaments of the face

. . . , so a woman, though rich and beautifull, deserveth smal prayse or favour, if the course of her life be not directed after her husbands compasse.[36]

The same idea is expressed in a simpler way by Orazio Lombardelli in his instructions to his young wife, *Dell'Uffizio della Donna Maritata* (1574): "Just as a mirror is bad if it makes a cheerful image seem gloomy or a mournful one joyful and festive, so a woman acts wrongly if when her husband is discontented, she ignores him, laughing, or if she is gay when he is melancholy."[37]

There is little to be gay about here; the mirror emblem totally suppresses any autonomy in the wife. In fact, it calls for an obedience so extreme that it appears to have been open to question. Even men writers acknowledge that objections could be raised to the reflector role, although they do so in passages designed to forestall resistance. In Edmund Tilney's *A briefe and pleasant discourse of duties in Marriage, called the Flower of Friendshippe* (1568), the lady Julia tells the younger Isabella that her husband's "face must be hir dayly looking-glass, wherein she ought to be always prying, to see when he is mery, when sad, . . . wherto she must alwais frame her own countenance."[38] Isabella responds by reducing the metaphor to absurdity: "Why, what if he be mad, or drunke, must we then shew the like countenance?" This is a pointed riposte, implying that men are seldom the perfect models their role in the family assumes. But Julia restores law and order by arguing that the wife of a madman or drunkard must speak gently to her husband and cajole him into recovery: shrewish criticism will only harm them both. Likewise, in Robert Snawsel's *A Looking glasse for Married Folkes* (1631), the objections of Margery the "malapert" are raised in order to be silenced. When Eulalie, the good Puritan wife, quotes the mirror *topos*, Margery bursts out with questions that pinpoint the abolition of personality demanded by the metaphor: "Are you a woman, and make them such dishclouts and slaves to their husbands? came you of a woman, that you should give them no prerogatives, but make them altogether underlings?"[39] Here, too, however, the text positions the angry woman as a defeatable devil's advocate. Eulalie assures Margery that she habitually performs such obedience, secure in the knowledge that it is "warranted by the Word of God." The mirror image posits a purely receptive and imitative role for women. Rather than asserting their difference or distance from the men they love, a rhetorical prerequisite for any sort of poetic performance, they are urged to shape their moods and words to their husbands' wills, to disappear into the specular limbo of the empathetic wife.

All in all, conduct books written outside court milieux demonstrate that a woman who composed love poetry was likely to be seen as transgressing a multitude of rules. She was speaking rather than listening. She was not working in a private household for a family but in a public literary world, going after recognition for herself alone. If she had trained herself in the conventions of Neoplatonism or Petrarchism, she was exercising argument and eloquence for her own ends. Above all, she was entering into public discourse, exposing the beauty of her language, akin to her body, to the masculine gaze. Rather than mirroring a man whose power over her was ratified by her culture, she was refocusing, escaping, or shattering that mirror. She was not only familiar with shameless "Sonnetes and Epigrames"; she was producing them herself. Her signature as a poet asserted her own claim to fame rather than her subservience to masculine ideals or to divine inspiration. It is no wonder that so few women took up the pen in sixteenth-century Europe.

Nor is it any wonder that two mythological figures, Echo and Philomel, were frequently invoked by women poets as figures for enforced speechlessness. Gaspara Stampa (*Rime*, 1554) identifies with both these victims of men's power in Ovid's *Metamorphoses*. In Ovid, Jove's infidelities cause Juno to punish Echo for her chatter, which prevents the queen of the gods from discovering her husband's misdeeds: Juno dooms Echo to speak nothing but the words of her disdainful lover, Narcissus. Philomel's brother-in-law, Tereus, king of Thrace, rapes her and cuts out her tongue so that she cannot tell her sister Procne what has happened, but she weaves her story into a tapestry that prompts Procne to free her and take revenge on the king.[40] The horror of such founding anecdotes was persistently repressed by a culture engaged in suppressing the verbal activity of women. To sixteenth-century men writing on women's conduct, Echo could even seem an ideal figure. Robert Cleaver in *A godly forme of household government* (1588) wrote: "as the echo answereth but one word for many, which are spoken to her, so a Maid's answer should be in a single word."[41] Male poets of the period typically condensed both myths into decorative formulae: they used Echo to emblematize a spirit of pastoral melancholy and named Procne and Philomel, the swallow and the nightingale, as shorthand for the coming of spring. Stampa, however, focuses on both figures with empathetic intensity. She uses the figure of Echo as a parallel to her own state, wasting away to a bodiless ghost because of her lover's indifference: "di donna serbo sol la voce e 'l nome"[42] (I retain nothing of a woman but the voice and the name). Further, she allies herself with Procne and Philomel as co-poets: if they help her to sing out her grief, she promises to reciprocate their choral role.

ENABLING DISCOURSES:
DEFENSES OF WOMEN AND
PRAISE OF POETS

The fates of the Ovidian heroines may seem to align them with the silent women of the conduct books. Yet Echo and Philomel, victims of speechlessness and violation, are commemorated in the poems of a woman who persisted in her will to write. Other women poets also persisted, typically because, like Philomel, they found ways to compromise with interdictions.

The range of their negotiations with ideological pressures on their sex is the subject of the analyses in my next chapters. The context for such negotiations was a spectrum of interdictions and permissions for women's writing, delimited at either end by two positions: "all public discourse is forbidden" and "you may at least do this much." The most submissive response was to deal only with the domestic and religious concerns considered appropriate for women and to write without any ambition for publication. This path was taken in England in posthumously published texts such as Elizabeth Grymeston's advice to her son in *Miscelanae, Meditations, Memoratives* (1604) and in Katherine Stubbes's *Confession* (1592).[43] Slightly farther along the spectrum, women translated religious texts, sheltering under the masculine authority of their originals; Margaret More's translation of Erasmus is a case in point. Other women wrote religious meditations themselves: Marguerite de Navarre's *Miroir de l'âme pêcheresse*, Vittoria Colonna's *Rime religiose*, Amelia Lanyer's *Salve Deus Rex Judaeorum*. But secular scholars such as Isotta Nogarola and Laura Cereta found their writing curtailed by vicious criticism and supported only to the extent that they suppressed their femininity or could be praised as exceptions to their sex.[44]

Such suppression of gender was impossible in love poetry. Amorous discourse played a central role in the courtier's rhetorical training; court culture encouraged improvisatory wit, provoked the display of learning, and rewarded erotic casuistry, even (or especially) at its most outrageous—in men.[45] But the lyric of seduction was a far less acceptable mode for women. Courtesans were the one exception. For them, erotic verse was a central requirement of a career built on self-display and verbal elegance. Veronica Franco occupies the radical end of the spectrum: in her *Rime*, she declares her profession openly through dialogues with clients in which she proclaims her sexual skills and uses challenging rhetorics to defend other courtesans and the female sex in general. But Franco's erotic invitations would have been scandalous in a woman not practicing her profession. In fact, far less erotic poetry elicited ferocious attacks. Gaspara Stampa insisted throughout her *canzoniere* on her fidelity to a distant and indifferent man, yet an obscene epitaph published immediately after her death attacked her as equally promiscuous in body and texts. The anonymous author characterized her as a common whore, sleeping with any man, plagiarizing everything she wrote from an early cohort in sin, and inviting a phallic salute from men passing by her grave.[46] An insulting link between poetic performance and sexual excess was also used by a Jacobean courtier to attack Mary Wroth. Edward Denny called her a "Hermaphrodite in show, in deed a monster" and recommended that she redeem her transgression of gender decorum by "writing as large a volume of heavenly lays and holy love as you have of lascivious tales and amorous toys."[47] Although the Englishman blamed the woman writer less for promiscuity than for monstrous nonconformity (perhaps a result of the rarity of women poets in England, compared to Italy), in both cases, the woman's life and works are equated as symptoms of deviant sexuality and social rebellion.

Where, then, could a woman who was not a courtesan find ideological justification or literary models for writing love poetry? Unless we posit an innate or mystical will to write, we have to expect that some sort of encouragement and resistance was available to women during this period. I have stressed the prohibitions imposed on women by gender ideology because its effects need to be recognized in the poems women succeeded in publishing. But the early modern complex of social and ideological shifts also worked in women's favor. Defenses of women, dedicated to noblewomen in court circles in Italy and France, celebrated learned and literary heroines. The rise of cities produced civic loyalties that were exploited by enterprising publishers, in Venice and Lyon, for example, who advertised women's texts as evidence of the cultural superiority of their towns. And humanists and popular pamphleteers profited by writing in favor of women, adding weight to the pro-woman side of the *querelle des femmes*.[48]

A central text for this debate was Christine de Pisan's *Le Livre de la Cité des Dames* (1405). The book was known only in manuscript in the sixteenth century, but it established three lines of argument that reappeared in defenses of women throughout the three centuries after it was written. In the opening scene of the book, an allegorical figure, Lady Reason, points out that male bias rather than philosophical objectivity has motivated misogynistic treatises on women. That is, rather than attempting to refute charges of female inferiority, Christine analyzes the social and psychological causes of men's assumption that women are inferior. Reason explains that misogynist writers have been rejected, aged, or envious men or poets who know no better than to repeat "what others have written in books."[49] Second, she states categorically that women are not only the equals of men but superior to them in certain ways, of "sharper and freer minds" (63). Culture, not nature, produces women who appear less intellectually able than men. If a boy and a girl were educated in the same way, no difference would exist between their literary or military skills; in fact, the girl would soon outstrip the boy. Finally, she offers a long list of illustrious women, culled from Boccaccio's *De claris mulieribus* but also from more recent times, including Sappho and Cornificia, a medieval Latin poet (64–65). Christine denies the truth of misogyny by exposing its cultural politics: as long as men have owned the means of representation, the figure of woman has been their undisputed invention. Reason concludes, "Whoever goes to court without an opponent pleads very much at his ease" (118).

These strategies are taken up again in France in women's texts of the middle sixteenth and early seventeenth centuries. Hélisenne de Crenne in her *Epistres invectives* (1534) responds to the misogynist Elenot by using examples of ancient and contemporary women to refute his claim that women have "dull and troubled minds." *Ad hominem*, she adds that only his willed ignorance of women's literary accomplishments could lead him to conclude that they are fit only to "spin wool": "I find the speed with which you come to this conclusion amazing. It certainly proves to me that if you could, you would forbid literary privileges to the feminine sex, criticizing us for being incapable of writing well. But if you had seriously studied the range of published books, your opinion would be different."[50] Like Hélisenne, Louise Labé substitutes the pen and the printing press for Bruto's emblems of housewifery. In her famous preface to Clémence de Bourges (*Euvres*, 1555), she blames the "harsh laws of men" for closing women out of the arts and sciences and encourages women to raise their minds above their "distaffs and spindles," to "show men the injustice they have done us in depriving us of the honor that could have been ours through study."[51] Half a century later Marie de Gournay in *L'Egalité des hommes et des femmes* (1622) argues, as Christine had, that nurture and education rather than innate ability determine the quick-wittedness of men and women alike.[52] In a second essay, *Le Grief des femmes*, she reinforces the *ad hominem* analysis of misogyny, in this case, men's ignorant dismissal of women writers: "Among men, dead and living, who have acquired fame as writers in our century, often in grave long gowns, I have known some who absolutely disdained the works of women, without, however, deigning to read them to see what they are made of."[53] All three of these women take one step further Christine's exposure of masculine self-interest in silencing women. They also insist that women, if educated, can write as well as men, a claim proved through their own and other examples of feminine publication.

In courtly circles after Christine's time, defenses of women were often written by men, who dedicated them to royal or noble patronesses from whom they were seeking favor. Castiglione lists a series of heroic and chaste women from the past and the present in Book III of *The Courtier*, although he names no women scholars or poets, probably because he is constructing an appreciative rather than a productive role for the *donna di palazzo*. But François Billon, in a vast volume dedicated to the queens and princesses of France, *Le Fort inexpugnable de l'honneur du sexe femenin* (1555), ends his list of mythic and royal women with praise for contemporary writers: in Italy, Olimpia Morata and Isabella di Vilmarini; in England, the princesses Anne, Margaret, and Jane, who wrote a hundred Latin couplets in honor of the queen of Navarre; in France, Claudine and Jane Scève and Jeanne Gaillarde of Lyon, as well as Pernette du Guillet, Hélisenne de Crenne, and Anne Tullone of Mâcon.[54] Billon's use of examples from his own decade puts him firmly on the side of women's writing in the present, in contrast to humanists' allusions to ancient heroines whose texts had been lost for centuries.

Billon's consistent labeling of contemporary French women writers according to the cities from which they come typifies another positive pressure on women to write: the civic and patriotic fervor intensifying in ascendant cities and nation states as they consolidated their autonomous identities. Louise Labé was celebrated as the jewel of Lyon, and Venetian poets praised their women colleagues as glories of the Republic. In other cities of Italy and in England, as well, men's attitudes toward women's literary efforts depended on what they saw as their potential contribution to the international reputation of the local culture. Ariosto, in the first twenty-four stanzas of Book 37 of *Orlando furioso*, offers a critique like Christine's and Hélisenne's of the erasure of women's texts: jealousy and spite have prompted "lying, envious and impious writers" to suppress the names and accomplishments of women throughout history.[55] But now, he says, many writers in Italy defend the accomplishments of women and women themselves claim the glory due them. By praising women, Ariosto actually praises men: his examples of properly appreciative readers include Tullia d'Aragona's admirers Bembo and Molza as well as Ercole d'Este, the son of his patron (xiii, 1–2), and these men vastly outweigh his single example of a woman poet, Vittoria Colonna. Although he praises her at length, he does so in terms affirmed in every conduct book: like a second Artemisia, she has drawn her dead husband "forth from the grave" through her undying chastity and loyalty. But Ariosto turns from the exemplary Colonna to exhort women in general to abandon "the needle and the cloth" and join the Muses on Parnassus (xiv). Indeed, he writes, his countrywomen are already earning fame for themselves and the Italian poets who celebrate them.

Italian women's fame reached England more problematically; there commentators cited women's writing as a negative example. Richard Mulcaster argued in 1581 that English girls were as capable of learning classical languages as their German and French counterparts. But his patriotism stopped there. The Protestant stress on female modesty took over in his advice to Englishwomen not to go as far as Italian women, "who dare write themselves, and deserve fame for so doing." He warns his countrywomen that the Italian women's "excellencie is so geason [uncommon, amazing], as they be rather wonders to gaze at, then presidentes to follow."[56] Nonetheless, writing was recognized as crucial to local and national patriotism: it was by writing—or not writing—that women were exhorted to raise the reputation of their cities and countries.

Billon's and Arisoto's use of contemporary examples reappears as a strategy in two energetically written defenses published by Italian women at the end of the sixteenth century. In Italy, the Counter-Reformation refueled the fires of misogyny: tracts attacking women proliferated during the 1570s and eighties, especially around Padua. A particularly rancorous book by Onofrio Filarco, *La Vera narratione delle operationi delle donne* (Padua, 1586), prompted two women to respond.[57] Moderata Fonte published a dialogue, *Il Merito delle donne* (1600, written during the late 1580s), in which seven women of different ages and marital status discuss the defects of men. One is envy, which has driven them to obliterate women's accomplishments and potentials. Fonte constructs a central character, Corinna (named after the Greek poet who defeated Pindar in lyric contests), to break down the traditional opposition between chastity and learning in women; she describes her heroine as simultaneously "filled with chastity and excellent in poetry."[58] In a rousing final poem, Corinna, like Labé, calls on her fellow women to aim for fame beyond the private household, in spite of hostile responses:

E rivolgendo il vostro alto desire
A' miglior opre, e a' più bei studi intorno,
Ornatevi d'un nome eterno, e chiaro
A' onta d'ogni cuor superbo, e avaro.

(147)

And, turning your high ambitions
To worthier works and fairer fields of study,
Adorn yourselves with eternal, brilliant fame,
To shame every proud and niggardly heart.

This willed linking of chastity and ambition is recast in Lucrezia Marinelli's *La nobiltà e l'eccellenza delle donne* (Venice, 1600). In a long chapter, "Delle donne scienziate e di molti arti ornate," Marinelli celebrates many ancient women writers but almost as many contemporary ones: Laura of Brescia, who wrote "elegant epistles" to Savanarola; Catherine Parr, wife of Henry VIII, who wrote meditations on the Psalms; and—more to the point for secular women poets—Veronica Gambara, "dottissima nella poesia" and immortalized by Ariosto.[59] Like her predecessors, Marinelli claims that men's envy has caused admirable women to disappear from cultural history. In a strategic correction of many humanists' use of classical authorities, she also argues that philosophers invoked as critics of women (Plato, Aristotle) were actually more sympathetic to her sex than the pseudophilosophers who cite them in support of their own misogynist notions.

The predominance of men in the reading public and writing elite of early modern Europe meant that women were much more likely to define themselves through their relationships to male celebrities than to identify with other women of their time. Evidence of mutual citation among women is hard to come by, given the repetition of Petrarchan and Neoplatonic tropes throughout Europe. Occasionally, however, women poets exchanged complimentary poems in praise of writers of their own sex. One example of female intertextuality is a set of sonnets written by three Italian women. Veronica Gambara addressed the second sonnet of her *Rime* (1554) to Vittoria Colonna, widow of the Marquis of Pescara and one of the most admired poets of the century, partly because her constant theme, her love for her dead husband, transgressed so few gender dictates. (Fifteen editions of her *Rime* were published between 1538 and 1558.) Gambara opens by naming Colonna as a woman poet: "O de la nostra etade unica gloria, / Donna saggia, leggiadra, anzi divina"[60] (Oh, unique glory of our age, / Wise, lovely, even divine lady). In her conclusion, she calls a chorus of women readers to honor Colonna: "Il sesso nostro un sacro e nobil tempio / Dovria, come già a Palla e a Febo, alzarvi" (Our sex should raise a sacred and noble temple to you / As we did in the past to Athene and Phoebus). Colonna responded by addressing a sonnet to Gambara in the last edition of her own *Rime* (1558). In Sonnet 79, she echoes Gambara's conventionally modest ending, in which she regrets the gap between her admiration and her ability to praise

Colonna. Colonna, too, says that her means fall short of her motives—
although she invokes her love for her husband as her justification: "Onde
l'alto dolor le basse rime / Muove, e quella ragion la colpa toglie"[61] (Thus my
high grief inspires my lowly rhymes, / And this motive removes any blame).
Finally, a poem appended to Gambara's *Rime* praises both Colonna and
Gambara by invoking them as models. Luciana Bertani, a Bolognese poet,
compares her countrywomen to Sappho and Corinna—seen now as heroines, not as Bruto's women of easy virtue—and praises them for their
"unique and exquisite works," which "banish every false and dangerous
custom." She concludes:

> Quest'alme illustri son cagion che ogni arte
> Tento per tôrre alla mia luce l'ombra,
> Sol perche al mondo un dì si mostri chiara.[62]

> These distinguished souls inspire me to try
> Every art to remove dark ignorance from my mind,
> So that, one day, my own fame may shine forth.

Both younger poets write with a clear sense of their gender and of the value
of an older woman as model. Although they cite ancient and distant examples of feminine power, they also praise a contemporary poet face to face in
a dialogue that shows that women were beginning to take one another seriously as participants in literary culture.

In their forays into the debate over female intelligence, then, as in their
rarer acknowledgment of one another in their lyrics, women resisted their
exclusion from cultural production. By drawing on ideological support outside their texts and by compromising with limits on women's speech within
them, poets who were not courtesans found ways of mediating social dictates and the conventions of love poetry. To publish without facing accusations of unchastity or presumption, some adopted a technique of mixing
genres, of inserting conduct-book discourses into their lyrics as justification
for their writing: Isabella Whitney and Catherine des Roches are cases in
point. Less humbly, Louise Labé appropriated the fame to which male humanists entitled themselves by addressing her love sonnets to a scholar-poet
and claiming international esteem for her own eloquence.

Other writers drew out the ideologically sanctioned feminine virtues encoded into reigning conventions of love poetry. By 1540, women poets confronted a system of vocabularies, rhetorical patterns, and *topoi* dominated by the
male gaze built into love lyrics written by men. Yet it is also important to recognize that niches for acceptable feminine positions could be found in most pre-
vailing conventions. The Petrarchan mode, in which a male poet yearns for an
unattainable lady, could be regendered to guarantee the chastity of a woman
poet. Petrarch and his followers dramatized involuntary separations from their
ladies because distance provided the occasion for their poems; Ronsard and Sidney, for example, composed intricate arguments to persuade their ladies to

lessen the gap. In the case of a woman poet, the absence of the male beloved fulfilled a social as well as a rhetorical requirement: it guaranteed the speaker's purity. In addition, the actual situation of a woman poet, isolated from coterie or court by choice or necessity, might literalize the Petrarchan convention of pastoral solitude. Both of these conventions shape Mary Wroth's position in *Pamphilia to Amphilanthus*. Pamphilia's wandering beloved elicits an outpouring of sonnets and songs from her, but her physical separation from Amphilanthus forecloses speculation about the sexual dimension of the relationship. The same is true of Gaspara Stampa's *Rime*. Although she recalls passionate nights in the past, in the dramatic present of the sonnets her lover is physically distant in battle or emotionally remote because of his indifference to her.

Women poets in coteries found a highly usable set of conventions in Neoplatonism. Socrates' theory of love between men as an ascent to spiritual vision, Christianized by Ficino and heterosexualized to suit sixteenth-century courts, stressed the equality of the lovers and the mutual refinement they stimulated in each other. Actively practiced as a code of courtly etiquette, Neoplatonism could be made into a liberatory discourse by a woman poet, as Pernette du Guillet's *Rymes* show. The traditional form of Neoplatonism, the dialogue, also established the literary credentials of the woman poet addressing her texts to men. Tullia d'Aragona, a courtesan, manipulated the mode to assemble a set of Neoplatonic letter-sonnets through which she incorporated clients and admirers into an idealized group portrait of poet-philosophers analyzing love theory with her.

Yet the history of gender ideologies I have offered here suggests that such solutions were never simple. The assumptions and fantasies of the culture left open only a narrowly circumscribed area for women's self-representations; to occupy it required wit and energies traditionally ascribed to men. And because women, restricted to the ostensibly private genre of love lyric, were excluded from the political orientation of genres higher in the Renaissance hierarchy—tragedy and epic—they condensed a whole range of demands and desires, protest and longing, into love poetry. Neoplatonism's code of equal relations between men and women, the fantastic transformations of Ovidian myth, and the open eroticism of Roman elegy provided channels for representations of female autonomy, revenge on men and solidarity among women, and sexual bliss. Even so, a woman poet disrupted the presumed intimacy of love lyric by publishing her work. However she insisted on the purity of her affection, she was likely to alarm the mentality that connected open female speech to open sexuality. For the woman poet, eros was fraught with perils. In the chapters that follow, I analyze how those perils were negotiated by writers responding to masculine discourses of love from diverse circumstances of class and culture. My readings are based on the theory that because language and literary convention embody ideological power, they are also media through which such power can be appropriated, challenged, and rewritten.

TWO

Writing to Live

Pedagogical Poetics in Isabella Whitney and Catherine des Roches

To be a professional writer and a woman in the sixteenth century was a very rare thing. Aristocrats of either sex rarely published. Class decorum required them to circulate their work privately in manuscript and to agree to let a printer have it only if a pirated edition had been published without the writer's consent—or at least to claim that this was what had happened.[1] Even stricter modesty surrounded women's writing, which was often published only after their deaths. Pernette du Guillet's husband and Gaspara Stampa's sister, for example, presented their wife's and sibling's work posthumously, as family homage to the dead. The professional writer was free from the demands of genteel amateurism, but he faced a publishing system far less hospitable to writers than to the purveyors of their work. Typically, a publisher paid one small fee for a manuscript; no copyright went to the writer and no royalties were paid, however many editions were printed.[2] For a woman writer, negotiations with a publisher were likely to go forward under an even greater power imbalance, given the scarcity of women colleagues in the book trade. Private patrons' approval of a writer's work was as unpredictable as the sums that could be expected from them. For poets such as Marot and Spenser, persistence and good timing as well as calculated flattery in poems and dedications were necessary to win royal support. Gender decorum encouraged women writers to seek women patrons rather than men (Tullia d'Aragona, for example, dedicated her *Rime* to Eleanora of Toledo, the duchess of Florence), but far fewer women than men had the independent wealth to act as patrons.[3]

Nonetheless, I begin this study with two professional women poets because their responses to these economic and social circumstances bring the dialectic of gender ideology, lyric convention, and self-representation in women's poetry during this period into clear view. Isabella Whitney, writing in London during the middle 1570s, and Catherine des Roches, writing in Poitiers from 1575 to 1586, both made their living through their pens. Their intention of winning a large audience can be seen in the maneuvers through which they produced an unimpeachably chaste and carefully popularized love poetry. Both poets were *bricoleuses*, improvisatory jugglers of materials they found already in place in their culture:[4] they recombined didactic and lyric genres in new ways to guarantee the respectability of their texts. But their need to profit from their writing also led them to less conformist strategies. By constructing newly active speaking positions, they transformed the roles assigned to women in the Ovidian and Neoplatonic modes they inherited from an androcentric literary system; and they wrote to and for women as a group.

ISABELLA WHITNEY:
A COUNTRY GENTLEWOMAN IN LONDON

Isabella Whitney published two short collections of poems, *The Copy of a letter lately written in meeter, by a yonge Gentilwoman: to her unconstant lover* (1567) and *A Sweet Nosgay, Or Pleasant Posye: contayning a hundred and ten Phylosophicall Flowers* (1573). Both were printed in cheap pamphlet form by Richard Jones, a London printer who specialized in popular manuals and poetic miscellanies.[5] Information about Whitney's background and her life in London comes mainly from the set of "Certain familier Epistles and friendly Letters by the Auctor: with Replies" in *A Sweet Nosgay*. These reveal that she was writing out of financial necessity, and the subject matter in both her collections suggests that she and her publisher wanted to attract a wide London readership.

Whitney came from a gentry family in Cheshire, that is, from the middle-ranking landowning population of the countryside. She dedicated *A Sweet Nosgay* to George Mainwaring, a member of a prominent Cheshire family, reminding him of their childhood together and describing herself as his "welwilling Countriwoman."[6] Her brother Geffrey Whitney was the author of *A Choice of Emblemes* (1586), which included a stunning total of ninety-three dedications to potential patrons.[7] Obviously, brother and sister both promoted their writing by any means possible. Like many women of her class, Isabella Whitney appears to have gone to London to work as a lady's companion; in a letter to her brother she mentions losing a position with "a vertuous Ladye, which tyll death I honour wyll" ("Epistles," sig. C6v). She names her two younger sisters, also working in London households, as her audience for an epistle on the duties of women servants, "A modest meane for Maides." The poem suggests that they all did fairly menial labor. She tells them to keep working after "Your Masters gon to bed, / your Mistresses at rest,"' to lock up the family plate and be sure windows and doors are secure. The poem is typical of Whitney in its simple form (twelve-syllable lines alternating with her usual fourteen-syllable lines, in couplets divided typographically into quatrains) and its advertisement of its practical advice:

> Good Sisters mine, when I
>   shal further from you dwell:
> Peruse these lines, observe the rules
>   which in the same I tell.

> So shal you wealth posses,
>   and quietnesse of mynde:
> And al your friends to se[e] the same,
>   a treble joy shall fynde.
>
> (Sig. C7v)

Whitney's warnings about how a maidservant should behave with the family of her employers imply that misjudgments of her character and unfair treatment are to be expected:

> Of laughter be not much,
>   nor over solemne seeme:
> For then be sure th'eyle [they'll] coumpt you light
>   or proud wil you esteeme.
> Be modest in a meane,
>   be gentyll unto all:
> Though cause thei geve of contrari
>   yet be to wrath no thrall.
>
> (C8v)

In her conclusion, she congratulates her sisters on having found secure positions and quotes a popular proverb to suggest that her own luck has not been as good:

> And sith that vertue guides,
>   where both of you do dwell:
> Geve thanks to God, and painful bee
>   to please your rulers well,
> For fleetyng is a foe,
>   experience hath me taught:
> The rolling stone doth get no mosse
>   yourselves have h[e]ard full oft.

Did Whitney lose her London job because of slander? Most of the "Certain familier Epistles" turn around her lack of fortune, by which she means both luck and money. In "A carefull complaynt by the unfortunate Auctor," she writes of ill health and "malice." A friend replies by refusing to believe gossip about her. C. B. writes: "Thy friends who have thee knowne of long, / will not regard thy enemies tong," and continues:

> The vertue that hath ever beene,
> Within thy tender brest . . .
> Doth me perswade thy enemies lye,
> And in that quarell would I dye.
>
> (D7r)

A cousin also mentions her financial and physical difficulties: "Indeed, I se[e] and know to[o] wel, how fortune spites your welth: / And as a tirant

Goddesse, doth disdain your happie health" (E1r). The details of how Whitney became a "rolling stone" remain obscure, but it seems certain that she turned to writing as a source of income when she became, as she says, "Harvestlesse, / and serviceless also" (A5v).

Her preface, "The Auctor to the Reader," is an exemplarily modest woman's intellectual autobiography. Whitney explains that she began to read and write because of enforced leisure: illness kept her indoors. She is self-taught, she says, through "such Bookes, wherby I thought / my selfe to edyfye." These included the Scriptures, which she abandoned because she had no "Divine" to guide her, and "Histories," which she found disillusioning because the "follyes" they record still plague "this our present time." In both remarks, Whitney observes gender decorum: women were warned against interpreting Scripture on their own authority and against reading that failed to provide uplifting examples.[8] She also mentions two widely read classical poets, Ovid and Virgil, and the contemporary Italian writer of neo-Latin pastoral, Mantuan. Altogether, her narrative of her preliminary reading establishes the persona of a practical and modest woman who has taken on serious books but always with a sense of her own limits.

Whitney subscribes further to women's roles as they were defined in her time in a poem to her sister, "Misteris A. B." (Anne Baron). Anne, married and a mother, was carrying out the proper duties of a woman; only her own single state, says Whitney, explains her career as a writer. Her expression of affection for her nephews and respect for the value of her sister's housekeeping makes her definition of her writing as a merely temporary career sound less like a declaration of independence than a bow to necessity:

> . . . Your Husband with your prety Boyes,
> God keepe them free from all annoyes. . . .
>
> Good Sister so I you commend,
>   to him that made us all:
> I know you huswyfery intend,
>   though I to writing fall:
> Wherefore no l[o]nger shal you stay,
> From businesse, that profit may.
>
> Had I a Husband, or a house,
>   and all that longes therto
> My selfe could frame about to rouse,
>   as other women doo:
> But till some houshold cares me tye,
> My bookes and Pen I wyll apply.
>   (D1v–D2r)

But the statement in the last stanza also has strategic value. Whitney is reassuring her readers that they are in the safe hands of a woman writer loyal to the bourgeois ideal of dedication to the household—although she foresees that role for herself, conveniently, only in the future.

Betty Travitsky praises Whitney's "Wyll and Testament," a rollicking farewell to London printed at the end of the *Nosgay*.[9] It is an engaging and unusually publicly oriented poem for a woman. Whitney lists the streets and neighborhoods of the city with a precision and breadth that suggest she moved through them much more freely than class decorum permitted the noblewoman or the citizen's wife. She names the artisans inhabiting each neighborhood (tailors, goldsmiths, fishmongers, wine merchants) and mentions some of the darker spectacles of the city: prisons (Newgate), public punishments such as the burning of criminals' thumbs (E5v), the panders of Ludgate (E6r), and the lunatics of Bedlam, who "out of tune do talke" (E7r). She also invents marriages for the benefit of the young and dispossessed, representing the economics of coupling with realistic humor:

> To Maydens poore, I Widdoers ritch,
> > do leave, that oft shall dote:
> And by that meanes shal mary them,
> > to set the Girles aflote.
> And wealthy Widdowes wil I leave,
> > to help yong Gentylmen:
> Which when you have, in any case
> > be courteous to them then: . . .
>
> > > > > > > (E6v)

Whitney also advertises herself and her printer in a salute to "all the Bookebinders by Paulles / because I lyke their Arte." She specifies:

> Amongst them all, my Printer must,
> > have somwhat to his share:
> I wyll my friends there Bookes to bye
> > of him, with other ware.
>
> > > > > > (E6v)

In her concluding conceit, in which she personifies her writing instruments as witnesses to her will, she keeps an eye on her audience even as she imagines her death:

> [I] Did write this Wyll with mine owne hand
> > and it to London gave,
> In witnes of the standers by,
> > whose names yf you wyll have,
> Paper, Pen and Standish [inkwell] were:
> > at that same present by.
>
> > > > > > > (E8v)

By aligning herself with the city in which she says she was "bred," Whitney builds a link to London readers. Her invitation to them to listen in on ostensibly private occasions (the composition of a will, the penning of a letter to a lover) is typical of her writing. The isolated melancholy of Petrarchism and the metaphysics of Neoplatonism are equally foreign to the direct, confiding posture of this working city poet.

Whitney's colloquial directness contrasts strongly to Thomas Berrie's highflown epistle for the *Nosgay*, in which he attests to the poet's obedience to gender expectations. He opens with a scene of "Ladies fresh," walking where "the Laurell branch doth bring increase" (A8v), by which he appears to intend a sort of female Parnassus. But he doubles this fantasy setting in order to work out a compromise between domestic and literary labor: by carrying out household tasks ("some did twist the silke of lively hewe"), the laurel forest's inhabitants guarantee the virtue of their companions who pursue literary fame: "Some others slipt the Braunch for prayses dew." Berrie also insists on moral philosophy as a proper woman's genre. Whitney, he points out, has avoided epic and tragedy, modes reserved for male poets: "She doth not write the brute or force in Armes, / Nor pleasure takes, to sing of others harmes."[10] Instead, his metaphors for Whitney's text stress feminine orderliness and nurture: she has "mustered" her flowers and "wrapped" them "in a packe"; she refreshes "the brused mynde." He ends by promising that the simple style of the *Nosgay* corresponds to the intellectual limits of Whitney's female audience, whom he reminds of her earlier "Copy of a letter": "And for her second worke, she thought it meete, / Sith Maides with loftie stile may not agree" (B1v).

Whitney, too, has an eye to gender decorum. At the end of her preface, she modestly acknowledges that her course of reading, which left her with a "mazed mind" and "brused brayne," finally led her to "Plat his Plot," that is, Hugh Plat's collection of pseudo-Senecan proverbs, *The Floures of Philosophie* (1572). In her dedication to Mainwaring, she adopts the role of the woman who conserves what the man has acquired: "though [these flowers] be of another's growing, yet considering they be of my owne gathering and making up: respect my labour and regard my good wil[l]." Moreover, by setting Plat's prose aphorisms into verse, Whitney appears to be working in the tradition of women as translators, serving a male writer's text rather than producing a new one. But her "makeing up" of the prose mottoes in fact adds a great deal to them: lively rhythm, memorable rhyme, a colloquial energy lacking in the original. Whitney also adds pro-woman modifications to Plat's proverbs on gender relations.

A typical revision occurs in her version of Plat's "Floure 74," "The love of wicked persons can never be gotten but by wicked meanes." Whitney expands the general observation into a pointed warning aimed directly at her reader (Flower 75):

> The love of wicked persons must,
>   be got by wicked meanes:
> Make thine accompt, when thou hast done
>   and geve the devil thy gaines.
>
>   (C1v)

She also revises Plat's maxims about love in directions that undercut masculine claims to rationality. To his "Floure 63," "The lovers teares will soone appease his Ladies anger," she adds a contrasting statement about gender imbalance (65):

> The lovers te[a]res, wil soone appease
>   his Ladyes angry moode:
> But men will not be pacified,
>   if Wemen weepe a flood.
>
>   (B8v)

She decenters the masculine perspective in another of Plat's *sententiae* on love (66: "The best Phisition to heale the lovers wound, is she that stroke the blowe"):

> If love hath geven thee a blow,
>   and that thou art unsound,
> Make meanes that thou a plaster have,
>   of them which gave the wound.
>
>   (68, B8v)

In her "them," Whitney generalizes the proverb to include both sexes. Her neutral pronoun takes away the blame attached to the beloved, presumed in Plat's "she that stroke the blow" to be a dangerous woman.

Why did Whitney decide to versify Plat? Richard Panofsky points out that Plat's *Floures* belonged to a potentially profitable genre, the collection of moral commonplaces popular with Tudor audiences. Plat had scanned late Roman and medieval philosophers as well as contemporary English books for extractable proverbs, which he arranged in a set of 883 prose "Floures," lacking any principle of organization. Whitney transformed this arid and rambling series of *sententiae* in several ways. She cut it down enormously; she organized maxims into thematic groups (fortune, friendship, love); she expanded Plat's terse sentences into metrical mottoes written in a memorizable iambic heptameter. All of these were devices calculated to increase the popularity of Plat's material. Most important, Whitney combined three genres into a new structure: she framed Plat's maxims with the story of her discovery of his book and with the group-composed letter anthology of the "familiar Epistles." As Panofsky puts it, she thereby created "a strong narrative occasion from the beginning, placing the sentences from Plat's book into the context of a personal experience," and she produced a text "original . . . in its application of life to literary convention."[11]

It is important to recognize how literary that "life" is, however, because the consciousness of an audience in the autobiographical narrative of the *Nosgay* restropectively clarifies Whitney's strategies in her love poem "The Copy of a letter." *A Sweet Nosgay* is original because Whitney inserts complaints about her poverty and illness into an emerging literary mode, the Ovidian lament, and joins to that mixture a set of responses from friends who are capable of writing presentably salable rhymed epistles. The group authorship and the consoling advice of the "Familier and friendly Epistles" illustrate two central themes in Plat: the importance of friendship and the necessity for enduring the blows of fortune patiently. So the Senecan maxims Whitney versifies from Plat dignify the group portrait she assembles from the epistles, and, conversely, the local specificity of the portrait dramatizes a situation in which stoic patience has evident value. Whitney makes her *Nosgay* into a three-way intersection of literary genres in order to characterize herself as an unfortunate but virtuous woman writer, energetically engaged with her family and friends and enlightened by ancient counsels of wisdom in adversity.

She uses a similar strategy of mixed genres in her lover's lament "The Copy of a letter lately written in meeter, by a yonge Gentilwoman: to her unconstant lover." In this poem and its sequel, "An Admonition to al yong Gentilwomen, and to all other Mayds in general to beware of mennes flattery," Whitney maneuvers for a positive position as a woman speaker. This is not easy, given that she adopts the newly fashionable mode of Ovid's *Heroides*, in which the Roman poet represented attempts by seduced and abandoned heroines to reclaim the men who had betrayed them. Ovid's Dido, Medea, and Ariadne were well known to English readers. The publisher William Caxton had printed a translation of the *Heroides* among his first offerings in the fifteenth century, Erasmus had recommended using the poems as models for letterwriting, and George Turbervile had just resuscitated the text in his 1567 translation, *The Heroycall Epistles . . . of Ovidius*.[12] Whitney shifts the voices of Ovid's solitary heroines into the speaking position of a marriage counselor whose opinions are legitimated by decades of advice books. As a result, she writes to her "unconstant lover" not as his victim but as his superior. She then turns to an audience of women as a social and literary critic, to expose men's deceptions of women. Her protest against her own mistreatment in "The Copy of a letter" becomes in "An Admonition" a generalized protest against gender arrangements in the society at large.

One strategy in "The Copy of a letter" is that it purports to be a private communication: Richard Jones's title invites the reader to eavesdrop on the "lately" abandoned fiancée as she pleads with her beloved to return. But the fact that the letter is "written in meeter" proves that it was a literary performance from the start, not a text meant only for the lover's eyes. Jones added two further poems to the set, epistles addressed by men to unfaithful mistresses. His title page, announcing that Whitney's poem is "Newly joyned to a Loveletter sent by a Bacheler, (a most faithfull Lover) to an unconstant and faithles Mayden," promises a kind of debate that was extremely popular in the sixteenth century. Examples included Thomas Elyot's *The Defence of Good Women* (1540), which pits the misogynist Caninius against the scholarly Candidus and the admirable Zenobia, and Edmund Tilney's *The flower of friendshippe* [1568], which sets Lady Julia and Erasmus, the defenders of husbands' authority, against the less orthodox Isabella.[13] Whitney's first poem, then, drew on a newly fashionable classical mode for its form and tied in thematically with a popular debate. Jones advertised the collection in a poem, "The Printer to the Reader," in which he promised both journalistic truth and literary invention to a male audience:

> What lack you Maister mine?
>   Some trifle that is trew?
> Why, then this same will serve your turne
>   the which is also new. . . .
>
> The matter of it selfe,
>   is true as many know:
> And in the same, some fained tales
>   the Auctor doth bestow.
>
> Therfore, bye this same Booke
>   of him that heere doth dwell:
> And you (I know) wyll say you have
>   bestowed your mon[e]y well.

This appeal to a sensation-seeking public helps to explain the mixed tones of Whitney's "Letter," which shifts between dramatically intimate accusations in the Ovidian mode and a cooler, well-wishing camaraderie. She begins aggressively by forestalling her lover's denial that he plans to marry another woman:

> As close as you your wedi[n]g kept
>   yet now the trueth I he[a]re:
> Which you (yer [ere] now) might me have told
>   what nede you nay to swere?

But then, less predictably, she pulls back to wish him luck:

> You know I always wisht you wel
>   so wyll I during lyfe:
> But sith you shal a Husband be
> God send you a good wyfe.
>
>   (A2r)

Rather than dwelling on the miseries of the past and present, as Ovid's heroines do, Whitney negotiates the position of the betrayed woman by concentrating on the future. An attitude of detached counsel prevails throughout most of the poem, reinforced by a grammatical oddity that emphasizes the distance between Whitney as speaker and her fiancé as listener: she uses the formal "you" rather than the intimate "thou." After her wistful reminder of her loyalty, she represents herself accepting the man's departure in a spirit of practical realism:

> And this (where so you shal become)
>   full boldly may you boast:
> That once you had as true a Love,
>   as dwelt in any Coast. . . .
> But yf that needes you marry must,
>   then farewell, hope is past.

But she then challenges the man in a transition that allows her to begin deploying her "fained tales" in a list of masculine betrayals drawn from familiar classical sources. She begins by daring him to distinguish himself from Sinon, the Greek who deceived the Trojans into taking the wooden horse into their city: "Now chuse whether ye wyll be true, / or be of SINONS trade." This is a curious analogy; Sinon's treachery had nothing to do with love. Whitney seems to be implying that all's unfair in love and war as men wage them. As the capital letters show, she is also heaping up the classical allusions advertised in Jones's preface. From Sinon, she moves on to a threat. Her public exposure of her lover's unfaithfulness will shame his sex by placing him in the category of earlier traitors to women:

> Whose trade if that you long shal use
>   it shal your kindred stayne:
> Example take by many a one
>   whose falshood now is playne.

> As by ENEAS first of all,
>   who dyd poore DIDO leave,
> Causing the Quene by his untrueth
>   with Sword her hart to cleave.
>   (A2r)

After Aeneas, Whitney deconstructs other classical heroes by applying a prowoman rather than an epic criterion to their careers: Theseus, Jason, and Paris, whom she blames rather than Helen for the fall of Troy, "all through the Grecian Rape" (A3v). Her allusions to classical couples fulfill Jones's promise of an entertaining "trifle," but the stanza in which she concludes her list of betrayals is written in a register of righteous indignation very different from a mere rehearsal of Ovidian anecdotes. Here Whitney speaks neither as a pathetic victim nor as a humanist poet, but as a judge who has seen through the antique glamor of these heroes to their moral failing:

> For they, for their unfaithfulnes,
>   did get perpetuall fame:
> Fame? wherfore dyd I terme it so?
>   I should have cald it shame.
>   (A3v)

The same kind of confident moral judgment is the norm for the next section of the poem, in which Whitney advises the man on how to choose a wife. A clear reversal of the power relations encoded into contemporary discourses on gender occurs in her move from rejected fiancée to marriage expert. Describing the ideal wife with all the authority of a male divine, Whitney appropriates the position of sermonizers such as Edward Hake and William Gouge. In a more secular vein, she also uses "fained tales" as models of the feminine ideal, much as Robert Greene would soon do in his *Penelope's Web* (1587), in which he cites heroines of romance as illustrations of obedience, chastity, and silence.[14]

Whitney represents herself as a model of moral conduct in a stanza preceding her portrait of the ideal wife as though she were demonstrating her own worthiness for the position. She claims a sensible resignation unimaginable in the passionate diatribes of Ovid's heroines:

> But if I can not please your minde,
>   for wants that rest in me:
> Wed whom you list, I am content,
>   your refuse for to be.
>
>   (A4r)

Whitney's phrasing of the stanza that introduces her portrait of the good wife might imply jealous mistrust of her lover's choice:

> For she that shal so happy be,
>   of thee to be elect:
> I wish her vertues to be such,
>   she nede not be suspect.

But as treatises on femininity demonstrate, women were "suspect" by reason of their sex whether their actions justified it or not. Whitney's language here echoes Protestant ideology: the notion of "election," the sense that a woman's purity is always under scrutiny. What is striking is that the *woman* poet adopts the traditionally masculine position of surveillance over women.

She goes on to list predictable wifely virtues, embellishing them with classical allusions:

> I rather wish her HELENS face,
>   then one of HELENS trade:
> with chastnes of PENELOPE
>   the which did never fade.
>
> A LUCRES for her constancy,
>   and Thisbie for her trueth:

Clearly, some table-turning is going on here. Rather than accept her lover's power to reject her because she lacks desirability, Whitney offers him a portrait of what feminine desirability ought to be. The portrait is actually an assignment, a reminder of the proper basis for a young man's courtship. Further, Whitney intends to be overheard giving this advice; it is written to impress

readers who share reigning views on love and marriage. Rather than repro-
ducing the pleading of Ovid's abandonèd mistresses (and providing pleasure
to male readers by representing men's power over such women), Whitney
delivers a mini-sermon. By replacing eros with didactic ventriloquism, by writing to the world through the mediating figure of the faithless man, she escapes from the Ovidian discourse of dead-ended feminine passion and courts
a readership of contemporary Londoners. The success of her pamphlet is indi-
cated by Jones's willingness to publish her *Nosgay* six years later.

She also adopts a masculine position to argue for herself as the right
woman for the man, which allows her to do so in a sober rather than a
seductive vein. The witty casuistry of an aristocratic love poet like Philip
Sidney would have been shocking in a woman poet. Especially in middle
sixteenth-century England, few women would have been willing to risk representing themselves as seductresses. Instead, Whitney invokes the virtues
of the bourgeois wife to win back her lover. In the quatrain following her
portrait of Penelope/Lucrece, she claims that she has depicted herself in it
(with the modest qualification that she lacks Helen's beauty):

> Perchance, ye will think this thing rare,
> 　in on[e] woman to fynd:
> Save Helens beauty, al the rest
> 　the Gods have me assignd.

All Whitney's terms in this argument turn around merit and rights. She invokes public concepts of justice rather than the private intensities of passion
to make her case:

> These words I do not spe[a]k, thinking
> 　from thy new Love to turne thee:
> Thou knowst by pro[o]f what I deserve
> 　I nede not to inform thee.

If the poem is read at a surface level, as a woman's letter to the man who
has jilted her, its purposes seem muddled. The writer appears to have in-
compatible goals. Does she want to expose the villainy of her betrothed or to
win him back? Is she writing to prove her forgiveness or to set up a public
vendetta against the man who has abandoned her? The contradictions become understandable, however, if we recognize that Whitney is, rather, attempting to win multiple literary admirers, more valuable in the long run
than a fickle fiancé. This is the interpretation that makes most sense of the
poem in its sociocultural context.

In her conclusion Whitney returns to her realistic, even insouciant acceptance of fate. She writes the farewell of a woman who intends to survive
rather than succumb to poverty, a lover's betrayal, or disempowering literary
convention. Her detached charity toward the man aligns her with the divine
perspective she prays for as his final reward:

> But let that passe; would God I had
> Cassandraes gift me lent:
> Then either thy yll chaunce or mine
> my foresight might prevent.
>
> But all in vayne for this I seeke,
> wishes may not attaine it
> Therefore may hap to me what shall,
> and I cannot refraine it.
>
> Wherfore I pray God be my guide
> and also thee defend:
> No worser then I wish my selfe,
> untill thy lyfe shall end.
>
> Which life I pray God, may agayne
> King Nestors lyfe renew:
> And after that your soule may rest
> amongst the heavenly crew.
>   (D5r)

I have been arguing that this combination of classical allusion and sturdy self-sufficiency was better calculated to appeal to readers of both sexes in Whitney's London than were the translated histrionics of Ovid's heroines. Similarly assertive in her final stanzas, Whitney refers her beloved to the "Admonition by the Auctor" for a further understanding of her state of mind. That is, the farewell to the lover is also an invitation to the literary sequel of the "Letter." In each "you" that Whitney ostensibly addresses to her private lover, she speaks to her public audience:

> And now farewel, for why at large
> my mind is here exprest:
> The which you may perceive, if that
> you do peruse the rest.

Many of the devices Whitney uses in the "Letter" reappear in her "Admonition," especially her combination of classical allusion and contemporary gender discourse. But the differences between the two poems are revealing, too. Because she is speaking to "mayds," members of her own sex, her attitude is less detached and judgmental, more a demonstration of solidarity with other women in danger from men.[15] And rather than rewriting male heroes, she attacks male poets, exposing Ovid as a teacher of deception. In this, she sides with educators such as Vives and Bruto, who were equally hostile to what they saw as the amorality of Roman love poetry. But the fact that Whitney is writing as a woman to women brings a newly gendered cultural politics into play; she represents herself as sharing her readers' vulnerability to neoclassical rhetoric. She also wrestles with the inherited language of denunciation that targeted women as temptresses and deceivers by allying herself with "mayds" whom she shows how to avoid temptation by men. As in "The Copy of a letter," she presents her disillusionment not as a spectacle of pathos but as a basis for practical advice.

The poem opens with a mixed-class address to "all yong Gentilwomen: And to al other Maids being in Love." Whitney establishes herself as a modest helper rather than a preacher from above, but she also points out the value of her text, written by a woman who knows the situation of her readers well enough to give them useful advice:

> To you I speake: for you be they,
>   that good advice do lacke:
> Oh, if I could good counsell geve,
>   my tongue would not be slacke.
>   (A5v)

> But such as I can geve, I wyll,
>   here in few wordes expresse:
> Which if you do observe, it will
>   some of your care redresse.

In her warning about men, Whitney uses a pair of images that demonstrate how saturated with suspicion of *women* the language available to her is. To criticize men's falsity, she has at hand the cultural stereotypes of the woman who paints her face and the Sirens who attempt to seduce good men from the paths of virtue.[16] With unsettling effect, she takes up the discourse evolved by moralists and satirists, from Solomon and Juvenal to Vives and Hake, and turns it against men:

> Beware of fayre and painted talke,
>   beware of flattering tonges:
> The Mermaides do pretend no good
>   for all their pleasant Songs.
>   (A6r)

If the male mermaid is a troubling mixture, Whitney's attack on traditional masculine literary discourse is also complex. She cites Ovid's *Ars amatoria* not to do homage to the Latin past but to expose the text's use against women:

> Some use the teares of Crocodiles,
>   contrary to their hart:
> And yif they cannot alwayes weepe,
>   they wet their Cheekes by Art.

> Ovid, within his Arte of love,
>   doth teach them this same knacke
> To wet their hand & touch their eies:
>   so oft as teares they lacke.

This, too, is a curiously mixed passage: Whitney simultaneously signals her knowledge of Roman poetry and rejects it as morally suspect. The double strategy results from her double audience: the women to whom the poem is ostensibly addressed and the "Maisters" to whom Jones advertises his "new trifles," that is, the majority of bookbuyers. Her attention to this second set of readers becomes explicit in her sudden shift from advice to women to an attack on their enemies:

> Why have ye such deceit in store?
>   have you such crafty wile?
> Lesse craft then this god knows wold soone
>   us simple soules begile.
>
> And wyll ye not leave of[f]? but still
>   delude us in this wise?
> Sith it is so, we trust we shall,
>   take hede to fained lies.

The source of such "lies" is ambiguous: does she mean poets' lies or lovers' lies? Both. She goes on to list a series of women misled by men in the *Metamorphoses* and *Heroides*: Scylla, rejected by Minos; Oenone, abandoned by Paris; Phyllis, deceived by Demophoön. As a counterexample, she mentions Leander, a true lover whom Hero "did trie . . . / before that she did trust" (A7v). Whitney shares her countrymen's fascination with Ovid, but she interprets him to a feminine audience whom she encourages to be suspicious readers, both of ancient texts and of the men who follow their suggestions in the present. While in "The Copy of a letter" she refuses the role of tragic victim and rejects the epic criteria by which such heroes as Aeneas are glorified, here she goes on the offensive, inviting her women readers into a group identity, a "we" armed against men's sexual strategies by a knowledge of their literary model. "The Admonition" is imitation with a difference.

The poem ends with a fanciful apostrophe to a trusting fish trapped by a false lure. Although Whitney uses the masculine pronoun to describe the fate of the fish, it is clear that she is displacing the amorous misadventure she dramatizes in "A letter" onto this piscatory alter ego:

> The little fish that carelesse is,
>   within the water cleare:
> How glad he is, when he doth see,
>   a Bayt for to appeare.
>
> He thinks his hap right good to bee,
>   that he the same could spie:
> And so the simple foole doth trust
>   to[o] much before he trie.

Why transform the lament of the forlorn mistress into the proverbial tale of a captured fish? The analogy allows Whitney to accomplish two things. She avoids the spectacular self-pity she also refuses in "A letter," although she can speak sympathetically, even tenderly, to this victim, imagined as a member of another species; and she can propose a happier fate for her sex, a secure life shared by the "mayds" of her title. Whitney's fancy and humor are as much a part of her protofeminist rhetoric as her direct assaults on the masculine complicity built into literary tradition:

> O little fish what hap hadst thou?
>   to have such spitefull fate:
> To come into ones cruell hands,
>   out of so happy state?

> Thou diddst suspect no harme, when thou
>   upon the bait didst looke:
> O that thou hadst had Linceus eies
>   for to have seene the hooke.

> Then hadst thou with thy prety mates
>   bin playing in the streames,
> Wheras Syr Phebus dayly doth,
>   shew forth his golden beames.

Whitney concludes the poem not on an elegaic note, as might be expected, but with a confident statement of her will to survive, as in the brisk farewell of "A letter." The similarity is no accident. This is the resolution of a woman determined to write, and, by being both useful and amusing, to fulfill the criteria of teaching and entertaining repeated throughout sixteenth-century poetics citing Horace's theory of the *dulce et utile*. Whitney also asserts the rationality of women against Renaissance arguments that they lacked it, and she repeats the solid female "we" of her early stanzas:

> And since the fish that reason lacks
>   once warned doth beware:
> Why should not we take hede to that
>   that turneth us to care.

> And I who was deceived late,
>   by ones unfaithfull teares,
> Trust now for to beware, if that
>   I live this hundreth yeares.

>   (A8v)

Taken together, Whitney's poems show how a woman writer could revise the subject positions of Ovidian tradition by drawing sixteenth-century demands upon women into both the thematic and performative levels of her lyrics: she writes about the good woman in the persona of a good woman. She also writes with a constant alertness to a double public: the male readers her publisher invites to buy *A Sweet Nosgay* and an audience of women likely to appreciate her confident self-representation and subversive humor. Whitney composes for groups; in the *Nosgay*, in fact, she composes as a member of a group, building the responses of her friends and family into her collection. She works outside the category of poet as solitary genius, a status to which postromantic critical opinion has assigned canonized writers in a serious misunderstanding of the common literary practice of the Renaissance. Whitney demonstrates the networks of need and appeal, of creative accommodation and subtle critique, through which women poets (like men) constructed texts acceptable to the system of gender expectations and publishing practices that governed early modern writing.

CATHERINE DES ROCHES: LAWYER'S DAUGHTER, POET'S DAUGHTER, COTERIE HEROINE

Catherine des Roches wrote in Poitiers during the 1570s, the decade after Isabella Whitney's publications in London, but the French and the English poet shared the same ambition: both wrote to make a living. Catherine des Roches was the daughter of Madeleine Neveu, who had outlived two lawyer husbands, André Fradonnet, who died in 1547, five years after Catherine was born, and François Eboissard, whose death in 1578 left his widow embroiled in lawsuits that lasted thirteen years.[17] (The quasi-noble surname used by mother and daughter came from a landholding called Les Roches, owned by Madeleine). Madeleine also lost two houses in Protestant attacks on the city of Poitiers in 1569. Although she began petitioning for recompense for this loss to Henri III in 1578, the year she was widowed, she received a royal grant for two thousand livres only in 1587. Both women managed the property remaining to them, collecting rents, suing debtors, and making loans. Such negotiations indicate that the Dames des Roches were much more prosperous than Whitney ever hoped to be.

Still, inherited property alone was not enough to support them. The publication of their first Oeuvres occurred in the same year as Madeleine's second widowhood, and in their final publication, Les Missives (1586), Madeleine commented gratefully that Catherine had supported them both with her pen, "sans mendier l'aide d'autruy" (without asking help from anyone else).[18] Letters from Madeleine also suggest that both mother and daughter accepted commissions as poets. In one, she sends a sonnet, as requested, to a noblewoman of Poitiers; in another, she thanks another woman client for her liberal payment to Catherine for an epitaph for her husband.[19] How much Abel L'Angelier, their publisher, paid them for their collections is not known, but they were obviously eager to sell him what they had. In the final letter of Les Missives, Catherine leaves the selection and the order of the letters entirely up to the printer: "Give them whatever title you think best, Missives or Letters or Epistles, for readers' curiosity will perhaps mean more rapid sales . . . and whichever of my writings you find least worth reading, throw them into the fire."[20]

The mother-daughter pair worked successfully to make their poems known. Both Les Oeuvres (1578, 1579) and Les Secondes oeuvres (1583,

1586) went into a third printing in Rouen in 1604, and *La Puce* (1582), a collection of poems by Catherine, Madeleine, and lawyers from Paris who had spent several months in their salon in Poitiers in 1579, went into a second and larger printing in 1583. Madeleine and Catherine also aimed for a readership beyond Poitiers. They offered their first collection to L'Angelier, a Parisian printer, because he could give them better access to court readers; they also addressed poems directly to the French king and queen, Henri III and Louise of Lorraine. This search for patronage did not go unnoticed. Catherine eventually felt the need to publish a sharp little epigram defending herself against charges of venality toward her rulers (*Oeuvres*, 1578, 147):

> A G. P.
> Vous dictes que je vends ces vers à leurs hautesses,
> Non, je ne les vends point: le present est entier,
> Car je proteste Dieu que Princes ny Princesses
> Ne m'ont jamais donné la valeur d'un denier.[21]

> You say that I sell these verses to their Highnesses,
> No, I sell them not at all: they are wholly a gift,
> For I call on God to witness that Princes or Princesses
> Have never paid me so much as the twelfth of a sou.

The Des Roches's court connections are recorded in an elegant handwritten anthology of poems addressed to members of the royal family, collected between 1578 and 1584, which includes several poems by both of them.[22] It seems likely that the king's grant to Madeleine finally came about as a result of royal appreciation of their poems. When Jehan Maignen, a councillor and secretary to the king, sent a notice that the sum had been authorized, he wrote to the Des Roches's lawyer that he had intervened "in order to show mesdames des Roches" how much he "honored their virtue."[23] Various scholars and writers celebrated the poets, including the humanist Joseph-Juste Scaliger, the lawyer-poet Etienne Pasquier, the court poet Pierre de Ronsard, Marie de Romieu in her *Discours de l'excellence de la femme* (1581),[24] François Billon, and Agrippa d'Aubigné.

The Des Roches held a salon for lawyers, doctors, and other highly placed professionals in their city house for years,[25] but their major entry into cultural life beyond Poitiers came when Les Grands Jours, a special session of the Poitiers lawcourts, began in the fall of 1579. Because the legal structures of the city were overwhelmed as a result of battles between Catholics and Protestants, Henri III decreed that lawyers from the Paris courts should go down to Poitiers to help finish the term's work. Some of these men, aware of the Des Roches's reputation as learned and witty women, made their way to their salon as soon as they arrived in the city. Etienne Pasquier wrote a long letter describing the afternoon and evening meetings there, which included competitions in improvising poetry. He singled out Catherine in a passage that reveals a typically sixteenth-cen-

tury surprise at seeing eloquence and wit combined with chastity in a
young woman:

> We still cannot cease talking. She is an unassailable Rock [Rocher], this woman
> I contend with in verse. I cannot challenge her without receiving a brilliant
> defense in return, from a pen so daring that I hesitate ever to write to her
> again. Not only does she refuse to owe a thing, she pays her debts with exces-
> sive interest, and she asks for no delay at all in acquitting them. I have never
> seen a mind as quick or as steady as hers. She is a woman who never lacks an
> answer. And yet no word ever comes from her that is unsuitable for a well
> behaved girl.[26]

This remark defines precisely what Catherine des Roches needed to accomplish in her self-representation as a poet. Like Whitney, she combined
wit with feminine propriety in ways that earned her admirers rather than
critics, drawing on reigning cultural discourses to claim permission for her
career and to expand her audience. Unlike Whitney, she moved in the haut-
bourgeois, semiprivate sphere of an urban coterie, chaperoned by her
mother but open to "civil conversation" with professional men who cultivated one another while watching the spoken and written performances of
their hostesses. Judging from La Puce, the group publication of this coterie,
its ambience was closer to the erotic, hyperverbal atmosphere of Castiglione's Urbino than to Whitney's working London. Pasquier's pretext for the
Poitiers collection was that he had seen a flea on Catherine's breast. By addressing compliments on the insect's good luck and good taste to Madeleine
des Roches, he opened a contest as to who could compose the most intricate
or amusingly salacious poem on the occasion. A wild rivalry ensued, in
which learned doctors composed verses in Greek, Latin, Italian, and Spanish
to produce more than eighty pages of mock heroic, punning, precious, and
obscene lyrics in honor of Catherine's flea (fig. 2).[27]

What was Catherine's role in this group game? Very much what it had
been and continued to be in the poems she published with her mother. Putting Castiglione's requirements for the donna di palazzo into practice in her
less aristocratic milieu, she maintained a reputable decency in a context of
generalized flirtation: she balanced witty affability with modesty by means
of an imperturbable Neoplatonism and a didactic rather than participatory
attitude toward love. The balance was especially delicate in La Puce, as a
comparison of Catherine's and Pasquier's first poems shows: gender permissions and prohibitions determine their underlying scenarios. Pasquier describes the woman's body in cartographic detail, following a long tradition
from Greek lyric through the Romance of the Rose, a tradition that had produced a similar contest, initiated by Clément Marot in 1536, in which male
poets competed in composing blasons, poems in praise of feminine body
parts, later published in a group text, Blasons anatomiques du corps femenin.[28]
Pasquier identifies with the flea as sexual aggressor in a fantasy of sucking,
biting, and penetration:

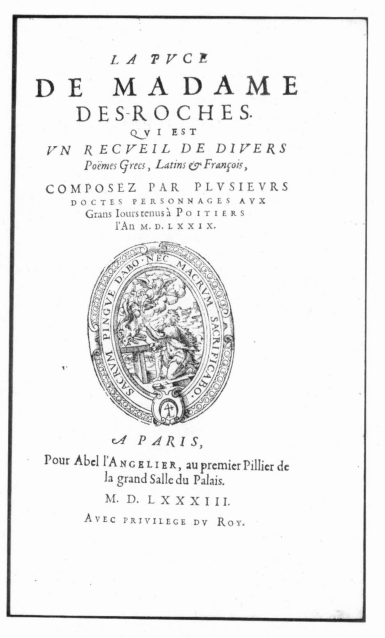

LA PVCE

DE MADAME

DES-ROCHES.

QVI EST

VN RECVEIL DE DIVERS

Poëmes Grecs , Latins & François ,

COMPOSEZ PAR PLVSIEVRS

DOCTES PERSONNAGES AVX

Grans Iours tenus à POITIERS

l'An M. D. L X X I X.

A PARIS,

Pour Abel l'ANGELIER, au premier Pillier de
la grand Salle du Palais.

M. D. L X X X I I I.

AVEC PRIVILEGE DV ROY.

Fig. 2. Title page of *La Puce*. (By permission of the Houghton
Library, Harvard University.)

> Puce qui te viens percher
> Dessus cette tendre chair,
> Aux milieu des deux mammelles
> De la plus belle des belles:
> Qui la piques, qui la poins,
> Qui la mors à tes bons poins. . . .
> O que je te porte envie
> A l'heur fatal de ta vie.[29]

> Flea, which comes to perch
> Upon this tender flesh,
> In between the breasts
> Of the fairest of the fair:
> You prick her, you stick her,
> You nip her where you like. . . .
> O how envious I am
> At the last hour of your life.

The male poet makes his identification with the flea explicit in his next lines by addressing the woman in the voice of the flea. Ever more risqué, he leaves her body parts suggestively unmentioned and flirts with hyperbolic blasphemy:

> Plust or à Dieu que je pusse
> Seulement devenir Puce:
> Tantost je prendrois mon vol
> Tout au plus beau de ton col,
> Ou d'une douce rapine,
> Je succerois ta poitrine,
> Ou lentement pas à pas
> Je me glisserois plus bas,
> Et d'un muselin folastre
> Je serois Puce idolatre,
> Pinçoittant je ne sçay quoi
> Que j'ayme trop' plus que moy.

> If only God now willed that I
> Might in turn become a flea,
> I'd immediately take flight
> To the fairest spot on your neck,
> Or, in sweeter thievery,
> I would suck upon your breast,
> Or else slowly, step by step,
> I would slide yet farther down,
> And there, with a merry muzzle
> I'd become a flea idolator,
> Lightly pricking I'll not say what,
> Which I love more than myself.

It is hard to imagine how Catherine would have responded to hearing this poem read aloud; it was doubtless a good thing that she already had a poem of her own ready. George Diller, a 1930s critic of the Des Roches, takes the entire collection as proof that strict morality could coexist with the complete absence of prudery in the sixteenth century.[30] But the differences between the man's poem and the woman's suggest to me that the "coexistence" was problematic. Discursive segregation seems a more accurate term: the voyeuristic gaze and the enumeration of caresses were reserved for the men in the Poitiers coterie. Catherine works out a different fantasy entirely, using Ovid's *Metamorphoses* as a model to invent a female flea interested not in seduction but in self-protection. The flea, she imagines, was once a nymph pursued by Pan; now, changed by Diana into a safer if lower form of life, she preserves her innocence through a physical agility that parallels the verbal agility the woman poet needs to negotiate the sexual fireworks going off all around her. In her speeches to the flea, she replaces male rivalry with female empathy:

> Pan, voyant voz perfections,
> Sentit un feu d'affections,
> Desirant vostre mariage:
> Mais quoy? vostre vierge courage
> Aima mieux vous faire changer
> En Puce, à fin de l'étranger. . . .
> Depuis fuyant tousjours ce Dieu,
> Petite, vous cherchez un lieu
> Qui vous serve de sauvegarde,
> Et craignez que Pan vous regarde.
>
> (2)

> Pan, seeing your perfection,
> Felt the fire of affection,
> And desired to marry you:
> But then your virgin's bold resolve
> Preferred to change you to a flea,
> So as to leave him far behind.
> Since then, fleeing from the god,
> Little one, you seek a place
> Which can promise you safekeeping,
> And still you fear that Pan can see you.

Although Catherine's eight-syllable lines echo the racy, shifting meter of Pasquier's couplets, she uses rhythm to suggest flighty panic rather than furtive sexual exploration:

> Bien souvent la timidité
> Fait voir vostre dexterité,
> Vous sautelez à l'impourveuë,
> Quand vouz soupconnés d'etre vue,
> Et de vous ne reste, sinon
> La crainte, l'adresse, et le nom.

> Often, your timidity
> Demonstrates your dexterity:
> You leap about unexpectedly
> When you suspect that you've been seen,
> And nothing of you remains behind
> Except your fear, your skill and name.

That final line is emblematic of Catherine's performance throughout the group-composed text. Fear of scandal leads her to quick and witty improvisation, through which she hopes to win a name, fame for literary virtuosity rather than "defame," as Thomas Salter put it, for imitating the lascivious wordplay of her male interlocutors.

Throughout her poems in *La Puce*, she continues to distinguish herself from her male companions in the coterie. To turn aside the jocular eroticism permitted to them by social and literary convention, she uses Neoplatonism as a counterconvention through which she can demonstrate the high-minded chastity she is constrained to display. But she also builds subtle self-advertisement into the contrasts she sets up between the men's racy texts and her own Neoplatonic rhetoric. One example is her response to Claude Binet. He follows Pasquier by writing a poem in which he identifies with the flea as it voyages around "le sein de la Pucelle" (the maiden's breast) to her armpits and nipples, although he shifts into a loftier gear toward the end by linking Catherine to Minerva, who, as Neoplatonic creator-goddess, has given birth to her as the "unique marvel of this time" (27). Catherine responds only on this second level, ignoring the close bodily focus of the *blason du tétin* that makes up most of Binet's poem. She insists that she does not deserve the elevated praise of his last lines, but she appropriates it in order to elaborate the creation of the exemplary woman Binet praises in her:

> Dy moy Rochette que fais tu?
> Ha tu rougis, c'est de la honte
> De voir un portraict qui surmonte
> Ta foible et debile vertue.
>
> BINET a voulu dextrement
> Representer une peinture,
> Qui est de celeste nature,
> Et la nommer humainement.[31]
>
> (30)
>
> Little Rock, what's your response?
> Aha, you're blushing; it's from shame
> At seeing a portrait that exceeds
> Your minor, negligible worth.
>
> Binet has deigned, with witty skill,
> To represent to us here below
> A painting of heavenly origin
> And to give it a human name.

Her closing repetition of her pun on her name likewise asserts a counteridentity to the female body so erotically figured by Binet:

> ROCHE tu ne sçaurois user
> D'un autre plus evident signe
> D'estre de tant d'honneurs indigne,
> Que ne pouvoir t'en excuser.

> Rock, you could not provide
> A more self-evident sign
> Of being unworthy of such honor
> Than the feebleness of your demurral.

Does Catherine's blush function as a reproach for Binet's wanton talk? In Castiglione's *Courtier*, Giuliano recommends precisely this symptom of embarrassment to women when group conversation becomes risqué.[32] But Catherine's response is more deliberate. Like the heroine of another courtly manual, Phausina, the model of womanly wit in Agostino Nifo's *De re aulica* (Naples, 1534),[33] she simply ignores the indecency of the man's remarks, changing the subject as though he had written nothing obscene.

In her response she capitalizes Binet's name as well as her own, to call attention to her participation in a game played by well-known men. Similarly, her response to another poem, "La Puce d'Odet de Tournebu, Advocat en la cour de Parlement," clarifies the process of mutual self-glorification that motivated the oral exchanges in the Poitiers salon and in this literary record of them. Turnèbe's title emphasizes his professional status, while his poem emphasizes the distinction of other members of the salon, to whom he declares his inferiority. Catherine responds with a graceful compliment: Turnèbe's "wise and beautiful soul" is reflected in his praise of her. But she adds a phrase to her title to call attention to her professional skill: "Response au sonet precedent faite sur le champ" (Response to the preceding sonnet, composed on the spot). In this game of compliment, refusal of compliment, and countercompliment, Catherine takes the role of an equal to her Parisian admirers.

But many of her other poems show her awareness of the double standard by which she risked being condemned for her ambition to write. Like Whitney, she took shelter against potential criticism by citing conventional ideals of womanly behavior, particularly the bourgeois emphasis on useful household work. In her first *Oeuvres*, she included "La femme forte descrite par Salomon," a paraphrase (loose translation) of the portrait in Proverbs 31 of the "virtuous woman" whose "price is far above rubies." Catherine's situation as woman poet in a suspicious era led her to write a much livelier version of the biblical text than the spare literal translation by Théodore de Bèze (published in Lausanne in 1556 and anthologized frequently thereafter), which she may have used as a starting point. His version of the passage is concise and unadorned:

Laine et filasse amassera
Pour entretenir son mesnage
Puis elle mesme filera,
Et des ses mains besognera
Franchement de bon courage.

Devant le jour se levera
Pour voir sa despense ordonnée
A sa famille pourvoira
Aux servantes ordonnera
Les ouvrages de leur journée.[34]

She'll gather wool and flax
To keep her household supplied,
Then spin wool herself
And labor with her hands
Openly, with a stout heart.

Before daybreak she'll rise
To arrange the day's spending;
For her family she'll provide;
To her servants she'll assign
Their tasks for the day.

The language of Catherine's expansion of the biblical passage counters the assumption that women's domestic and literary activities contradict one another. In "La femme forte descritte par Salomon," she implies that housewifely work and the writing of poetry have something in common by describing the processes of cloth making with the term used to justify poetry in contemporary aesthetics, the Horatian *dulce et utile*:

Ell' se leve au matin premier que le soleil
Monstre ses beaux rayons, et puis faict un ouvrage,
Ou de laine, ou de lin, pour servir son mesnage,
Tirant de son labeur un utile plaisir.

(148)

She rises in the morning early, before the sun
Shines forth its bright rays, and then sets to work
On wool or on flax, for her household's advantage,
Gaining from her labor a useful enjoyment.[35]

She also expands the portrait of the good woman to include various tools used by a mid-sixteenth-century housewife and her servants. In fact, she improves upon ritual invocations of the distaff and the spindle (*le quenouille* and *le fuseau*) as emblems of feminine virtue in conduct books. By naming the bundle of wool used in spinning and the bobbin used to wind up the fibers of the flax plant in linen making, she sets up a scene of domestic textile-work through which she demonstrates a more than conventional knowledge of household techniques:

Ses servantes aussi qu'elle a bien sçeu choisir,
Chassant l'oisiveté, sont toutes amusées
A cherpir, à peigner, à tourner leurs fusées
Faire virer le trueil, comme un petit moulin,
Le Chastelet aussi pour devider le lin.

Her maidservants, too, whom she's carefully chosen,
Chasing off idleness, entertain themselves all
By shredding flax, combing wool, twisting out skeins of it,
Twirling their spindles like miniature windmills,
And using the bobbin to wind up their fibers.

An engaging balance is worked out in this poem between the formal solemnity of the alexandrine lines and the familiar vocabulary. Catherine's method resembles Whitney's. By grafting popular contemporary material onto a prestigious ancient source, she shows that she is a good daughter of the bourgeoisie, expert in the details of womanly duty, and also a knowledgeable poet, able to organize them into the elevated meter appropriate for a translation from the Scriptures.

She works out a similar balance in a sonnet addressed to her distaff, the wooden baton on which a mass of wool was set in order to be spun. By juxtaposing the emblem of housewifery to the tools of the poet, she resolves an apparently irreconcilable ideological opposition. The poem's cajoling tone and shifting vocabularies are symptoms of the challenge Catherine confronts in balancing conflicting discourses to write her defense of poetry. As in Whitney's "Copy of a letter," a double audience is envisioned for this poem. Catherine speaks to the distaff as an intimate familiar, the symbol of domestic responsibilities she knows well, but she also uses it as a medium to placate a wider audience likely to be hostile to literary ambition in a woman:

> A ma quenoille
> Quenoille mon souci, je vous promets et jure,
> De vous aimer toujours, et jamais ne changer
> Vostre honneur domestic pour un bien etranger,
> Qui erre inconstamment, et fort peu de temps dure.
>
> (122)

> Distaff, my care, I promise you and swear
> That I'll love you forever and never exchange
> Your prestige in the household for an external good
> That wanders at random and lasts but a short time.

The circumlocution of the fourth line is significant. Desire for fame is so unthinkable in this domestic context that Catherine alludes to it only through periphrasis. Her declared preference for an alliance with the distaff rather than ink and paper is an equally defensive move, as spelled out by the military vocabulary in the second quatrain and by her attribution of autonomy to pen and paper, as though she dares not represent herself actively using either:

> Vous ayant au costé je suis beaucoup plus seure
> Que si [e]ncre e[t] papier se venoient à ranger
> Tout à l'entour de moy, car pour me revanger
> Vous pouvez bien plustost repousser une injure.

> With you at my side I am far more secure
> Than if ink and paper surrounded me
> In my defense, for in a counterattack
> You can much better repel an assault.

The tone becomes ever more propitiatory as Catherine proposes a truce with the distaff, in an apostrophe intended to persuade her audience that writing poetry need not oppose domestic virtue but can in fact celebrate it:

> Mais quenoille m'amie il ne faut pas pourtant
> Que pour vous estimer, et pour vous aimer tant
> Je delaisse du tout cest' honneste coustume
> D'escrire quelquefois[;] en escrivant ainsi
> J'escri[s] de voz valeurs, quenoille mon souci,
> Ayant dedans la main, le fuzeau, et la plume.

> But distaff, my love, it's still not required
> That because I admire you, and love you so much,
> I must give up entirely this honorable habit
> Of writing at times; for by writing as I do,
> I write of your value, distaff, my care,
> Holding spindle and pen together in my hand.

Some readers of the sonnet have seen a sly humor in it, as though Catherine were exaggerating her obedience to conflicting demands as a way of mocking their intransigence.[36] There is certainly comic potential in the image of a woman with both hands full of pens and spindles, distaffs and inkwells. But the propitiatory tone of the sonnet and its concluding compromise, its synthesis of the spindle *and* the pen against the either/or of bourgeois gender ideology, are more characteristic of what Anne Larsen calls Catherine's "conciliatory feminism"[37] than a parodic self-portrait would be.

Like Whitney, Catherine is more likely to aim her wit at men than at herself. For example, in a long prose text defending education for women, her "Dialogue de Placide et Severe," in her *Secondes oeuvres*, she mocks the misogynist Severe with high comic glee. She brings this straw man onstage "avec la face merveilleusement refrongnée"[38] (with an amazingly scowl-ridden face) and represents his misery at home as a clear case of well-deserved misfortune. His wife is bad tempered and disdainful, his daughter affected and rude, and he is too blind to see that his refusal to let them educate themselves is the cause. Instead, he absurdly declares himself superior to "ces petites Bestioles," whose imbecility cannot be compared to the rationality he attributes to men. When Severe says that if he found his wife reading, he "would soon let her know that her hand should reach for the distaff, not the book," Placide, the defender of women, denies the truth of this familiar opposition: "Each of these activities aids the other. Pallas Athene practiced them both" (37). Placide goes on to quote a song in which Severe's assumption that a learned woman will be immoral is pithily defeated:

> Les Dames qui veulent bien vivre
> Desireuses d'aprendre et voir
> Hantent les vertus et le livre,
> Mariant les meurs au sçavoir.
>
> (40)
>
> Ladies who wish to live well,
> Desiring to learn and to see
> Dwell both in virtue and books,
> Marrying morals to learning.

Less politely, Catherine, through Placide, wishes Severe the woman he deserves and compliments him ironically on his civility:

> Si pourtant vostre gentilesse
> Veut suivre le commun erreur,
> Puisse quelque sotte Maistresse,
> Bien tost vous dérober le cueur.
>
> Qu'en tout ce que vous pourrez faire,
> Soit pour servir, prier, crier,
> Jamais vous ne puissiez luy plaire,
> Ny de ses mains vous delier.
>
> (41)
>
> If, still, genteel sir, you persist
> In this common misjudgment [of women],
> May a thoroughly stupid mistress
> Soon run away with your heart.
>
> May everything that you can do,
> Serving her, praying or shouting,
> Never succeed in pleasing her
> Nor in freeing you from her grasp.

Such detachment and mockery are easy to manage in a dialogue, in which Catherine need not identify herself wholly with any character. When she writes love poetry, however, she faces a different set of problems, related to her gingerly performances in *La Puce*: how to maintain the appearance of chastity and intellectual self-sufficiency in the framework of amorous convention, which calls for a confessional or at least a first-person stance. Her solution is twofold. In a series of sonnets entitled "Sincero à Charite" and "Charite à Sincero," she adopts the position of stage manager or director, presenting a dialogue between two lovers rather than identifying herself exclusively with the woman. Her adoption of Charite as a nickname (meaning Grace, as in the Three Graces) was well known to members of the Poitiers coterie,[39] but she draws upon a rigorous version of Neoplatonic theory in order to teach rather than seduce the hero. Like Whitney, she establishes herself as advisor rather than passionate partner to the man in the case.

Catherine's preface to the series of sonnets is clearly intended to forestall any suspicion about her chastity. Addressing her remarks to her mother but aiming them at hostile critics, she responds to the objections she imagines being raised to a woman love poet by insisting that she is portraying an ideal rather than confessing a personal history:

> Ils diront peut estre que je ne devois pas escrire d'amour, que si je suis amoureuse il ne fault pas le dire, et si je ne suis telle il ne fault pas le feindre: je leur respondray à cela, que je ne le suis, ny ne feins de l'estre: car j'escry ce que j'ay pensé et non pas ce que j'ay veu en Syncero, lequel je ne connoy que par imagination. Mais comme il est advenu à quelques grands personnages de representer un Roy parfaict, un parfaict orateur, un parfaict courtisan, ainsi ai-je voulu former un parfaict amoureux. (*Oeuvres*, 53)

> Perhaps they will say that I shouldn't have written about love, that if I am in love, I must not say so, and if I am not, I mustn't pretend to be. To this I'd answer that I am neither in love nor pretending to be; for I write what I have thought, not what I have seen in Sincero, whom I know only through imagination. But just as it has happened that certain great men have represented a perfect king, a perfect orator, a perfect courtier, so I have tried to fashion a perfect lover.

In other words, Catherine is writing a verse courtesy book for men. What follows will be not only a sequence of Neoplatonic love poetry but an exemplary double portrait written to encourage masculine self-improvement.

In fact Catherine accomplishes more than this in the twenty-six sonnets she writes for Sincero and Charite. Although Sincero is given the opening lines in the preliminary prose dialogue and the first twelve sonnets, the collection as a whole gives conceptual and rhetorical control to Charite. She determines the vocabulary Sincero uses, she sets up a series of norms for him to follow, she mocks and threatens him, and she uses him as a mirror to reflect her own articulate perfection. One reason that Catherine insists in her preface that fantasy rather than fact has ruled as she composed the poems may well be that the symbolic world of Sincero and Charite so totally reverses the power relations in the social world the poet inhabited.

George Diller argues that the poems to Sincero were written to Claude Pellejay, the son of a lawyer from Poitiers, whose family was close to relatives of the Des Roches. Pellejay went to Paris to study mathematics, worked for a time as secretary to the Duke of Anjou, soon to be Henri III, and spent most of his later life as a financial officer for the court. He was known to have written two early collections of songs and sonnets to Catherine des Roches; although these were never published, she wrote him thanks for sending her another poem, his "Hymne de la Beauté."[40] Diller's case strikes me as plausible, especially his citation of a line in Charite's tenth sonnet in which she asks whether her lover's faithfulness to her is now rivaled by his loyalty to the king of Poland (Henri's title before he became king of France). But the "historical" identity of Sincero raises more questions than it solves, as is the case with attempts to identify the lovers addressed in other women's texts. Whatever Catherine's relationship to Pellejay was, Sincero is a literary construction, possibly almost entirely a fantasy character. The degree of resemblance between the French man and the Neoplatonic hero of the lyrics is impossible to ascertain in our time.

Moreover, Catherine goes to great pains to deny the biographical element in her sonnets. Why, if she wanted to publicize her love for Pellejay, does she insist that her portrait of Sincero is purely imaginary? Motives more self-protective and more ambitious than autobiographical revelation shape her sonnet-dialogue. And the possibility that Sincero was modeled on Pellejay does not mean that the sonnets from Sincero are his. Diller concludes that Catherine's is the principal voice in the sonnets, although he defines the dialogue that precedes them as a "collaboration" between her and Pellejay. The directions in which she took that collaboration are extremely interesting for a study of relations between social power, gender, and literary production. I believe that Catherine des Roches wrote the poems of both characters in the sequence in order to construct the model of a courteous private man, as she claims in her preface, but also, and principally, to put into practice the tenet of Neoplatonic theory according to which a virtuous woman could dominate and refine her male lover. By taking that tenet literally and using it as the basis for a two-voiced sonnet sequence, Catherine constructs a literary realm in which she is undisputed ruler.

The main difference between Catherine's relationship to the men in the coterie and her relationship to the fictional man to whom she assigns and addresses love sonnets is that Sincero is her creature, both an ideal admirer and a mouthpiece through which she can ventriloquize masculine poetic convention. The *blason* is a case in point. For more than a century in Europe, men writing love poetry had described the perfect woman. They had also set her up as an in-text audience for their arguments and pleas and drawn on religious and satirical traditions to write recantations or farewells to love. Catherine appropriates that position by writing as a man in the persona of Sincero and by describing him as the perfect man in the persona of Charite, who is not only the male lover's muse but a writer herself. Catherine represents Charite as the controller of the male poet's attitudes and gives her the last word by setting her poems after his in the sequence. The final sonnet is by Sincero, but it echoes Charite's terms and preserves her for posterity.

In the opening "Dialogue de Sincero et de Charite," Charite takes a critical stance toward the male lover's narration of his enamorment. This narration is built on a familiar Neoplatonic topos. Sincero says that Destiny called on the Fates to design the most beautiful living creature possible; Nature and God helped; Charite was the result. Charite responds to this idealizing tale with playful mockery. She recognizes that poetic convention rather than providential creation is the real source of lovers' portraits of their ladies: "I think, rather, that through the grace of your words, you take my name up to Heaven, Sincero, and bring it back down when it suits you" (96). She accepts his homage with exemplary detachment, through which she clears herself of any sensual involvement with him but allows him to go on playing the Neoplatonic game: "But since you want to be admired as a lover and a poet, you can pretend without being reproached for it; and I, who have nothing to do either with poetry or with love, can certainly hear you out without putting much faith in your words." Charite will be a skeptical audience, allowing Sincero to experiment with lovers' language but implicating herself in the process only as an amused critic. Here again, Catherine takes a role close to Castiglione's assignment for the court lady: she challenges men to impressive verbal performances without committing herself to any one man. As a result, she gives no onlooker (or reader) any reason to think she is "suspect."

The twelve "Son[n]ets de Sincero à Charite" work through a series of Neoplatonic and Petrarchan commonplaces. As a good Neoplatonist, Sincero insists on Charite's celestial virtues: the gods are fighting him over her because they want to take her back to heaven (1); her superiority to him makes him fear that she will reject him (3). He also proves that he is fluent in the imagery and syntax of Petrarchism: he burns and freezes in her presence (12); the intricate parallelism of the correlative sonnet analyzes the process through which her eyes, hands, and hair allure, imprison, and delight him (6). Some of the poems add a particular emphasis to the lexicon of praise, however. Sonnet 4 Neoplatonizes the *blason* by adding intellectual agency to physical beauty in the lady: we hear that Charite's mouth is lovely not only as an object to look at but as the source of her laughter, sighs, and "sages discours." And Sonnet 9 substantially revises Petrarch's metaphor of the lover's life as a ship blown wildly off course by passion.[41] Sincero claims, as many of his literary predecessors did, that he has erred in love, but he announces as early as the first quatrain that Charite has been his savior:

> Ma nef au gré des vens dedans l'onde poussee,
> Erroit de toutes parts quand vostre heureuse main,
> Piteuse de mon mal me retira soudain,
> En me sauvant des flotz de la mer courroucee.
>
> (101)

> My ship, tossed at random among the waves,
> Veered every way until your blessed hand
> Pitying my suffering, suddenly released me,
> Saving me from the waters of the wrathful sea.

This speaker transforms the desperation represented in Petrarch's famous ship sonnet in the *Canzoniere* into the rational equilibrium that Charite has taught him:

> Follement aveuglé d'une erreur insensee
> Monstrant que la raison m'estoit donnée en vain,
> Je me laissois guider d'un erreur incertain
> Lors que vostre bel oeil arresta ma pensee.

> Insanely blind, in meaningless error
> Proving that reason had been given me in vain,
> I let myself go into unstable wandering
> Till your lovely eye centered my thought.

Catherine ventriloquizes this self-portrait through the figure of Sincero because its emphasis on the exemplary virtue and intellectual clarity of the beloved woman is very much in her interest:

> Ainsi le sainct honneur de voz perfections
> Conduisant sagement toutes mes actions
> Commande sur mes sens, mes pensers, et ma vie.

> And so the holy honor of your perfections,
> Wisely controlling all of my acts,
> Rules over my senses, my thoughts, and my life.

A similar vision of the woman's power to form the lover dominates the next to last sonnet in the series, 11, in which the speaker declares that Sincero and Charite, joined in love, are one and the same (a point I have been arguing literally, on the level of literary composition). Here, however, contrary to Charite's claim in the "Dialogue" that she does not practice poetry, the male lover declares that his fame arises entirely from her writing, through which she will win eternal life for them both. Such statements of confidence in the lovers' endless fame are typical of conclusions to Neoplatonic sequences,[42] but the homage to the female beloved as a poet is new. Through Sincero, Catherine is establishing an identity not only as a chaste mistress but as the creator of her lover's public persona:

> Je me sens tres-heureux de me voir estimé
> Par voz doctes ecris, et connoy bien, Madame,
> Que vous pouvez ordir une excellente trame
> Qui rendra par voz vers mon renom animé.
> (102)

> I feel my good fortune when I see myself praised
> In your learned writing, and I know well, Madame,
> That you can weave an excellent tissue
> Which, through your verses, will give life to my fame.

The metaphor of the poet's text as interwoven threads is rich in associations. "Ourdir une trame" has come to mean "hatch a plot" in French, and Catherine is certainly constructing a plot, in the sense of a self-adulatory love story, in this sequence. "Trame" more literally means woof or warp, that is, the substructure of a woven cloth—or text; and it can also mean the course of a life, as spun out by the Fates. To Sincero, then, Charite is a benign fate, who saves his life through texts contrived to increase his fame—and above all, to preserve hers, as the savior and idol of the lover who acknowledges her role in producing a literary identity for him. The end of the poem takes up the textile imagery again to represent Charite as a life- and self-preserving goddess rather than a self-sacrificing Alcestis. By positioning Sincero as a mouthpiece for the combined domestic and literary vocabulary crucial to Catherine's self-defense as a poet, the poem concludes in a narcissistic triumph for her. The woman poet here guarantees the man's afterlife, and he echoes her characteristic synthesis of household and aesthetic terms:

> Alceste rachesta de son mary la vie
> Voulant mourir pour luy, mais vous avez envie
> De racheter la mien[n]e avec plus heureux sort.
> Pource que sans mourir[,] chaste, sçavante et belle,
> Vous filez pour nous deux une vie immortelle
> Qui vaincra les efforts du temps et de la mort.

> Alcestis won back the life of her husband
> By offering to die for him, but you desire
> To redeem my life through a happier fate.
> For without dying, chaste, learned and beautiful,
> You spin out for both of us life everlasting,
> Which will conquer the forces of time and of death.

If it is true that there is no love like self-love, Sincero is certainly the perfect lover. He mirrors back to Charite the public image Catherine invents for herself. By shaping the discourse of the lover as well as the lady, she produces a duet sung in her own honor. The balance of power written into the sonnets from Sincero is much less conventional than the Neoplatonic mistress they celebrate.

Catherine's dominant role in the Neoplatonic couple is obvious in Charite's sonnets to Sincero. Indeed, this part of the sequence disturbs Diller, who objects to it (and to Catherine) as egotistical, sensually underendowed, and "too rational by half."[43] If we read the poems as part of a self-representation intended to win readers rather than lovers, however, they look very different. Catherine writes didactically, even imperiously, in the sonnets, but by doing so, she produces a manual for proper behavior in the Neoplatonic salon. As a result, her sequence carries out an extraordinary redistribution of the power relations encoded in male-authored love poetry. Catherine/Charite uses Plato, Plotinus, and their Renaissance adaptors as the base for a campaign to regender love lyric.

Her first move is to write the *blason* of a perfect man. But Sonnet 1 does more than describe a masculine ideal; it is phrased as a series of nonnegotiable demands. She uses the volitive subjunctive to emphasize that such a man *ought* to exist and that she will be satisfied with no less:

> Je veux que Sincero soit gentil et accord,
> Né d'honnestes parents, je veux que la Noblesse
> Qui vient de la vertu orne sa gentillesse
> Et qu'il soit temperant, juste, prudent et fort.

> I want Sincero to be polite and quick-witted,
> Born of honorable parents; I want the nobility
> That virtue provides to adorn his gentility,
> And I want him temperate, just, prudent and strong.
>
> (106)

So far, this seems closer to the portrait of a perfect courtier than to that of a lover. Catherine's ideal of the virtuous suitor is equally demanding:

> Je veux que Sincero m'ayme jusqu'à la mort,
> Me retenant du tout pour unique maistresse,
> Je veux que la beauté avecques la richesse
> Pour le favoriser se trouvent d'un accord.

> I want Sincero to love me until death,
> Keeping me forever as his one and only love,
> I want beauty, together with wealth,
> To grant him their favor in perfect agreement.

The frank avowal of financial interest in this quatrain is muted by the shift to physical attractions in the tercets, but the list of requirements is daunting here, too, as is the insistent summary in the last line:

> Je veux en Sincero une douce eloquence,
> Un regard doux et fin, une grave prudence,
> Un esprit admirable et un divin sçavoir.
> Un pas qui soit gaillard, mais toutefois modeste,
> Un parler gracieux, un agreable geste,
> Voila qu'en le voyant, je desire de voir.

> I want in Sincero a caressing eloquence,
> A gaze soft and clever, a dignified caution,
> A wonderful mind and heavenly learning.
> A step that is lively, but nonetheless steady,
> Speech full of grace, agreeable gestures,
> This is what, seeing him, I want to see.

The firmness of these demands may well shock Diller. Catherine is writing a new kind of poetry, a hybrid between conduct-book prescription and erotic description. At the same time, she is exploiting the traditions she inherits: she takes literally the humble pose of the male Petrarchan and the Neoplatonic lover. Men writing in these modes conventionally

declared their awe and obedience to their mistresses; Catherine now codi-
fies that pose into a detailed etiquette. It is one thing for a man writing
love poetry to repeat formulas of service and devotion; it is quite another
for a woman poet to turn those formulas into imperatives uttered in a
feminine voice. She also transforms the criteria for feminine beauty built
into the *blason* as genre. By voicing this set of desiderata, she gives an
unequivocal answer to the question "What do women want?" Her *blason*
is daunting partly because it is so commandingly phrased and also because it includes practical considerations foreign to Petrarchan and Neoplatonic praise of the lady. It is hard to imagine Ronsard listing wealth
among the attractions of Marie or Cassandre: he expected to make his
own fortune. Because Catherine des Roches was equally obliged to make
hers, she includes among the threads she ties together in this first sonnet
the ideologically sanctioned assumption that the husband will support his
wife.

The plot of Catherine's sequence is minimal: Sincero goes off to court
and Charite begins to suspect that he loves another woman. In a sonnet
midway through the set (5) Catherine conflates the private world of love
with the public world of proverbial morality: she cites popular *sententiae* to
persuade her lover to return. In men's love poetry proverbial statements usually functioned as a form of wit: the reader was invited to laugh at the skill
with which a poet quoted moral mottoes in a recognizably amoral argument.
Philip Sidney, for example, in Sonnet 107 of *Astrophil and Stella* (1591), uses
a proverb about masters' responsibility for their servants to convince Stella
to give him her attention again. He is the servant:

> On servants' shame oft Maister's blame doth sit;
> O let not fooles in me thy workes reprove,
> And scorning say, "See what it is to love."[44]

Charite uses the same proverb less playfully to correct her lover and to insist
on her virtue in the world beyond the poems: she warns Sincero that any
blot on his reputation will blacken hers as well. However pure a Neoplatonic
relationship may be, doubts about the woman's chastity hover at its margin;
therefore Charite's self-protective move is urgent. The poem opens with a
concealed threat:

> Amy je ne sçaurois rompre ce doux lien,
> Ce doux lien d'amour, dont vous me tenez prise,
> Aussi ne veux-je point faire une telle entreprise
> Puis que tous mes efforts n'y serviroient de rien.
>
> Je vous ayme et honore, et voy assez combien
> La troupe des neuf soeurs sur tout vous favorise,
> Mais si dessus voz moeurs on faict quelque reprise
> Le blasme n'en sera non plus vostre que mien.
>
> (108)

My friend, I could never break this sweet bond,
This sweet bond of love, in which you hold me fast,
I don't even want to attempt such a thing
For none of my efforts would be any use.
    I love you and honor you, and I recognize, too,
How much the nine sisters grant you their favor,
But if some objection is raised to your morals
The blame will fall not on you but on me.

Charite goes on to imagine herself as the wise enchantress who saves the lovelorn hero of *Orlando furioso* from his excesses, and it is in this role of kindly omnipotence that she quotes the proverb about masters and servants. Thus she uses conventional wisdom not to win Sincero back (the veiled threat of dismissal hangs over the whole sonnet) but to reinforce her position as director of his behavior:

Pour vous retirer donc de l'ecole du vice,
Je voudroy ressembler une sage Melice,
Et vous pouvoir conduire en plus heureux sentier.
    Pour les fautes d'un serf on s'en prend à son maistre,
Et si vous estes mien, ou desirez de l'estre,
Soyez donc, Sincero, en moeurs pur et entier.

So to retrieve you from the school of vice,
I would like to resemble Melissa the wise,
And be able to set you on a happier path.
    For the faults of a servant, his master is blamed,
And if you are mine, or still want to be,
Sincero, be pure and wholeheartedly good.

Catherine resembles Whitney in her refusal of the role of pathetic abandoned mistress: it is neither dignified nor chaste to plead with an indifferent man.

The threat implicit in Sonnet 5 turns to outright menace in later poems. Rather than begging her lover to return, Charite exemplifies outraged virtue. She opens Sonnet 7 with what sounds like a gentle request for information, but she turns immediately to her suspicions. Then, violently rejecting the double standard, she threatens to return the man's fickleness in full measure:

Mais d'où vient, Syncero, qu'estant si loing d'ici,
Vous ne m'escrivez point, la douce souvenance
De nostre chaste amour, est elle en o[u]bliance?
N'avez vous plus de moy pensement ny souci?
    Vrayment si j'apperçoy que vous soyez ainsi,
Volage et indiscret, vous n'aurez la puissance
De me vaincre en oubly, car pour vostre inconstance
Je veux estre inconstant et le seray aussi.

(109–10)

> But how is it, Sincero, being so far away,
> You do not write to me? Is the sweet memory
> Of our chaste love now totally forgotten?
> Do you no longer think or care for me?
>   Truly, if I discover that you have become
> Fickle and indiscreet, you will be powerless
> To outdo me in forgetting, because in exchange
> I want to be faithless, and faithless I'll be.

The sonnet shifts to a fierce competition in hostility, for which Charite frees herself from blame by pointing out that the man's betrayal forces her to such extremes. This is not sweet melancholy but spectacular denunciation:

> Doncques si vous m'aymez, pensez que je vous ayme
> Autant comme mon cueur, autant que moymesme:
> Mais si vous ne m'aymez je ne vous ayme point,
>   Si vous me haissez, je hay plus que la rage,
> Je hay plus que l'enfer, vostre mauvais courage,
> Ainsi l'amour me bleçe, et la hayne me point.

> If, then, you love me, believe I love you
> As much as my heart, as much as myself;
> But if you don't love me, I love you not at all,
>   If you hate me, I hate you more than fury,
> I hate more than hell your cowardly weakness,
> Thus does love wound me and hate stab my heart.

Catherine compensates for this outburst, a bravura piece if ever there was one, with several poems in which she takes up her role as judicious advisor again. In 9, she masters the possibility that Sincero has changed "des moeurs et de langage" (in morals and language) by proposing lightheartedly that they both start over with new lovers. But even here, she retains the right to advise him about his choice by defining a courtly feminine ideal, and in her last line she returns to the demanding tone and stern rhythm of Sonnet 1:

> Si vous m'estes constant, je vous seray constante,
> Si vous voulez changer, e[h] bien j'en suis contente,
> Cherchez une autre amie, et moy un autre amy:
>   Cherchez une maistresse honneste, aymable et belle,
> Et moy un serviteur sage, accort et fidelle:
> Car je ne veux jamais que l'on m'ayme à demy.
>
>   (111)

> If you are true to me, I will be true to you,
> If you want a change, then I am quite content.
> Look for another love, I'll find another, too.
>   Seek out a chaste mistress, who's gracious and lovely,
> I'll look for a suitor wise, witty and true;
> For I refuse to be loved only halfway.

In Sonnet 12 she gives Sincero further advice on how to become a model courtier-intellectual. She demonstrates her own urbanity in her remarks on his new surroundings:

> La plus grand part du temps demeurez à l'estude,
> Puis quand vous serez las de vostre solitude,
> De raisonner en vous, et de penser en moy:
>   Allez voir le Palais, et la paume, et l'escrime,
> Et les Dames d'honneur, de vertu et d'estime,
> Gardant tousjours l'amour, l'esperance, et la foy.
>
> (112)

>   Most of the time, remain at your studies,
> Then, when you're tired of being alone,
> Of talking to yourself and thinking of me,
>   Visit the Palace, watch tennis and swordplay,
> And ladies-in-waiting, esteemed for their virtue,
> But stay true to your love, your hope, and your faith.

The local details here (the tennis courts and fencing galleries of the Paris palace) may support the argument that Sincero was Pellejay. But they are more interesting as an indication of the audience Catherine was attempting to impress: not only the *gens de robe* of Poitiers but readers familiar with the entertainments of the capital city and the court.

Charite's final sonnet confirms that Catherine's portrait of Sincero is essentially a portrait of herself. She bases the poem on the conventional conceit by which a lover is said to carry the portrait of his lady in his heart, engraved there by Love. In a humorously literal vein, Charite demands a look into Sincero's picture gallery, where she sees herself reflected with satisfying brilliance. From the beginning, this inner visual portrait is linked to the verbal portrait of Charite that Sincero has given to the public. The poem sets up a gallery of mirrors in which Catherine studies herself:

> Ouvrez moy Sincero, de voz pensers la porte,
> Je desire de voir si l'amour de son traict
> Vous engrave aussi bien dans le cueur mon pourtraict
> Comme vostre beau vers à mes yeux le rapporte. . . .
>   Ouvrez donc s'il vous plaist: ha mon Dieu je me voy,
> Ha mon Dieu, que de bien, que d'honneur je reçoy[!]
> Apres que vous m'avez par mille vers chantée,
>   Je me voy dans voz yeux, et dedans voz escrits,
> Et dedans vostre cueur, et dedans voz esprits,
> Par la Muse, et l'amour, si bien representée.
>
> (112–13)

>   Open to me, Sincero, the door to your thoughts,
> I want to see whether love with his arrow
> Etches my portrait as deep in your heart
> As your beautiful verse sets it forth for my eyes. . . .

> Open up, open, please: ah, my God, I see myself!
> Ah, my God, what delight, what honor I am given.
> After you've sung me in thousands of lines,
>   I see myself now in your eyes and your writing,
> And within your heart and within your soul,
> By the Muse, and by love, so well represented.

Image, mirror image, literary representation, self-representation, specular production of the self by means of an other:[45] the sonnet spells out what this sequence of poems has been. Sincero's function is to bring Charite into being, to reflect her opinions in his actions, and to mirror her perfection in his poems.

The reflexivity of the sequence stands out in its final poem, Sincero's "Responce au dernier sonnet de Charite," which centers on feminine self-love. Extending the conceit of the lover as receptacle for the beloved's image, Sincero invites Charite to use him as a looking glass. The complimentary description that ensues is conventional on the thematic level, but if, as I think, Catherine produced it herself, it is also an act of literary autoeroticism. The self-effacement in Sincero's offer of himself as Charite's mirror sets up a dizzying series of narcissistic gazes, at the center of which stands the woman poet:

> REGARDEZ vous en moy, Charite ma Deesse,
> Regardez vostre front, heureux siege d'amour,
> Regardez voz beaux yeux, ma lumiere, et mon jour,
> Qui commandent mon coeur d'un oeillade maistresse.
>
> (115)

> Look at yourself in me, Charite my goddess,
> Look at your forehead, the blessed seat of love,
> Look at your eyes, my light and my sun,
> Which rule my heart with a powerful glance.

He goes on to enumerate her beauties, prefacing each one with the imperative "Regardez" in a paean to justified vanity. The curious linking of sight and sound in the tercet (does one mainly see a laugh?) signals the degree to which seeing and being seen dominate the fantasy of the poem:

> Regardez l'or frisé de vostre blonde tresse,
> Regardez voz sourcils courbez d'un demi-tour,
> Regardez mille traicts recelez à l'entour
> Pour servir le tyran de ma jeune allegresse.
>   Mais surtout regardez vostre gracieux ris,
> Qui par sa grand'douceur ouvre le Paradis,
> Où veullent demeurer les bien-heureuses ames:

> Look at the filigreed gold of your hair,
> Look at your brows, arched in half-circles,
> Look at the thousand arrows hidden all around
> To serve [love,] the tyrant of my youthful delights.

But above all, look at your graceful laugh,
Which, in its sweetness, reveals the Paradise
Where all blessed souls desire to dwell.

In a witty change of direction, the poem concludes with a warning: Catherine should look no further because she risks becoming a rival for her own affection, replacing Sincero entirely. The joke of the final lines is to the point: the poem envisions a self-love so total that it dispenses with the lover entirely:

Ha n'y regardez plus, Madame, car j'ay poeur
Que vous connoissant si parfaicte en mon coeur,
Vous mesme ne brulez dans voz propres flames!

Ah, look no longer, Lady, for I fear
That knowing yourself so perfect in my heart,
You yourself will catch fire from your own flames!

In Catherine's Neoplatonic system of visual and verbal exchange, mannered and artificial as it is, a quiet revolution is being carried out. In a complete reversal of the ideological processes through which men of a particular class set up legitimating ideals for their women, the woman poet constructs a man to legitimate herself. Sincero's *raison d'être* is to obey and to praise her, to guarantee her virtue and poetic force by serving as a medium through which she proves her chastity and demonstrates her refinement. In this inversion of gender hierarchy, Sincero's is the sex that needs correction and rebuke; Charite speaks as the arbiter of morals and of elegance. No wonder Diller finds Catherine des Roches troubling as a love poet! Rather than exploring passion as its ingratiating victim, she is exploiting chastity to justify herself as a writer—in a radical revision of the speaking position inscribed in a poetic discourse that had included women mainly as stimuli for masculine self-display.

Catherine's insistence on her purity may seem obsessive to a later era, but her biography as well as her poetry shows that she was conscious of the social usefulness of chastity. She never married, and she never stopped writing. Confronted by the intense surveillance over women's sexuality and the subjection expected of them in marriage, she associated herself with Diana and the Amazons rather than accept a role as Alcestis. She defines Neoplatonic love as a guarantee of feminine autonomy in a pastoral play, "La Bergerie," in which she gives the following verses of a song to two female characters:

ROSE.
Chantons de la liberté
Car la liberté des Dames
C'est la plus belle clarté
Qui puisse luyre en leurs Ames.

PENSE.
Roseline, les espris
Ne se treuvent tous de mémes;
L'un se plaist bien d'estre pris,
L'aultre de vivre à soy memes.

Mais une sainte amitié
Ne fait perdre la franchise:
Le Ciel est d'amour lié
Quand la Terre il favorise.
(Secondes oeuvres, 30)

Rose:
Let us sing of liberty,
For the liberty of ladies
Is the brightest light
That can shine in their souls.

Pensé (Pansy, Thought):
Little Rose, our minds
Are not all the same;
One is happy to be in love,
Another to live on her own.

But a holy and chaste love
Does not deprive us of freedom,
Heaven is linked to such love
Whenever it blesses the earth.

"Sainte amitié," the Neoplatonic term for love in the sense of the spiritual training through which each lover puts the other, means freedom. From Pensé's remark, we can see why. Quasi-religious, defined in opposition to both erotic and married love, Neoplatonism leaves the woman poet free to represent herself and her lover according to a system of rules that rewrites gender relations as defined in the society at large. Catherine appropriated a central prohibition in her culture ("an unmarried woman shall not write of sexual love") and turned it into permission for a lifelong poetic career: "if a woman must write of love, let chaste love be her subject." Such propriety gave authority to the sonnets of Charite and carried Catherine unscathed through the erotic skirmishes of La Puce. Catherine's militant chastity is not, as Diller would have it, a symptom of neurotic frigidity but a negotiated position from which she draws the reserves she needs to pass the barricades erected against women writers in her time.

THE FISH AND THE FLEA:
CONCESSIONS AND VICTORIES

Taken together, Isabella Whitney and Catherine des Roches make visible certain processes of compromise and challenge through which a professional woman poet made her way into public view in the sixteenth century. Each writer offers her audience two attractions: apparent compliance with gender expectations and a text advertised as useful. Whitney's modest narrative of how she came to versify Hugh Plat promises homely wisdom, while Catherine's claim to chaste detachment supplies her with credentials as a tutor of Neoplatonic etiquette. Both poets appeal further to their readers through a technique of mixing modes, allying the pleasures associated with erotic tradition to emerging class ideals: bourgeois prudence, coterie brilliance. These are poems intended to please a public and make a profit.

But Whitney and des Roches also construct fantasy images of themselves as ingenious animals alert to danger: the fish that learns to mistrust the hook, the flea that escapes male pursuit. The jumpy ingenuity attributed to these alter egos signals both poets' invocation of mainstream demands for proper womanly behavior to camouflage their unconventional ambitions. Whitney accedes to Protestant insistence on wifely obedience; Catherine des Roches affirms the courtly obsession with women's chastity. But the survival of Whitney's fish and the agility of Catherine's flea also point to their refusal of the gender positions they confronted in a male-dominated system of literary representation. Whitney transforms the pathetic victim role of Ovid's heroines into the self-control of a woman mastering betrayal through detachment, popular wisdom, and socioliterary critique; Catherine des Roches gives a commanding voice to the perfect beauty called upon but rarely heard in Neoplatonic lyric. And both poets imagine and appeal to a community of women, although des Roches does so more fancifully than Whitney: Rose and Pensé are pastoral fictions, while "yong Gentilwomen and Mayds in general" were among the actual readers of Whitney's verse letters.

The differences between the two women's class situations account for several other contrasts in their collections. Whitney's realism, her dependence on friends and family for encouragement and for additional pages in her pamphlet, her simple language and down-to-earth humor arise from a more popular milieu than the Poitiers coterie, which encouraged Catherine's use of an amorous code practiced by upwardly mobile professional men. The bone of contention in Whitney's "Copy of a letter" is socially specific: a broken engagement as it illustrates the disadvantages faced by women in love. Des Roches's elaborate orchestration of gazes and lyric conventions in the hall of mirrors through which she represents her own perfection is a much more symbolically mediated attempt to escape gender constraints.

But Catherine, like Whitney, wrote in dialogue, in an actual collaboration with her mother and in a fictional one with Sincero as ideal lover. This group composition, the inclusion of other voices and other texts in a woman's oeuvre, is a consistent pattern in the poems of urban and coterie writers. The birth of the author, to reshuffle terms from Foucault and

Barthes,[46] was not yet complete, and women's marginal status in the world of literary production made them even more likely than men to call upon other writers for support. Self-representation through dialogue was more central still in two collections of poems written by women in coteries in France and Italy. Whitney's and Des Roches's strategies of concession and revision appear again, in different forms, in Pernette du Guillet's *Rymes* and the *Rime* of Tullia d'Aragona.

THREE

The Poetics of
Group Identity

Self-Commemoration through Dialogue in
Pernette du Guillet and Tullia d'Aragona

"Dialogue" is a term with such various meanings in recent criticism that I should begin by explaining what I mean by it in sixteenth-century women's poetry. As a classical genre taken up by Renaissance writers, dialogue meant speech represented as occurring between two or more people and directed at an audience beyond them. In one form, it moves toward a foregone conclusion. This is the case in the *Symposium*, in which Plato records the responses of interlocutors such as Phaedrus and Agathon in order to show Socrates examining and rejecting ideas opposed to his own as the text builds the argument that prevails at the end. "Dialogue" in this case means dramatized logic organized through the defeat of false propositions. This authoritative mode was often adopted in Renaissance texts. In Sperone Speroni's first *Dialogo d'amore* (1542) for example, the writer assigns Tullia d'Aragona and Bernardo Tasso the articulation of mistaken attitudes about jealousy, while Nicolo Gratia and Francesco Molza enlighten them about the emotion's proper place in Neoplatonic theory.[1] On a more popular level, the second book of Guazzo's *La civil conversatione* (1574) sets the untutored Guglielmo against the urbane Annibal in a dialogue that consists mainly of Annibal's corrections of Guglielmo's rustic assumptions.[2] Here dialogue is a rhetorical structure through which straw men and women are set against the speaker shown to know the truth.

A more equal and less predictable kind of dialogue was theorized by Mikhail Bakhtin in his 1920s work on Rabelais and Dostoevsky.[3] For Bakhtin, dialogism is the unresolved tension between opposing ideas and vocabularies characteristic of novelistic discourse. Rather than subsuming popular dialects and correcting errors, Bakhtin argues, the dialogic writer includes a variety of polemical positions in his text, a field in which "heteroglossia," the interplay of each attitude and the style of speech corresponding to it, reinforces the particularity of different discourses rather than moving toward a last word that supersedes all others in the debate. This kind of dialogue, although less common in early modern writing than the directive Socratic mode, structures some of the best-known Renaissance texts.[4] Bakhtin argues for Rabelais as an illustrative case, and Castiglione's *Courtier*, in which many questions are discussed without necessarily being resolved, is another example. In another important text for love'poets, Leone Ebreo's *Dialoghi d'amore*, the voices of the impulsive Filone and the detached Sofia work antiphonally to clarify Neoplatonic theory.[5]

Jacqueline Risset, in her study of the *Ecole lyonnaise*, the loose literary grouping in which Pernette du Guillet wrote and recited her poems, argues that the relationships among the Lyon writers were genuinely dialogic. They participated in a collaborative and open-ended exploration of philosophy, love theory, translation, and linguistic experiment different from the pursuit of individual fame through adherence to a group program that linked the poets of the Pléiade.[6] One reason for the collective spirit of the Lyonnais, she argues, was that they shared similar class positions, belonging either to the rising bourgeoisie or to the petty nobility, and to a city that enjoyed a certain freedom from royal and religious control, in contrast to the poets of the Pléiade, who typically came from the middle nobility and depended on court patronage.[7] Lyon had no court and no Sorbonne; it stood at the crossroads of Italy, Switzerland, and Germany; and it was rich in international literary activity because of annual book fairs and a great number of Italian and local publishing houses. Altogether, this was a beneficial situation for women writers. Welcomed in independent literary coteries as they never were in official institutions such as universities, they could further their private educations through contact with a variety of male intellectuals at the same time that the absence of a unified social group or dominant aesthetic allowed them relative autonomy as poets, as it did to the men in the fluid urban circuit.

Circuit, in fact, seems a better word than coterie to describe the fluctuating, multicentered associations among men and women such as Pernette du Guillet, the wife of a nobleman and the subject of Maurice Scève's long poetic sequence, *Délie*; Scève and his sisters, Catherine and Sibylle, also poets;[8] the Neoplatonist Pontus de Tyard, an ally of Scève's and later a member of the Pléiade; Clémence de Bourges, a nobleman's daughter to whom Louise Labé dedicated her *Euvres*; the humanist theologian Etienne Dolet; the printer Jean de Tournes, a specialist in Neo-Latin and scholarly texts; Clément Marot, the court poet who organized a contest of *blasons* in which Scève won first prize; Jehanne Gaillarde, who wrote a response to Marot's rondeau in her honor.[9] Contemporaries described Labé as holding open house for literary men and Pernette's publisher recalled her performing her poems for appreciative hearers, but neither woman appears to have taken on the role of salon hostess in as constant or stellar a way as Madeleine and Catherine des Roches in Poitiers. Pernette, a woman poet among several others, was probably less constrained than Catherine des Roches by the constant scrutiny against which the des Roches's Neoplatonism was a defense.

Risset sees Pernette's poems as an instance of genuine dialogue, that is, an exchange that affirms the differences between the speaker and her interlocutor(s):

The *Rymes* are situated in a literal dialogue with *Délie*, . . . and the dialogue extends as a structuring principle to texts in the *Rymes* not directly addressed to Scève: dialogue form underlies the entire work, the form of a genuinely "dialogic" dialogue, that is, one open to the *otherness* of the interlocutor (thus the opposite of a purely subjective outpouring), in three alternating modes: the other text (Scève, "mon Jour"), the reader (the "Dames"), the author (who is also the recipient), all within a deductive process of questioning the nature of love. (25)

Why should this practice of dialogue be central to the work of a woman poet during the 1540s? One answer is that she herself was the other. Because she confronted a poetic system that had historically excluded women as speakers, she had no authorized position from which to write; no poetic tradition of her time positioned a woman writer as the suitor of a man. On the spot, she was vastly outnumbered by literary men whose conventions and critical judgments set the terms for any poet's practice. How could she not be aware of her marginal relationship to the literary establishment when all her predecessors were men (Petrarchism and Neoplatonism record the names of male writers, as do the Anacreontic and Marotic modes Pernette also used), when her mentor and publisher were men, and when her future history as woman and as poet seemed certain to be written by men? Faced with the asymmetry between men's ownership of poetic discourses and literary fame and her limited access to both, the woman poet had to take the differences between herself and her male counterparts seriously.

But a woman poet could turn this imbalance in cultural power to her own ends: she could advance her career by invoking the names and imitating the vocabularies of famous male colleagues. By naming a master, she could construct a literary self through her affiliation with his circle and citation of his work. Presenting her poems as a series of responses to a famous man reflected favorably on the woman whose lyrics demonstrated her familiarity with his texts and testified to the social bond implied by her choice of him as addressee. In such a case, the woman writer not only recognizes the otherness of the man; she appropriates his difference—that is, his public reputation—for herself. This strategy of self-representation through published dialogue lies at the heart of Pernette du Guillet's *Rymes* and Tullia d'Aragona's *Rime*.

Pernette spent her entire short life in Lyon, where she was married to the aristocratically named Monsieur du Guillet (about whom nothing else is known), while Tullia was a courtesan, making her living through sexual liaisons with wealthy clients in a career that took her from Rome to Siena and Florence. These differences in class and culture produce striking contrasts in their poems. Pernette centers her lyrics on one man, Maurice Scève. Although she works in a variety of lyric modes different from Scéve's *Délie*, most of her eighty *Rymes* involve a subtle alternation of imitation and critique through which she assumes the prestige of the male poet and the Neoplatonic love theory he invokes, although at times she positions herself against both. Tullia rarely defines herself in opposition to her interlocutors;

she is more involved in cooperating in a constellation of cultural stars. Her strategy is to draw many men into an epistolary group portrait, at the center of which she shines as the companion to northern Italy's intellectual elite.

Both writers, however, show how women poets constructed an identity for themselves by calling attention to their participation in male-dominated cultural groups. Although they were not writing primarily to earn a living, their situations as women required them to establish visible bonds to male celebrities, to personalize their intertextual relationships by naming their colleagues in poetry. Circumscribed by the social and literary primacy of men, they manipulated male-authored texts and reputations in order to claim fame for themselves. Pernette and Tullia regendered the masculine perspective built into Neoplatonism; in addition, they reworked classical myth to imagine freedom and power more directly, reversing the subject positions written into Ovidian metamorphoses.

PERNETTE DU GUILLET:
IMITATION AS SELF-CELEBRATION

Pernette du Guillet's first biographer and critic, Verdun Saulnier, recognized in 1944 that the few comments her contemporaries made about her often contradict one another. Not even her date of birth has been fixed with any certainty. But she was probably born in the early 1520s in Lyon, into a family highly placed enough to allow her to study Italian, Spanish, Latin, and Greek and to play the spinet and the lute, accomplishments praised by her editor, Antoine du Moulin, who mentions in his dedicatory preface that she recited her poems in "many a good company."[10] She met Maurice Scève, who was already making a name for himself in literary circles in France, in 1536; she married Monsieur du Guillet in 1537 or 1538; she died in 1544, probably of the plague raging in Lyon that summer.

Although Antoine du Moulin remarks that her *Rymes* were found in a disorderly pile after her death, Pernette wrote over seventy carefully finished poems in a variety of forms. Two of her *chansons* were published in songbooks in Lyon and Paris in the early 1540s; one was well enough known by 1549 to be defended by Barthélemy Aneau and Guillaume des Autelz in their response to Joachim Du Bellay's attack on medieval verse forms in *La Deffence et illustration de la langue françoyse*.[11] She occasionally takes up themes similar to Scève's in *Délie*: the exchange of a ring, a meeting by water, calumnies by the couple's observers. But she also experiments with love riddles, medieval forms such as the *coq à l'âne* and *mommerie*, and *résponsifs*, that is, critical revisions of poems written by her contemporaries. Her *Rymes* were published posthumously by Jean de Tournes, one of the best printers of Lyon, in 1545, a year after the publication of Scève's massive love sequence *Délie*.

The publishing circumstances of Pernette's *Rymes* reveal a good deal about the ideological climate in which she wrote. Antoine du Moulin dedicates his preface, "Aux Dames Lyonnoizes," to women readers, friends and mourners of Pernette, whose civic pride he appeals to by holding the local poet up as a model for her *concitoyennes*:

> . . . les Cieux nous enviantz tel heur la nous ravirent, ô Dames Lyonnoises, pour vous laisser achever ce qu'elle avoit si heureusement commencé: c'est à sçavoir de vous exerciter, comme elle, à la vertu: et tellement, que, si par ce sien petit passetemps elle vous a monstré le chemin à bien, vous la puissiez si glorieuse-ment ensuyvre, que la mémoire de vous puisse testifier à la Posterité de la docilité et vivacité des bons esprtiz, qu'en tous artz ce Climat Lyonnois a tous-jours produict en tous sexes, voire assez plus copieusement, que guere autre, que l'on sache. (2–3)

> Heaven, envious of our good fortune, snatched her away from us, oh ladies of Lyon, in order to let you finish what she so admirably began: that is, to train yourselves in virtuosity, as she did, and so well that, if she has shown you the road to success through this modest pastime of hers, you may follow her in such a praiseworthy way that your fame will demonstrate to posterity the docility [teachability] and vivacity of mind, suited to all the arts, which this Lyonnais climate has always produced in both sexes, far more abundantly than almost any other city known.

Du Moulin goes on to urge his city's women to international rivalry; they should be inspired by Pernette's example to "animate themselves in letters," to compete for "the great and undying praise that the ladies of Italy have acquired for themselves today" (3).

Du Moulin encourages women to new ambitions here, but elsewhere in his preface he is more ambivalent: he reproduces his culture's fixation on their sexual purity. He emphasizes the spotless life and reputation of his author, whom he describes as "vertueuse, gentile et toute spirituelle" (vir-tuous, high born, and entirely "spiritual," a word that did not yet have its primary later connotation of verbal quickness and wit). Scève and Pernette use the word "vertu" as praise for a lover-poet of either sex, to signify the power to achieve perfection in love and in poetry. In their dialect, it means amorous devotion, verbal brilliance, and high poetic style.[12] But du Moulin genders the term to praise Pernette's chastity. He adds that he is publish-ing her poems only at the insistence of her grieving husband, thus legiti-mating lyrics that might otherwise seem scandalous as the work of a married woman, and he counters mistrust of women writers by warning readers ready to blame him for publishing the *Rymes* that they will merely expose their corrupt suspicions, in contrast to the innocent curiosity of bet-ter readers, the "bonnes et vertueuses Dames" of Lyon. Men's poems in-cluded in the volume contribute further to the construction of an unimpeachable reputation for Pernette. The introductory *huitain* (eight-line poem), written by the publisher Jean de Tournes, stresses "affection saincte" as the theme of *Les Rymes*, and even Scève's epitaph links Pernette's "vertu" with her chastity:

L'heureuse cendre aultrefois composée
En son corps chaste, où Vertu reposa,
Est en ce lieu par les Graces posée
Parmy ses os, que Beaulté composa.

(111)

The blessed ashes formerly contained
In her chaste body, where Virtue lay,
In this spot are set down by the Graces
Amidst her bones, which Beauty composed.

Pernette, too, defines love as a chaste and spiritual union. But she is less docile and more vivacious in her poetic strategies than the presentation of her volume suggests. Scève's centrality as the addressee of her *Rymes* is a major principle of unity in the sequence: her epigrams to him construct a glowing portrait of the poet who had been circulating some of the 450 poems of *Délie* for years before its publication in 1544. But the brilliance of this portrait reflects directly onto Pernette as the beloved and disciple of the poet she eulogizes. Her attraction to his fame is revealed as early as her description of him in Epigram 3:

Ce grand renom de ton meslé sçavoir
Demonstre bien, que tu es l'excellence
De toute grace exquise, pour avoir
Tous dons des Cieulx en pleine jouyssance.

Your great renown for wide-ranging knowledge
Demonstrates clearly how far you excel
In every exquisite grace by having
All heaven's gifts freely at your command.

Pernette identifies her poet-lover with transparent puns on his name. In her fifth epigram, she builds a message about the man into capitalized words that encode his effect on her into the letters of his name: "Et par ta main, [il t'a pleu] le VICE A SE MUER / . . . En mon erreur CE VICE MUERAS" (And by your hand you were willing to transform [my] vice / . . . You will transform the vice of my wandering ways). The wit of the anagram turns Scève's name into a demonstration of Pernette's verbal skill at the same time that she claims that *he* metamorphizes her. In her sixth *chanson* and her thirty-fourth epigram, she puns on the word "severe," which echoes the Latinized form of Scève's name (Scève/*saevus*/*sévère*). By relating his name to his strictness ("en faict, comme de nom, severe": severe in deeds, as in name) she identifies herself as apprentice to a rigorous mentor.

Poetic discipleship is the subject of many of Pernette's epigrams. Her use of the epigram form itself (a short poem of four to twelve lines, written in ten-syllable verse and usually ending with a "pointe," a neat turn or witty summary)[13] is an homage to Scève's strict use of ten-line stanzas (*dizains*) throughout *Délie*. But if imitation is the sincerest form of flattery, it also produces a subtle form of self-aggrandizement. In Epigram 6, for example, Pernette's disclaimer of her own skills as a poet goes hand in hand with a reminder to her readers that she has been the object of Scève's praise. The poem is typically self-referential and typically alert to an audience beyond the Neoplatonic couple. Pernette begins by naming the verse form she shares with Scève and by stressing the public nature of her confession of inadequacy. Although the intimate "tu" suggests the closeness of their private relationship, she acknowledges her beloved's adulating public, as well:

> Par ce dizain clerement je m'accuse
> De ne sçavoir tes vertus honnorer,
> Fors du vouloir, qui est bien maigre excuse:
> Mais qui pourroit par escript decorer
> Ce qui de soy se peult faire adorer?

> In this ten-line poem, I openly admit
> That I am unable to praise your virtues,
> Except in intention, a feeble excuse:
> But who by writing could further embellish
> A man who makes himself adored on his own?

Pernette resolves the problem in an apparently self-effacing way by asking the master to teach her how to imitate him. Literary discipleship here sounds like complete self-abnegation, a poetic equivalent of the wifely mirroring recommended in conduct books: the disciple aspires toward total resemblance to her model. But Pernette specifies that the techniques of eulogy she wants to learn are those her mentor practices in her honor:

> Je ne dy pas, si j'avois ton pouvoir,
> Qu'à m'acquicter ne feisse mon debvoir,
> A tout le moins du bien que tu m'advoues.
>   Preste moy donc ton eloquent sçavoir
> Pour te louer ainsi, que tu me loues!

> I am not saying that if I had your power,
> I would not fulfill my duty to you,
> At least to return the good you vow to me.
>   Lend me, then, your eloquent savoir-faire
> To praise you in the way that you praise me!

Pernette's pact with her mentor turns the traditional portrait of lady as the object of masculine praise into an affirmation of her virtues as active poetic apprentice. She also shows that she can already imitate her mentor, in spite of her protestation to the contrary: the *dizain* form and the witty *pointe* demonstrate her skill in the Scèvian mode.

Pernette foregrounds herself as a poet in her second epigram, a narrative of enamorment as conversion. To trace her illumination by love, she begins with a scene of nocturnal confusion. The logic of the day-night cycle as psychological metaphor (often used by Scève to suggest the repetitiveness of his conflict between lust and love, despair and hope), together with the imperfect tense, might suggest that the midnight of her soul is doomed to repeat itself over and over:

> La nuict estoit pour moy si tresobscure
> Que Terre, et Ciel elle obscurissoit,
> Tant qu'à Midy de discerner figure
> N'avois pouvoir, qui fort me marrissoit.

> To me the night was so extremely dark
> That it obscured both earth and sky,
> So much that at midday I could not discern
> A single shape, which caused me great alarm.

But she stops the cycle with an image of expanding brightness, which she translates from visual dazzlement into vocal energy: she announces that her immediate response to the appearance of her Sun was an outpouring of praise. Spiritual illumination and poetic vocation are linked in the flow of clauses through which the narrative moves to its climax. In this history of a poet, love leads immediately to language:

> Mais quand je vis que l'aulbe apparoissoit
> En couleurs mille et diverse, et seraine,
> Je me trouvay de liesse si pleine
> (Voyant desjà la clarté à la ronde)
> Que commençay louer à voix haultaine
> Celuy qui feit pour moy ce Jour au Monde.

> But when I saw that the dawn was appearing
> In a thousand colors, both diverse and serene,
> I found myself so filled with delight
> (Seeing brightness everywhere around me)
> That I began to lift my voice in praise
> Of he who brought this Day into the world for me.

Du Moulin's placement of this poem second in the collection makes sense. In it Pernette announces the poetic program for *Les Rymes*: she will celebrate love, the man love brought into her life, and "saincte amytié" as the force that generates her text.

Pernette's praise of her beloved also affirms the truthfulness of the poems he has written in her praise. In Epigram 17, she lists her beloved's qualities, including the eloquence that convinces her of her own desirability. The simple, even naïve diction of the poem produces an impression of selfless gratitude, yet it turns the spotlight onto Pernette as the heroine of both Scève's sequence and her own. She calls attention to her own merit by re-

minding her readers that it has been commemorated by a lover-poet of recognized discernment:

> Je suis tant bien que je ne puis le dire,
> Ayant sondé son amytié profonde
> Par sa vertu, qui à l'aimer m'attire
> Plus que beaulté: car sa grace, et faconde
> Me font cuyder la premiere du monde.

> I am so happy that I cannot describe it,
> Having sounded the depth of his affection
> Through his virtue, which draws me to love him
> More than beauty would: for his grace and eloquence
> Make me esteem myself the first woman in the world.

Pernette transforms the passive position of the heroines of love lyrics composed by her male contemporaries by exploiting her Lyonnais public's familiarity with Scève's "loz tant requis" (*Chanson* 4: "praises so sought after").
She sets up an exchange of representations through which her self-portrait
as appreciative critic confirms her poet's praise of her. As the two halves of a
dialogue, Scève's *Délie* and Pernette's *Rymes* act like the outer wings of a
three-way mirror, arranged so that the two lovers and the readers beyond
them can observe the brilliant cross-reflections set in motion by their mutually self-referring texts.

Pernette uses Scève's *oeuvre* as an accrediting intertext for her own, then,
but she also diverges from it in gender-determined ways. She begins to make
distinctions as early as her first epigram, in which she transforms the visual
and verbal vocabulary with which Scève opens *Délie*. His title page includes
an emblem showing two winds blowing down upon a rock surrounded by
waves, a symbol for Délie's integrity, her resistance to passion, and the permanence of the love she inspires and shares. The image clarifies the full title
of the sequence, *Délie, object de plus haulte vertu* (Délie, object and example
of highest virtue). In the prefatory *huitain*, "A sa Délie," Scève describes the
poems that follow as "durs Epygrammes," meaning difficult or obscure, but
also hard and pure because they have been tempered in Love's flames.[14] He
also tells his addressee that she will be able to read "many errors" in his
poems—textual errors, as his use of the verb "lire" suggests, and also moral
ones, as the "jeunes erreurs" (youthful wanderings) mentioned in his first
dizain make clear.

Pernette's opening poem takes up Scève's lapidary image and his allusion to the "haulte" perfection of the beloved, but she turns both to self-
laudatory uses. She represents her first meeting with her beloved as a total
metamorphosis: losing all sense of her former self, she retains only the force
to record her suffering and happiness in love—an ennobling process, however, through which she suggests that love has imprinted upon her what she
now faithfully publishes to the world:

> Le hault pouvoir des Astres a permis
> (Quand je nasquis) d'estre heureuse et servie:
> Dont, congnoissant celuy qui m'est promis,
> Restée suis sans sentyment de vie,
> Fors le sentir du mal, qui me convie
> A regraver ma dure impression
> D'amour cruelle, et doulce passion,
> Où s'apparut celle divinité
> Qui me cause l'imagination
> A contempler si haulte qualité.

> The lofty power of the Stars allowed me
> (From my birth) to be lucky and well served:
> So that, recognizing the man promised to me,
> I lost the sensation of life,
> Except for feeling pain, which leads me
> To engrave my hard impression
> Of cruel love and sweet passion,
> In which the divine figure appeared
> Who causes me, in my imagination,
> To contemplate such lofty qualities.

Mirroring Scève's theory of love, she purifies his literary practice. She admits no error, either in her early life or in her poems. Her use of the verb "regraver" (l. 6: to carve out, to retrace in stone) allows her to claim the precision of a stonecarver and, by implication, the concision and durability of the first epigrams, the Greek and Roman poems cut into burial tablets.[15] So she appropriates Scève's genre but revises his persona in her own introductory poem.

Pernette's use of "imagination" at the end of this epigram implies that she has internalized the image at which she gazes, according to an axiom central to Neoplatonic theory. Marsilio Ficino in his commentary on the *Symposium* and Leone Ebreo in his *Dialoghi d'amore* both describe the process whereby each lover incorporates and becomes the other: as the image of the beloved fills the heart of each lover, both increasingly come to resemble each other.[16] Scève spells out the narcissism implicit in this search for a self through an ideal other in *Délie* at the end of *dizain* 271:

> Je quiers en toy ce, qu'en moy j'ay plus cher.
> Et bien qu'espoir de l'attente me frustre,
> Point ne m'est grief en aultruy me chercher.

> I seek in you what I cherish most in myself.
> And although any hope of attaining it is vain,
> I do not regret seeking myself in another.

But as the frustration Scève alludes to here suggests, the male poet also narrates moments of lust, doubt, despair, and bitterness, drawing on Petrarchan and Ovidian traditions to represent his struggle to rise above physical passion. Pernette, in contrast, dates the tranquility celebrated in her *Rymes* from her early conversion to an unchanging "amour saincte." Such a focus is understandable in a married woman writing poetry in 1540. Unlike Scève, Pernette could not risk confessing youthful indiscretions (as Guasco tells his daughter Lavinia, a woman's chastity, once besmirched, can never be restored)[17] or struggles with lust (as Scève does in *dizain* 161, for example, in which he represents himself as writhing in torment like a man trapped in nettles as he imagines Délie in bed with her husband). Demands for female chastity encouraged a theoretical bent in Pernette, leading her to emphasize the transcendental and contemplative elements of Neoplatonism. Rather than analyzing the "antiperistases" of love, by which Scève means the interaction of mutually reinforcing opposites, that is, of sexual will and spiritual desire,[18] she represents herself as the heroine of a Neoplatonic plot that begins with two positive discoveries—of the lover, of her ability to celebrate him—and provides her with stable contentment.

This position is evaluated negatively by one of Pernette's critics, Robert Griffin. He acknowledges her independence from Scève, but he judges her pattern of revising his statements of passionate desire into formulations of Neoplatonic theory as unnatural: "This theorizing of love has a detrimental effect on our impression of Pernette the woman. . . . Meeting Scève on an intellectual level where the man in man is neither desired nor fully developed is intelligible enough, but this symbiotic attachment causes her most womanly instincts to deteriorate."[19] There is a good deal wrong with this statement, not least the biologistic assumption that female "instincts" predispose all women in all circumstances to "desire the man in man." Two of Griffin's assumptions are especially debatable, given the historical context of Pernette's *Rymes*: first, his expectation that a thematic reading of poetry produced through the grids of sexual ideology and literary convention in the sixteenth century will reveal any writer's unmediated "instincts"; second, his certainty that Neoplatonic abstraction was a limitation rather than an enabling strategy for Pernette.[20] In fact, she uses the terms of "saincte amitié" to lay claim to a love as different as possible from the duties imposed on women in her time. The love she defines is based on reason, which sixteenth-century gender theory defined women as lacking; it assumes equal powers in the relationship, which contemporary family and legal codes rejected; and it dramatizes an intellectual intimacy militated against by the contrasting roles assigned to men and women. And Pernette's "amitié" is offered to public view as the work of a married woman, in opposition to the private/public dichotomy that positioned wives inside the house and outside literary production.

An early instance of Pernette's emphasis on reason is her sixteenth epigram, in which she corrects *dizain* 56 of *Délie*. Scève writes that Reason in him has been "asservie," enslaved, by his body, spirit, and senses; he sends all four to Délie to be cured. Pernette carries out this assignment obediently, aligning herself with Reason and offering an explanation of how the four elements of the psyche should be hierarchized. But her cooperation in the poetic exchange rewrites the gender hierarchy of her time. She speaks not as the irrational inferior of man but as an enlightened judge of this particular man:

> L'ame et l'esprit sont pour le corps orner,
> Quand le vouloir de l'Eternel nous donne
> Sens, et sçavoir pour pouvoir discerner
> Le bien du bien, que la raison ordonne:
>   Parquoy, si Dieu de telz biens te guerdonne,
> Il m'a donné raison, qui a pouvoir
> De bien juger ton heur, et ton sçavoir.
>   Ne trouve donc chose si admirable
> Si à bon droict te desirent de veoir
> Le Corps, l'Esprit, et l'Ame raisonnable.

> The soul and the mind are there to adorn the body,
> When the divine will gives us
> Sense and knowledge, so that we can perceive
> The highest good, over which reason reigns:
>   So while God rewards you with these qualities,
> He has given me reason, which has the power
> To assess your happiness and your knowledge.
>   Do not then think it such a wondrous thing
> That, rightly, all these in me desire to see you:
> The body, the mind, and the rational intellect.

The phrasing of the last two lines produces a double meaning. The adjective "raisonnable" can apply to the "you" of the line above, so that a second meaning would be "My body, mind, and soul desire to see you more reasonable." Either way, Pernette takes the role of expert counselor, through which she distinguishes herself sharply from the psychically disordered speaker of Scève's *dizain*. The male poet invokes the apparatus of Neoplatonic theory in order to confess that it is not operating as it should in his case; the woman poet responds that it is working perfectly in her case and ought to work better in his.

In fact, a curious destabilizing of traditional gender oppositions becomes visible when the two collections are read together. Scève's use of the name Délie (inhabitant of Delos, Diana, the goddess of the moon) carries a connotation of lunar instability, the inconstancy attributed to women, as does his description of Délie waxing and waning through terrifying stages (in d. 193, for example); Pernette's name for him, "mon Jour," like her comparison of him to Apollo (Epigram 2), participates in a conventionally gendered astrological system, which associates the light of the sun with the lucid power of masculinity. Marriage theorists frequently quoted Plutarch's dictum that a wife should be like the moon to her husband's sun, shining more brightly when he is near and vanishing from public view in his absence,[21] an image of proper order affirmed by a denunciation of its opposite in Juan Luis Vives's pedagogical treatise, translated in France as *Le Livre de l'institution de la femme chrestienne* by Pierre de Changy in 1542:

> En union de mariage l'homme est l'ame et la femme le corps: l'ung commande et l'autre sert. C'est chose ridicule et execrable, que la dame pervertissant et gastant les loix de nature, prefere sa reputation à celluy qu'elle a prins pour seigneur et maistre: comme le chevalier qui veult commander à l'empereur, le paysant à son seigneur, *la lune au soleil*, et le bras à la teste.[22]

> In marriage, the man is the soul and the woman the body; he commands, she serves. It is a ridiculous and blameworthy thing that a woman, perverting and destroying the laws of nature, should prefer her reputation over the man she has taken as lord and master: as if a knight should want to rule an emperor, a peasant his lord, *the moon the sun*, and the arm the head.

The dialogue between Pernette and Scève reverses the Plutarchan roles: Pernette writes in the reasoned Apollonian mode while Scève voices the inconsistency attributed to women. Does her policing ego somehow free his lyric unconscious? The repeated defeats of "debvoir" (duty) in Scève's nocturnal *dizains* and the public connotations of "pouvoir" (power) in Pernette's *Rymes* signal their different uses of idealizing love theory. The male poet disrupts his Neoplatonism with Petrarchan longing and Ovidian sensuality, producing an unruly text very different from his later, magisterial *Microcosme*; the woman poet uses Neoplatonic terms punctiliously to write the drama of her spiritual ascent because such philosophical/spiritual rigor allows her to claim the intellectual and moral authority reserved for men in her culture.

A striking demonstration of the contrasts between the two poets' versions of love is a pair of epigrams sometimes cited as proof of their parallel concerns: her Epigram 13, his *dizain* 136. I have been suggesting, however, that it is precisely through deviations in their use of a common vocabulary that each writer establishes a distinct textual identity. Critics have argued that Scève's poem was the catalyst for Pernette's and vice versa, but priority seems less important to me than the dialogic process through which differences between the texts clarify the focus and manner of each. This story of love's bliss is recounted from two contrasting and gender-reversed perspectives, the woman's rational and directed toward honor, the man's passionate and wishfully amoral. Pernette's efforts to control the relationship in the present and the future stand out clearly when her shorter, more causally explicit analysis of the event and hope for its outcome are read against Scève's celebration of amorous fusion.

Pernette begins by representing herself from a point of view outside the recently accomplished union. Her shift in tenses (from the immediate past to the present to a volitive oriented toward the future) clearly separates the

stages of the relationship from one another, as does the series of causes
and effects through which duty leads to honor, honor to permanence, and
"I" to "we." Pernette ends by bargaining with Love, arguing that the honorable outcome of the lovers' union obliges the god to preserve their
happiness:

> L'heur de mon mal, enflammant le desir,
> Feit distiller deux cueurs en un debvoir:
> Dont l'un est vif pour le doulx desplaisir,
> Qui faict que Mort tient l'autre en son pouvoir.
>   Dieu aveuglé, tu nous a faict avoir
> Du bien le mal en effect honnorable:
> Fais donc aussi, que nous puissions avoir
> En noz espritz contentement durable!

> The happy outcome of my suffering, inflaming desire,
> Distilled two hearts into one duty:
> So that one lives because of the sweet pain
> That allows Death to hold the other in his power.
>   Blind god, you have brought us both,
> From good, suffering honorable in its outcome:
> So make it possible, too, that we can share
> In our spirits long-lasting contentment!

Some critics have argued that Pernette's deathlike union (l. 4) alludes to the
ecstasy of orgasm; this is the view of T. Anthony Perry.[23] But it seems unlikely that a woman poet in Pernette's situation—married to a nobleman,
object of scrutiny in her city—would openly celebrate an act of adultery. The
paradox of bliss in misery, like the imagery of love's flames, is a conventional term in the Neoplatonic lexicon, and the verb "distiller" (l. 2) suggests
an alchemical process of purification as much as erotic liquefaction. Yet the
poem does exhibit a kind of anxious propriety. Pernette's rapid movement
away from "the sweet pain" of line 3 suggests an effort to redefine the experience as the basis of a decent and stable alliance. The emphasis of the poem
falls on the wish for rational security as a stage beyond problematic rapture.

Read with Pernette's poem, Scève's brings the differences between the
two into high relief. He sexualizes their encounter, uses repetition and alliteration to dwell on its pleasures, and returns from spiritual to physical terms
in his last line:

> L'heur de nostre heur enflambant le desir
> Unit double ame en un mesme povoir:
> L'une mourante vit du doulx desplaisir,
> Que l'autre vive a fait mort recevoir.
>   Dieu aveuglé tu nous a fait avoir
> Sans aultrement ensemble consentir,
> Et posseder, sans nous en repentir,
> Le bien du mal en effect desirable:

Fais que puissions aussi long sentir
Si doulx mourir en vie respirable.

The joy of our joy, enflaming desire,
Unites a double soul in a shared power:
One, dying, lives on the sweet pain
That brought death to the still living other.
  Blind god, you have brought us,
Without otherwise sharing identical feeling,
And made us possess, without repenting,
The pleasure of pain, desirable in its effects:
Allow us to feel such sweet dying
as long as the breath of life lasts.

Where Pernette focuses on duty, Scève celebrates physical pleasure; where she makes a distinction between two hearts (one lives because the other dies), he speaks of two souls' identity, with an overtone of the poetic code in which double death means mutual orgasm (one dies because the other has already died); where she defines honor as the outcome of regret, he denies any need for repentance; while she ends with a prayer for spiritual solidarity between the lovers, he ends with a lingering association between their longevity and their shared breathing, in a fantasy that this love will always retain its intense sensuality.

Critical opinion has generally taken Scève's poem as a revision of Pernette's and evaluated it more highly. But Saulnier and Risset account for the superiority of Scève's poem according to opposing criteria: he finds it more lucid and better balanced than Pernette's, she finds it more complex because so densely erotically charged.[24] Judgments of this kind seem to me to reveal more about critical preoccupations at different moments in literary history than about texts written in the present tense of a dialogue. When textual differences are produced by poets of different sexes, those differences reveal the effects of multiple determinants: the poets' selection of particular elements from the range of available erotic discourses is channeled through the gender ideologies of their era, and the dialogue intensifies the contrasts by inviting readers to look for distinctions in each poet's use of the same lyric mode.

As the process of textual differentiation goes on, Pernette consistently emphasizes her chastity as a point of contrast to Scève. She claims once, in her sixth song, that he is universally praised for his "austere chastity," but his poems complicate the picture. More often she invokes sexual purity when she is defining her own role in the relationship. In a witty *chanson* (7), she defends her chastity against possible accusations. The shift in refrain in the fifth stanza signals that this self-portrait is intended to counter censure, and the confusion of Danaë with Daphne may be symptomatic, as well. Can Pernette not bring herself to mention the Ovidian heroine used to condemn all women's venality in the Renaissance?[25]

Qui dira ma robe fourrée
De la belle pluye dorée
Qui Daphnes [Danaë] enclose esbranla:
Je ne sçay rien moins, que cela.
　　Qui dira qu'à plusieurs je tens
Pour en avoir mon passetemps,
Prenant mon plaisir çà, et là:
Je ne sçay rien moins, que cela. . . .
17　　Mais qui dira, que la Vertu
Dont tu es richement vestu,
En ton amour m'estincella:
Je ne sçay rien mieulx, que cela.
　　Mais qui dira que d'amour saincte
Chastement au cueur suis attaincte,
Qui mon honneur onc ne foula:
Je ne sçay rien mieulx, que cela.

If anyone says my dress is lined
With the lovely golden rain
That startled Danaë in her inner room,
I know nothing at all of that. . . .
　　If anyone says I flirt at large,
To amuse myself with many men,
Taking pleasure here and there,
I know nothing at all of that . . . .
　　But if someone says that it was Virtue,
In which you are so richly dressed,
That sparked me into loving you,
I know nothing better than that.
　　But if someone says that sacred love
Chastely has reached into my heart,
And never done my honor harm,
I know nothing better than that.

It is possible that Pernette was replying to specific charges against her in Lyon, although this defense sounds more like a contribution to the polemic around *L'Amye de court*: it systematically counters the vices attributed by Bertrand de La Borderie to the court lady.[26] In any case, unlike Scève, Pernette, had to write with a constant awareness of the risk of accusations provoked by suspicion of a woman poet's ambition.

But it would be a misreading to see Pernette's insistence on her chastity only as evidence of conformity to social expectation. Several of her poems show her redefining chastity, shifting it from an imposed constraint into a justification for claiming equal power with her partner. Like Catherine des Roches, she links chastity to serenity and to a firm sense of female merits and rights. In *Chanson 9*, for example, she plays off scenes of sinister darkness against the tranquility guaranteed by "saincte amitié." She opens by invoking a similarity-in-difference between herself and the beloved man, representing herself as the terrestrial materialization of his spiritual power:

> Je suis la Journée,
>   Vous, Amy, le Jour,
>   Qui m'a destourneé
>   De fascheux sejour.

> I am the day,
>   You, my love, the Daylight,
>   Which has turned me aside
>   From uneasy rest.

If she seems to accept a lesser status as a single day created by Scève as perpetual sun, she goes on to contrast the nocturnal frivolity of lovers to the lucidity of her love in order to insist on the equality of the commitment she shares with her Sun:

> On peult de nuit encor se resjouyr
> De leurs amours faisant amantz jouyr:
>   Mais la jouyssance
>   De folle pitié
>   N'a pas de puissance
>   Sur nostre amytié,
>   Veu qu'elle est fondée
>   En prosperité
>   Sur Vertu sondée
>   De toute equité.

(ll. 15–24)

> Night can still be delighful
> For making lovers take joy in love,
>   But the delight
>   That foolish pity grants
>   Has no potency
>   In our loving friendship,
>   For our love is founded
>   In prosperous fortune,
>   On Virtue, long tested
>   In loving fairness.

"Equité" is the crucial word here, a term meaning "equality" as well as fairness and instinctive justice (attention to the spirit rather than the letter of the law).[27] "Jour" may be masculine in Pernette's scheme while a single day is feminine, but she shifts the power relations encoded into this light imagery by insisting that the lovers discern each other's merit equally. She adopts a legal term to legitimate her ideal of the lovers' mutual respect: "equité" rewrites the unequal relationship authorized between men and women in early modern family theory.

A late epigram, 48, suggests'that Pernette herself sensed the transgressive qualities in her fantasy of reciprocity. The poem is a series of denials through which she simultaneously constructs the portrait of a disobedient woman and holds it at a distance. The vocabulary of the first six lines politicizes gender relations as relentlessly as did marriage manuals of the sixteenth century:

> Non que je vueille oster la liberté
> A qui est né pour estre sur moy maistre:
> Non que je vueille abuser de fierté
> Qui a luy humble et à tous devrois estre:
> Non que je vueille à dextre, et à senestre
> Le gouverner, et faire à mon plaisir:

> It's not that I want to take away the freedom
> Of the man born to be master over me:
> Nor that I want to lord it over him, from pride,
> I, who should be humble to him and to all men:
> It's not that I want, to left and to right,
> To rule over him and do just as I please:

But Pernette's concessions are only temporary. The poem fulfills the expectation set up by its denials: she is in fact going to issue a command. She does so in a response to Scève's *dizain* 202, in which he admits that he does everything he can to persuade her to love him—not merely, he claims, to satisfy his will (*vouloir*) but to win her in a way that leaves her "libre intention" undisturbed. Pernette simplifies his position by appealing to Neoplatonic theory, which held that desire was a higher form of longing than carnal will because desire aspired to a stimulatingly inaccessible perfection.[28] She corrects his will by linking it to her desire, that is, her wish that he could share her search for a higher form of union:

> Mais je vouldrois, pour noz deux cueurs repaistre,
> Que son vouloir fust joinct à mon desir.

> But I do wish, to nourish our two hearts,
> That his will were joined to my desire.

The absence of direct address in this poem is striking: there is no "I" and "you," but an "I" and "him." Pernette presents her self-restraint and her wish for her lover to an outside audience rather than speaking to him in the second person.

She also shows what she can do if the autonomy she constructs for herself in the Neoplatonic duo is threatened. In a rude short poem, Epigram 28, she rejects her beloved harshly, blaming him for the breakdown of the relationship:

> Si je ne suis telle que soulois estre,
> Prenez vous en au temps, qui m'a appris
> Qu'en me traictant rudement, comme maistre,
> Jamais sur moy ne gaignerez le prys.

> If I am no longer as I used to be,
> Blame time for it, which has taught me
> That by treating me harshly, as a master,
> Never will you gain supremacy over me.

Saulnier conjectures that this poem is a justification for Pernette's marriage; the autobiographical explanation is intriguing. But what is most striking in Pernette's rebellion is the colloquial diction and the political terms she adopts. With demystifying frankness, she blames the rupture on the man's attempt to wield the power of a master because such power is exactly what she has excluded from her definition of love. She may use a mythological discourse that implies the superiority of men to women, but the absolute domination of a "master" breaks the contract she has built into "amitié saincte." Hence the anti-Neoplatonic bluntness of these lines.

The poem ends with a concession, but one that depends on proof of reform on the man's part: his fidelity in spite of her rejection convinces her to return to the rituals of Neoplatonic compliment. Yet her last lines are as much a reminder of the rules the man must follow as a declaration of renewed devotion:

> Et toutesfois, vous voyant tousjours pris
> En mon endroit, vostre ardeur me convye
> Par ce hault bien, que de vous j'ay compris,
> A demeurer vostre toute ma vie.

> Nonetheless, seeing you still eager
> For my company, your ardor convinces me
> Through that high good which I understood through you,
> To remain yours all my life long.

The bargaining position here has become far more complex than the appeal for poetic teaching in Epigram 6. The disciple now exploits the vocabulary she has learned from her mentor to oblige him to prove his loyalty to the amorous system they share. Intellectual rigor, spiritual equality, reciprocal responsibility, fair exchange: Pernette makes all four mutually interdependent in her construction of an empowering feminine Neoplatonism.

Pernette's definition of "amour saincte" is persistently aimed at an audience beyond the single and occasionally imperfect lover. Her sense of readers outside the Neoplatonic couple is obvious in the epigrams she begins to address to her city as well as her "Jour" when she confronts evidence that he is courting another woman. The rhetorical power plays worked into these jealousy poems suggest that writing them was Pernette's attempt to master the traditional helplessness of the abandoned woman by framing her accusations for eyes other than Scève's. She begins to add a satiric edge to the poetic dialogue, to write epigrams exposing her "Sun's" mistreatment of her to outside observers. These are coterie poems with a vengeance.

Early on in the jealousy sequence, she adopts the syllogistic reasoning used in courtly love games to call her beloved to order by appealing to Neo-platonic axioms. In Epigram 26 she proceeds from a general premise to an irresistible conclusion. Her use of legal jargon is mock serious, but there is a curiously menacing tone in the final invocation of absolute law. Pernette's appeal to the rules of love suggests that she is writing not only for the eyes of her wandering "Jour" but for a jury of more loyal lovers whom she intends to win over to her side:

> Prenez le cas que, comme je suis vostre
> (Et estre veulx) vous soyez tout à moy:
> Certainement par ce commun bien nostre
> Vous me debvriez tel droict, que je vous doy.
> Et si Amour vouloit rompre sa Loy,
> Il ne pourroit l'un de nous dispencer,
> S'il ne vouloit contrevenir à soy,
> Et vous, et moy, et les Dieux offencer.

> Take as a premise that just as I am yours
> (And want to be), you are entirely mine:
> Certainly, then, according to our shared joy,
> You would owe me the same right that I owe you.
> And even if Love wanted to break his own Law,
> He could not free either one of us
> Unless he were willing to perjure himself
> And to offend you, and me, and the gods above.

Further jealousy poems confirm that Pernette is no longer writing a love duet but a denunciation meant to be overheard by a crowd. Her epistles expose the imperfections of her lover and her rival as well. She crosses the generic line that separates love lyric from satire in Epigram 37, addressed to a male friend, in which she invokes the end of the men's friendship as proof that her addressee shares her contempt for her lover and her rival alike: "Prenant sur luy esgard, et congnoissance, / Qu'il me delaisse, encor pour une moindre" (Since in spite of your esteem for him, you recognize / That he is dropping me, and even for a lesser woman). In other equally contemptuous dismissals of her rival, she turns again to outside audiences for support. Epigram 38, for example, opens with the claim that every onlooker shares her low estimate of the other woman: "Plus ne m'en chault, la congnoissant à l'oeil, / Comme chascun, non plus belle, que bonne" (I'm no longer upset, seeing with my own eyes, / As everyone does, that she is no more beautiful than good). The poem is constructed to declare Pernette's superiority, shored up by her claim that all of Lyon witnesses her beloved's bad judgment.

In *Chanson* 5, Pernette turns to a feminine audience to enlarge her attack. She invites the women in her milieu to boycott faithless men:

> Dames, s'il est permis
> Que l'amour appetisse
> Entre deux cueurs promis,
> Faisons pareil office:
> Lors la legereté
> Prendra sa fermeté. . . .

> 25 Ne nous esbahissons
> Si le vouloir nous change:
> Car d'eulx nous congnoissons
> La vie tant estrange
> Qu'elle nous a permis
> Infinité d'amis.

> Ladies, if it's allowed
> To love to sample
> Two faithful hearts at once,
> Let's do the same;
> Then [men's] fickleness
> Will take firmer form. . . .

> Let's not be surprised
> If our desires change:
> For we learn from men
> A life so unruly
> That it allows us
> Any number of lovers.

Like Epigram 28 ("Si je ne suis telle que soulois estre"), this poem ends with a statement of forgiveness. Although Pernette multiplies the targets of her critique, she repeats her pattern of promising to return to the fold on the condition that men change their behavior:

> Mais puis qu'occasion
> Nous a esté donnée,
> Que nostre passion
> Soit à eulx adonnée:
> Amour nous vengera
> Quand foy les rengera.

> But since the chance
> Has been given to us,
> Let us restore
> Our affection to them.
> Love will avenge us
> When faith has reformed them.

This is a comic poem, one that could circulate throughout Lyon and amuse a popular audience as well as the cognoscenti to whom Pernette read her texts aloud. It is also publicly oriented in its call to women to challenge the double standard. All in all, *Chanson* 5 exposes the multiple layers of readership to which Pernette appeals throughout the *Rymes*. The audience she calls upon is fourfold. The poem's dedicatees ("Dames") are invoked as women who share the speaker's misfortune. But beyond this feminine public, the poem aims at male readers: their transformation as lovers is the goal of Pernette's call to mass female rebellion. And as Neoplatonic disciple turned comic leader of her sisters, Pernette is showing her mentor and a larger literary audience the degree to which his betrayal prompts her to abandon the lyric conventions on which their dialogue has been based.

Many of the strategies I have been discussing are drawn together in Pernette's *Elégie* 2, a long narrative in which a protofeminist revision of Ovid opens up a fantasy of sexual power that modulates into an adroit appeal to her audience and Scève's. She opens with a pastoral setting and with a wish: she represents herself, like Diana, bathing nude in a fountain, luring her beloved toward her and holding him back at the same time. Even in its erotic aquatics, the poem at first conforms to Guazzo's portrait of the ideal mistress who maintains an alluring balance between seducing a lover and holding him at arm's length:

> Combien de fois ay-je en moy souhaicté
> Me rencontrer sur la chaleur d'esté
> Tout au plus pres de la clere fontaine,
> Où mon desir avec cil se pourmaine
> Qui exercite en sa philosophie
> Son gent esprit. . . .
> Puis peu à peu de luy m'escarterois,
> Et toute nue en l'eau me gecterois: . . .
> Mais si vers moy il s'en venoit tout droict,
> Je le lairrois hardyment approcher:
> Et s'il vouloit, tant soit peu, me toucher,
> Lui gecterois (pour le moins) ma main pleine
> De la pure eau de la clere fontaine,
> Luy gectant droit aux yeulx, ou à la face.

> How many times have I secretly wished
> To find myself, in summer's heat,
> As close as can be to the clear fountain
> Where my desire accompanies the man
> Who exercises his noble spirit
> In considerations of philosophy. . . .
> Then, little by little, I'd move away,
> And, entirely naked, I'd leap into the water. . . .
> But if he came straight toward me,
> I'd let him approach me boldly;

And if he wanted to touch me, however slightly,
I'd throw a handful, at the least,
Of the clear fountain's pure water
Straight into his eyes, or at his face.

But the poem carries out a startling revision of the Ovidian and Petrarchan versions of Actaeon's downfall: Pernette presents the meeting of divinity and mortal from the perspective of the goddess rather than her victim. The woman's pleasure in controlling the man comes through clearly in the leisureliness of the narration and in the fantasy of reducing the lover who claims to offer devoted service into an actual servant:

> O qu'alors eust l'onde telle efficace
> De le pouvoir en Acteon muer,
> Non toutefois pour le faire tuer,
> Et devorer à ses chiens, comme Cerf:
> Mais que de moy se sensist estre serf,
> Et serviteur transformé tellement
> Qu'ainsi cuydast en son entendement,
> Tant que Dyane en eust sur moy envie,
> De luy avoir sa puissance ravie.

> O that the water had the power
> To change him into Actaeon—
> Not, however, to have him killed,
> And devoured by his dogs, like a deer;
> But to make him feel he was my slave,
> So that he felt, and understood,
> That he had been transformed into a servant,
> So much that Diana herself would envy me
> For having stolen her power away.

Immediately after this avowal of her desire for erotic mastery, Pernette disavows it; she returns to a sense of literary and social obligation. Yet she makes no apology for the nudity, the erotic freedom, and the divine power the myth allows her to imagine. She withdraws the fantasy not to reassert her chastity but to assume another kind of power, the ability to protect her poet-lover's career:

> Mais, pour me veoir contente à mon desir,
> Vouldrois je bien faire un tel deplaisir
> A Apollo, et aussi à ses Muses,
> De les laisser privées, et confuses
> D'un, qui les peult toutes servir à gré,
> Et faire honneur à leur hault choeur sacré?

> But yet, to see my desire fulfilled,
> Would I want to cause such displeasure
> To Apollo, and also to his Muses,

> To leave them deprived and bereft
> Of a man who can serve them to perfection,
> And honor their lofty, sacred choir?

This focus on poetic productivity rather than sexual pleasure typifies *Les Rymes*. Pernette benefits from her role as Scève's muse and interlocutor throughout their dialogue; hence her identification with Diana and the Muses here. As the inspirer and guide of the male poet, she locates herself at the center of his oeuvre. Only her self-repression can lead him back to continued acclaim from the audience she herself woos by writing this poem of renunciation:

> Ostez, ostez, mes souhaitz, si hault poinct
> D'avecques vous: il ne m'appartient point.
> Laissez le aller les neuf Muses servir,
> Sans se vouloir dessoubz moy asservir,
> Soubz moy, qui suis sans grace, et sans merite.

> Give up, give up, my hopes, such a
> Lofty goal; it is not mine to ask.
> Let him go, to do service to the nine Muses,
> Without the desire to enslave him to myself,
> Myself, who lack both grace and merit.

Pernette's deference to deities whom she herself has invoked is less humble than it may seem. By raising the poet's vocation above her will to erotic sovereignty, she turns outward to a public of readers awaiting further texts by Scève and claims their gratitude:

> Laissez le aller, qu'Apollo je ne irrite,
> Le remplissant de Deité profonde,
> Pour contre moy susciter tout le Monde,
> Lequel un jour par ses escriptz s'attend
> D'estre avec moy et heureux, et content.

> Let him go, so that I don't anger Apollo,
> Filling him with divine force,
> To stir up the whole world against me—
> The world, which one day through his writing
> Expects, as I do, to be happy and fulfilled.

Even the self-abnegation in this conclusion includes a fantasy of power. As Pernette imagines what she will not do, she also imagines that she can outdo what Apollo does, that is, fill his mortal sibyls with prophetic powers: she represents herself filling the god with divine anger. Yet she registers less concern for the god's favor than for the favor of a secular public. Her attentiveness to the "world" of readers at the end of this elegy is consistent with the strategies she uses throughout the *Rymes*. She invites her public and Scève's to appreciate her control of her sexuality and his: by rejecting celebrity as a femme fatale, she lays claim to fame as a literary mentor. The former apprentice is now the mediator/midwife to whom the world will be indebted for further works of the master.

This persistent sense of an audience has been a central issue in my discussion of this urban poet. Whether Pernette is seeking fame as the feminine partner in an idealizing dialogue or defaming her lover and her rival, she writes outward. Her *Rymes* expose the public dimension of the conventions of solitary meditation and epistolary intimacy. She uses both modes to construct a self-portrait meant to be admired by a specific community of readers: the cultural elite of her city. *Les Rymes* construct an audience capable of recognizing the correctness of Pernette's Neoplatonism, the exemplary purity of her version of love, and the justice of her claim to a separate but equal identity in the dialogue she and Scève perform with each other—and always for the readers of Lyon.

TULLIA D'ARAGONA:
THE COURTESAN'S TEXT
AS GROUP PORTRAIT

Like Pernette du Guillet, Tullia d'Aragona appropriated the vocabulary of Neoplatonism to write poems to famous poets. But a major difference is that Tullia wrote to over thirty men, dukes and soldiers as well as poets, and she included their replies in her collection of poems, published in Venice in 1547. The title of the collection, *Rime della Signora Tullia d'Aragona; et di diversi a lui* (Poems by Tullia d'Aragona, and by various men to her), emphasizes its anthology aspect, and in fact, over two-thirds of the poems are signed by men. In a first section of thirty-eight poems, Tullia addresses twenty-five sonnets to male acquaintances. Some belong to the political elite of Florence: Duke Cosimo de' Medici, the ruler of Florence, and his brothers-in-law, the Spanish princes Pedro and Luis of Toledo. Many are humanist poets known throughout Italy: Pietro Bembo, Benedetto Varchi, Girolamo Muzio. Others are ecclesiastics, such as Ippolito de' Medici and Ugolino Martelli. The second section of the book consists of ten sonnets, organized into pairs that share the same rhyme schemes, the first of each pair written by Tullia, the second a response written by a man. This order is reversed in the third section of the book: in six pairs of sonnets, the man's *proposta* precedes Tullia's *risposta*. The fourth section of the book consists of Muzio's eclogue "La Tirrhenia," dedicated to Tullia and spoken by two shepherds who praise her as a poet and celebrate her admirers. And the fifth and final section of *Le Rime* is composed of fifty-five sonnets written to Tullia by male admirers.

What does the multiplicity of Tullia's interlocutors reveal about her literary project? As a courtesan, she made her living through contacts with highly placed men, whom she attracted through her reputation as a musician and writer. This cultural training distinguished her, as a *cortigiana onesta* ("honest" in the sense of honored: prosperous, highly placed), from less well-paid prostitutes.[29] To command high fees and the loyalty of aristocratic client-lovers, the elite courtesan had to be able to play and sing, to quote classical Italian poets, to initiate belleletristic and philosophical conversation. Tullia appears to have been particularly well known as a literary figure. Ludovico Domenichi described an evening at her house in Rome during which an energetic discussion of Petrarch's uses of Provençal and earlier Tuscan poets took place; Sperone Speroni assigned her a leading role in his Neoplatonic *Dialogo dell'amore* (1542), in which one of the speakers, Niccolo Gratia, compares her to Sappho and Diotima; Niccolo Martelli published a letter to her in which he played on her name to praise her as a female rival to Tully (Cicero): "Today there is in the world a Tullia d'Aragona, whom one can truthfully honour equally, and in whom the soul of Poetry and the nobility of Philosophy join in celestial company."[30] She herself wrote a philosophical dialogue, *Della Infinità di amore*, in which she represents herself learning the techniques of logical disputation from Varchi.[31]

Literary practice brought the courtesan positive publicity. But in Tullia's case, the rewards of poetry were more concrete than that. In 1547, the year she moved to Florence, she was threatened with the humiliation of being categorized as an ordinary prostitute. She was summoned before the magistrates for disobeying a sumptuary law recently proclaimed by Cosimo de' Medici, which required courtesans to wear yellow-bordered veils to distinguish themselves from the noblewomen whose rich costume they imitated. Tullia consulted two men who had participated in her literary salons: Pedro of Toledo, the brother of Cosimo's wife Eleonora, and Benedetto Varchi, a new lover and ally. Don Pedro advised her to appeal to the duchess; Varchi helped her to compose a letter to her. The strategy worked. Cosimo himself wrote on her petition, "Fasseli gratia per poetessa" (Be merciful to her, as a poet),[32] and a notice in the Florentine state archives explains the basis for the judgment as "la rara scientia di poesia e filosophia" that learned men attested to in her.[33] Her reprieve demonstrates the power of a literary reputation—and also its composite character, its dependency on recommendations from well-known men in the literary establishment. Courtesanship demanded timely manipulation of sexuality and patronage; Tullia coordinated both to win political safety at this moment of crisis.

Le Rime were the offering she made to the Medici clan in payment for her exemption from the law. Although few of Tullia's sonnets are love poems, in nearly all of them she courts fame. Most of the poems are prefaced with the name of the person to whom they are addressed, and the poems written for her make up a dossier of noblemen and literati whose textual presence dramatizes her prestige as the focus of so many eulogies. She builds her reputation upon the reputations of her poets, who benefit in turn from the homosocial bond they construct with one another through her.[34] Her text is like a hall of mirrors in which the woman and the men all bask in one another's reflected glory, rewriting the economic and sexual rivalry which actually set a courtesan's clients against one another. In *Le Rime*, masculine competition is displaced into a harmonious group portrait, an improving fiction through which the woman acts as a mediating figure for the men's self-representation as an elite unified by their connoisseurship of erotic and poetic codes. Given the mutual benefits such a text conferred on its writers, it is not surprising that it was republished three times before the end of the sixteenth century.

Her sonnets explore the erotics of fame rather than the conventions of passion. Like Pernette, when Tullia praises a poet who praises her, she praises herself. She pieces together an identity as a poet by addressing *laude* (poems of praise) to the great and by asking for *carte* (letter-poems) from her admirers, which she assembles into a self-glorifying autograph book. Her poems to Cosimo de' Medici and Eleonora di Toledo exemplify the first strategy; the *proposte/risposte* poems dramatize the second.

Tullia's humility toward the great is always double-edged, a way of elevating herself as poet at the same time that she insists on her indebtedness toward her addressees. In her dedication to Eleonora, for example, she apologizes for her poems as "small, unworthy efforts" but justifies offering them to the duchess by reminding her of the responsibilities of patrons: "the compositions of all writers, in all languages, especially those of poets, have always had such grace and preeminence that no one, however great, has ever refused them but always cherished them instead" (3).[35] In her seven sonnets to Cosimo de' Medici she demonstrates what a grateful poet can do in return for princely favors. She combines classical allusion, pastoral decor, and political praise into a language of ingenious compliment that brings credit to her as well as to the duke. In her first sonnet, she works out an architectural conceit. Recalling the garlands and incense that ancient shepherds took to Pan's temples, she deplores her own inability to offer Cosimo gifts worthy of his "rare virtues and priceless kindness"; his own breast and heart must replace the classical temples, and her soul must be her offering to him. The poem publicizes the benefits she has received at the hand of the duke of Florence, and its final line puts the focus on Tullia herself: "Vittima l'alma mia, se tanto vale" (Let the sacrificial victim be my soul, if it is worthy of so great an honor).

As chaste lover of Cosimo, Tullia writes with an eye to her own commemoration as well as his. In her fourth sonnet she addresses him as "the new Numa of Tuscany," thanks him for making his city so welcoming for her, and ends by promising to write him further praise. The last line of the poem spotlights her activity as a poet. She defines the lyric genre she will employ and emphasizes her own bid for fame as the player of the reed pipe emblematic of pastoral poetry:

> Così potessi un di farmi sentire
> Cortese no, ma grata con la mia
> Zampogna, ch'a te sol, bench'indegna, ergo.
>
> (4)

> So may I one day make myself heard,
>   Not courtly but at least pleasing with my pipe,
>   Which, though unworthy, I raise to you alone.

Tullia's most explicit representation of herself as Cosimo's poet, eternalized along with the ruler she commemorates, comes at the end of her fifth sonnet, in which she calls upon the Muses to weave a garland of praises for the duke. The apostrophe to the Muses arises from a conventional pose of modesty: Tullia denies her own capacity to compose *laude* worthy of her subject. But the sonnet ends with a line that grounds the poet in the future of literary immortality. Tullia eternalizes herself by speaking from the third-person perspective of a posthumous biographer:

> E per me lodi, e gratia a lui
>   Rendete, o Dive, che lingua mortale
>   Verso immortal virtù s'affanna indarno;
> Quest'è valor, quest'è suggetto tale,
>   Che solo è da voi sole, e non d'altrui,
>   Cosi dicea la Tullia in riva d'Arno.

> And give praises and thanks through me to him,
>   O goddesses, for a mortal tongue
>   Labors in vain, faced with immortal virtue;
> This is true valor, this is a subject
>   That belongs to you alone, to no one else—
>   So spoke Tullia on the banks of the Arno.

This signature line, like a painter's name written into the canvas of a nobleman's portrait, marks Tullia's awareness of the fame she is constructing for herself as the poet to the ducal family of Florence.

Enrico Celani condemns Tullia as a writer who "presents a sharply etched image of the fawning courtesanship [*strisciante cortigianeria*] that surrounded even the most minor princes" (xvii). But this courtesanship is exactly where Tullia's artistry lies, and it was required by her career—as it was by the careers of male courtier-poets, including Castiglione, the flattering portraitist of the Gonzagas of Urbino, and Ariosto, whose celebration of the Este family is central to *Orlando furioso*.[36] Rather than dismissing the discourses of courtly compliment as somehow subpoetic, I am interested in how women used them to consolidate their reputations. Frank Whigham, analyzing such codes in letters written to patrons in sixteenth-century England, points out the erotic vocabulary that accompanies pleas and expressions of gratitude between men.[37] In contrast, Tullia's poem-epistles suppress erotic turns of phrase. One reason must have been that readers were likely to take sexual invitation in a woman's text literally while they would accept the rhetorical function of amorous metaphor in a man's. Tullia also intended her poems to the Medici to demonstrate that she was no longer a courtesan, that their generosity had reformed her, and this is another explanation for the chastity of her language—although her male interlocutors, as was the case with Catherine des Roches's fellow poets in *La Puce*, labored under no such constraints. Tullia has it both ways: she publishes sonnets by Ippolito de' Medici and Muzio that frankly praise her for her physical desirability, but she herself uses a discourse of spiritualized Neoplatonism. To affirm her new status as a protégée of the Medici, she collects trophies from literary men whom she rewards by publishing her own poems of praise to them.

She is quite forthright about this process of exchange. In her fifteenth sonnet, for example, to Cardinal Bembo, she announces a conversion; following his example, she says, she has rediscovered the moral life. A Dantean echo is heard in her sixth line: "Scorger la strada di virtù smarrita" (I can discern virtue's path, strayed from until now). But her motive for returning to the path of honor is clearly as much a literary as a spiritual one: "Per lasciar del mio nome eterno segno" (To leave behind a sign that makes my name eternal). She defines one technique for garnering fame: naming the famous. To the military hero Ridolfo Baglioni, for example, she writes a sonnet (16) explaining that her Muse addresses him not only to praise his valor but to reflect his glory onto Tullia herself: "perch'in voi nomar conosce e sente, / sorger nel vostro onor la gloria mia" (for she knows and senses that, by naming you, / my glory takes your honor as its source).

Entire poems are structured according to rituals of gathering and returning praise. In one instance Tullia reminds Muzio of his past devotion in Rome as a way of asking him to write about her in Florence now. In her twenty-fourth sonnet, she asks him to compose a new declaration of his love:

> Visse gran tempo l'honorato amore
>   Ch'al Po già per me v'arse. E non cred'io
>   Che sia si chiara fiamma in tutto spenta.
> E se nel volto altrui si legge il core,
>   Spero ch'in riva d'Arno il nome mio
>   Alto sonar anchor per voi si senta.
>
>   (9)

> Long lived the famous love you burned with
>   For me by the Po. And I don't believe
>   That such a bright flame is now entirely spent.
> And if a man's heart can be read in his face,
>   I hope that my name, on the banks of the Arno,
>   Will be heard again, sung aloud by you.

Two cities, two audiences: Tullia demands repeated homage from her admirers, and she publishes it when and where she needs their support.

The dialogic layout of the *proposte/risposte* poems translates the system of mutual praise into visual terms: Tullia requests or responds to a sonnet, and the evidence of her success is there on the same page. An example from

the second section, "Sonetti della Signora Tullia, con le Risposte," sets up a
contest in apparent modesty: Tullia's humble request for poetic teaching is
paired with Varchi's claim that his merits depend entirely on her high esteem. The structural symmetry of the two texts strikes the reader's eye. Each
writer places the other's name, capitalized, in the same position, midway
through the fifth line of the poem. Varchi's image of Tullia as the light, that
is, the vision through which he is reflected to the world at large, comments
upon the mirroring exchange through which a flattering dual portrait is even
now being composed:

LA TULLIA
Quel, che'l mondo d'Invidia empie, e di duolo;
   Quel, che sol di virtute è ricco, e adorno,
   Quel, che col suo splendor un lieto giorno
   Chiaro ne mostra a l'uno e a l'altro polo,
Quel sete VARCHI voi: quel voi che solo
   Fate col valor vostro oltraggio, e scorno
   A i più lontan, non ch'ai vicin d'intorno;
   Ond'io v'ammiro, riverisco, e colo.
E di voi canterei mentre ch'io vivo,
   S'al gran suggetto il mio debile stile
   Giunger potesse di gran spatio al meno.
O pur non fosse a voi noioso, e schivo
   Questo mio dire scemo, e troppo humile:
   Che per voi renderassi altero, e pieno.

IL VARCHI
Se da i bassi pensier talhor m'involo,
   E me medesmo in me stesso ritorno;
   S'al ciel, lasciato ogni terren soggiorno,
   Sopra l'ali d'amor poggiando volo;
Quest'è sol don di voi TULLIA, al cui solo
   Lume mi specchio, e quanto posso adorno
   La've sempre con voi lieto soggiorno,
   Di santo e bel disio levato a volo.
E se quel, ch'entro 'l cor ragiono, e scrivo
   Del vostro alto valor Donna gentile,
   Ch'avete quanto puo bramarsi a pieno,
Ridir potessi, o beato, anzi Divo
   Me, per me proprio tutto oscuro, e vile
   Se non quant'ho da voi pregio, e sereno.
                          (Pair 3, 15)

He who fills the world with envy and regret,
   He who alone is rich and decked with merit,
   He who with his brilliance brings
   Joyful, clear daylight to either pole,
This man, VARCHI, is you: you, who alone
   By your merit bring contempt and scorn

To men both far and near;
 So that I admire, revere and worship you.
I would sing of you my whole life long,
 If my feeble style could rise to this
 Great subject, or even close. Oh, if only
This, my weak and all too humble speech,
 Does not annoy and repel you—it will,
 Through you, become lofty and eloquent.

If ever I fly above lowly thoughts,
 And rediscover myself in myself,
 If, leaving every earthly dwelling behind,
 I fly upward, soaring on the wings of love,
This is your gift alone, TULLIA; in your light
 I am reflected, and as much as I can, I praise
 That place where I stay, delighted, with you,
 Lifted into flight by holy and lovely desire.
And if I could declare aloud what I recite and write
 In my heart of your high worth, noble lady,
 Which you possess as fully as can be desired,
I could call myself blessed, no, even a god
 Although unknown and lowly in myself, except
 For the esteem and joy I win through you.

As lyrical diptych, the dialogue affirms typographically what it declares on the thematic level: each poet attributes his/her success to the other, and the juxtaposition of the two texts confirms that each provides a springboard for the other's virtuosity.

Collaboration of a similar kind goes on in the third section of *Le Rime*, "Sonetti di diversi alla Signora Tullia, con le risposte di lei." But Tullia needs more ingenuity when she writes in response to a preceding poem. One example is a sonnet in which the satirist Luigi Grazzini (nicknamed *Il Lasca*, "The Roach") breaks the rules of fame exchange by telling Tullia that she alone is capable of singing her praises in the style they require. In other words, he implies, "Do it yourself." While this invitation may be a compliment to her powers as a eulogist, it is also a refusal to play the game; Grazzini resists being organized into the chorus singing Tullia's praises. Yet his sonnet, like Varchi's, capitalizes the name of the woman whose reputation he confirms even in his claim of inadequacy:

Se'l vostro alto valor Donna gentile
 Esser lodato pur dovesse in parte,
 Uopo sarebbe al fin vergar le carte
 Col vostro altero, e glorioso stile.
Dunque voi sola a voi stessa simile,
 A cui s'inchina la natura, e l'arte
 Fate di voi cantando in ogni parte
 TULLIA, TULLIA suonar da Gange a Thile.

Si vedrem poi di gioia e maraviglia
    E di gloria, e d'honore il mondo pieno
    Drizzare al vostro nome altare, e tempi.
Cosa che mai con l'ardenti sue ciglia
    Non vide il Sole rotando il Ciel sereno,
    O ne gli antichi, o ne moderni tempi.

                                        (19)

If your high worth, noble lady,
    Were to be properly praised, even in part,
    Sheets of paper would have to be covered
    With your lofty and famous style [stylus].
Thus you alone equal to yourself,
    To whom nature and art bow down,
    Make yourself, resounding everywhere,
    TULLIA, TULLIA echo from the Ganges to Thule.
Then we will see the world, filled with
    Joy and wonder, with your glory and honor,
    Raise altars and temples to your name—
A sight that the sun, with his burning brows,
    Has never seen, wheeling through the calm sky,
    Either in ancient or in modern times.

However evasive Grazzini's compliment may be, Tullia turns it into the occasion for a floral conceit through which she thanks him for encouraging her in a moment of depression. Confessing that aging has made her lose faith in her skills as a writer, she rewrites Il Lasca as a revivifying force. By defining his refusal as timely inspiration, she celebrates her own renewal as a poet:

Io, che fin qui quasi alga ingrata, e vile,
    prezzava in me così l'interna parte,
    Come di fuor, che tosto invecchia, e parte
    Da noi ben spesso nel più bello Aprile,
Hoggi LASCA gentil non pur a vile
    Non mi tengo (mercè de le tue carte)
    Ma movo anchor la penna ad honorarte,
    Fatta in tutto a me stessa dissimile.
E, come pianta che suggendo piglia
    Novo licor da l'humido terreno,
    Manda fuor frutti, e fior, benche s'attempi,
Tal' io potrei, sì nuovo mi bisbiglia
    Pensier nel cor di non venir mai meno,
    Dar forse anchor di me non bassi essempi.

I, who until now have considered my inner
    And my outer self a useless, lowly weed,
    Which rapidly withers and vanishes
    From sight in the midst of the loveliest April,
Today, noble LASCA, I no longer
    Feel self-contempt, thanks to your poem,

> But I raise my pen again to honor you,
> Transformed entirely from my former self.
> And as a plant, drawing up new moisture
>   From the dampened earth,
>   Sends forth new fruits and blossoms even though it ages,
> So may I, since such a new thought whispers
>   In my heart that I need never decay,
>   Produce again not unworthy examples of my skill.

Like most of the poems in *Le Rime*, this is a sonnet about poetry: about the mutual compliments that keep it circulating and the roles of pathos and metaphor in embellishing the circuit of exchange. Pens, styluses, paper, and ink are the commodities that circulate in this poetic system, which exposes in its reciprocal complexity the processes by which any poet or group of poets acquires fame. Tullia's poets are also her patrons, as she is theirs, and their "polylogue"[38] makes explicit the mutual compliments and manipulation of public attention through which male poets as well as courtesans made names for themselves in the city-states of late Renaissance Europe.

Postromantic critical assumptions, however, have led to the effacement of Tullia's multiauthored text in favor of a focus on single poems that can be read as soliloquies. Enrico Celani, for example, who edited *Le Rime* in 1891, rearranged the original order so as to suppress the paired sonnets: he set all of Tullia's poems together, dividing them from the *proposte* and *risposte* of her interlocutors. His title advertises the poet's status as a courtesan (*Le Rime di Tullia d'Aragona, cortigiana del secolo XVI*) as her own did not, but his reordering of the poems replaces the collaborative process of fame building with poems that appear to have been composed in isolation. The same bias toward individual composition has meant that Tullia's most frequently anthologized lyrics have been those in which she speaks atypically to an unnamed lover rather than to a specifically named poet. In fact, the lover to whom she wrote her most famous sonnets first appears in *Le Rime* as a poet: Piero Manelli, a young Florentine nobleman, to whom she addresses a sonnet (27) comparing her writing to his. Conventional signs of sexual difference are absent from this poem. Tullia stresses the similarity of temperament and ambition between herself and Manelli in an opening challenge that sets up a poetic contest rather than an amorous duet:

> Poi che mi diè natura a voi simile
>   Forma, e materia; o fosse il gran Fattore;
>   Non pensate ch'anchor disio d'honore
>   Mi desse, e bei pensier MANEL gentile?
> Dunque credete me cotanto vile,
>   Ch'io non osi mostrar cantando fore,
>   Quel che dentro m'ancide altero ardore,
>   Se bene a voi non ho pari lo stile?

(10)

Since Nature gave me matter and form
   Similar to yours (or God was the donor),
   Do you not think that she also gave me
   The desire for honor and high intellect, noble MANELLI?
Do you really think me so worthless
   That I dare not reveal and sing forth
   The proud and killing passion within me,
   Even though my style is not equal to yours?

The conclusion of the sonnet is ambiguous: does its last word, "longing,"
refer to the speaker's desire for the man—or for the worldly fame she mentions at the end of the first tercet?

Non lo crediate, no PIERO, ch'anch'io
   Fatico ognihor per appressarmi al Cielo
   E lasciar del mio nome in terra fama.
Non contenda rea sorte il bel disio,
   Che pria che l'alma dal corporeo velo
   Si scoglia, satierò forse mia brama.

No, do not believe it, no, PIERO, for I, too,
   Labor every hour to prepare myself for heaven
   And to leave some fame for my name on earth.
May hostile fate not block this fair desire:
   That before my soul is released from the body's veil,
   I may perhaps satisfy my longing.

Tullia was in her forties and Manelli only twenty-four at the time this sonnet
was published. Her success in establishing a reputation for herself as "the
courtesan of the academicians" may explain her emphasis on poetic rivalry
rather than erotic union in the poem that includes his name.

   In the 1547 edition of *Le Rime* the following seven sonnets bear no addressee's name. Celani presents them as addressed to Manelli, entitling several "Allo stesso" (To the same man), but these texts are actually curiously
free-floating. Lacking capitalized names to identify their recipients, they invoke pastoral landscapes and feminine audiences in ways that contrast with
Tullia's more frequent apostrophes to the circle of male admirers. An audience is implied and often specified even in these poems, but the difference in
addressees—the figures of Love and hope, a small bird, a female pet grieving for her lost offspring—establishes a new position for the poet, less engaged in exchanging praise, more reflective and empathetic—although still
always engaged with at least a fictive audience.

   Her plea to an unnamed lover (Sonnet 31) and her description of him
(34) belong clearly to the Petrarchan tradition; either poem could have been
written by a man. In Sonnet 31 one adjective signals a feminine speaker
("priva / Della gratia, onde nasce ogni il mio ben" [deprived / Of the grace
that is the source of all my happiness]), but the poem otherwise closely imi-

tates Petrarch's *Canzone* 15, "S'i' 'l dissi mai, ch'i' venga in odio a quella" (*Canzoniere*, 206: "If I ever said such a thing, may I be hated by her"), in its denials of an unnamed act against the lover: "S'io 'l feci unque, che mai non giugna a riva / L'interno duol, che'l cor lasso sostiene" (If I ever did such a thing, may the grief my weary heart endures never reach an end). Likewise, the *blason* of Sonnet 34 lists beauties that could belong as well to a woman as to a man: golden hair, bright eyes, a white hand, and graceful manners. Tullia's portrait of the man leaves Petrarch's praises of Laura unchanged; only the title of this part of the collection, "Sonetti della signora Tullia," indicates that the person being described is a man. As in her poem to the radical preacher Bernardo Ochino, pointing out that the severity of his instructions deprives mankind of the free will God gave them (Sonnet 25), Tullia retains the authority of conventional discourses (Petrarchism, theology) by voicing them in a non-gender-inflected way.

But in other sonnets in this set she clearly identifies herself as a woman. In her thirty-second sonnet, for example, she sets up three analogies to define amorous despair. Two of her comparisons involve conventional masculine types, a captured warrior and a storm-tossed sailor, but she adds a new figure to the list: a mother who has lost a child. Her opening focus on the woman's loss establishes a feminine frame of reference, so that her comment on her own emotional state in the final tercet completes the pattern and reinforces the contrast the sonnet is designed to assert:

> Se ben pietosa madre unico figlio
>   Perde talhora, e nuovo alto dolore
>   Le preme il tristo e suspiroso core,
>   Spera conforto almen, spera consiglio.
> Se scaltro Capitano in gran periglio
>   Mostrando alteramente il suo valore
>   Resta vinto, e prigion, spera uscir fuore
>   Quando che sia con baldanzoso ciglio.
> S'in tempestoso mar giunto si duole
>   Spaventato Nocchier già presso a morte,
>   Ha speme ancor di riverdersi in porto.
> Ma io, s'avvien che perda il mio bel Sole,
>   O per mia colpa, o per malvagia sorte,
>   Non spero haver, ne voglio alcun conforto.
>   (11)

> If a devoted mother loses her only child,
>   And a new, deep sorrow oppresses
>   Her sad and sighing heart,
>   At least she hopes for comfort, for advice;
> If a shrewd Captain, in great danger,
>   Demonstrating his high courage,
>   Is conquered and taken prisoner, he hopes to escape
>   Sometime or another, maintaining a bold front.

If in a stormy sea, near death,
  A sailor groans in terror,
  He still has hope of returning safe to port.
But I, if I should lose my lovely Sun,
  Either by my fault or through malicious fate,
  I neither hope to have nor desire any comfort.

The poem invites its audience to appreciate how Tullia's variation on the Petrarchan pattern intensifies its refusal of consolation. It is possible that she envisioned women readers, although she probably did not intend the poem as a reference to her own motherhood (she had a daughter, Penelope, in 1535 and a son some years later); without a husband she had little to gain from publicizing this part of her past. To the extent that she was suppressing her sexual history in the *Rime* in order to establish her worthiness as poet to the Medici, however, referring to maternity in a general way may have been a safe strategy for appealing to readers of her own sex.

Pathetic maternity is also the theme of a later sonnet (35), in which Tullia addresses a bereaved female pet. By drawing an analogy between Lilla as grieving mother and herself as abandoned lover, she reverses the convention whereby a male lover speaks jealously to his lady's pet (Catullus to Lesbia's sparrow, for example, or Phillip Sidney to Stella's). Empathy, not rivalry, structures this poem:

Se materna pietate afflige il core,
  Onde cercando in questa parte, e in quella
  Il caro figlio tuo LILLA mia bella
  Piangi, e cresci piangendo il tuo dolore;
A te, ch'animal se di ragion fore,
  E non intendi (ohime) quanto rubella
  Sia stata ad ambe noi sorte empia e fella,
  Togliendo a te'l tuo figlio, a me'l mio Amore;
Che far (lassa) degg'io? qual degno pianto
  Verseran gli occhi miei dal cor mai sempre?
  Che conosco il tuo mal, e'l mio gran danno.

                    (12)

If maternal pity afflicts your heart,
  So that, looking everywhere
  For your beloved son, my pretty LILLA,
  You weep and by weeping increase your pain,
Although you are an animal, without reason,
  And do not understand (alas) how cruel
  Fierce and heartless fate has been to us both,
  Taking your son from you and Love from me,
What (unhappy woman) should I do? what fitting tears
  Shall my eyes weep, flowing from my heart forever?
  For I am conscious both of your pain and of my loss.

The ending of the poem returns to the realm of erotic exchange and self-glorification. Tullia's allusion to Psyche, a mortal woman who sang the beauties of Eros, flatters the man to whom she attributes the god's youth and divinity. Even Tullia's invocations of feminine alter egos contribute to the compliments the *Rime* direct toward male readers:

> Chi potrà di Psychì con alto canto
>   Cantar l'altere lodi? o con quai tempre
>   Temprar quel, che mi da sua morte, affanno?

> Who can share Psyche's lofty song
>   To praise her high beloved? Or with what cures
>   Diminish the anguish his death causes me?

But the mythological reference also raises the issue of poetry again, in a way that allows the woman poet to call attention to her own successes: Tullia compares herself to another woman, a poet-singer privileged by intimacy with a god.

Elsewhere, too, myth allows Tullia to imagine a freer and more powerful position for herself. Her twenty-ninth sonnet, like Pernette's *Elégie* 2, re-writes an Ovidian metamorphosis from a feminine point of view. Tullia's material looks considerably less promising: the story of Philomela (*Metamorphoses*, VI), raped by her sister Procne's husband, Tereus, who cuts out her tongue, hoping to keep his crime unspoken, and locks her up in a hidden cottage. But Philomela weaves an account of the assault into a tapestry, which Procne immediately understands; vengefully, she serves Itys, her son by Tereus, to his father at a banquet, in a three-way confrontation that transforms Philomela and Procne into the nightingale and the swallow. In men's poetry in the Renaissance, the violence of the Ovidian episode is usually repressed; Philomela and Procne are combined into a formula signifying a spring landscape. Sannazaro, for example, in Eclogue 11 of the *Arcadia*, turns Philomela's cries of anguish into "soavi accenti" and represents Procne as repenting her misdeed, thus suppressing Tereus's role as rapist and provoker of revenge.[39]

Tullia rereads the myth to emphasize Philomela's escape from the literal prison in which Tereus encloses her and also from the prison of silence. She equates the stone-walled cottage with the psychic prison of love: to be free from love is to resemble Philomela, liberated from the imprisonment through which Tereus hoped to maintain his reputation. But Tullia's Philomela escapes only temporarily. The sonnet tells a tale of recovery from one love followed by entrapment in another:

> Qual vaga Philomena, che fuggita
>   È da la odiata gabbia, e in superba
>   Vista sen'va tra gli arboscelli, e l'herba
>   Tornata in libertate, e in lieta vita;

Er'io da gli amorosi lacci uscita
 Schernendo ogni martire, e pena acerba
 De l'incredibil duol, ch'in se riserba
 Qual ha per troppo amar l'alma smarrita.
Ben havev'io ritolte (ahi Stella fera)
 Dal tempio di Ciprigna le mie spoglie,
 E di lor pregio me n'andava altera;
Quand'a me Amor, le tue ritrose voglie
 Muterò disse, e femmi prigionera
 Di tua virtù, per rinovar mie doglie.

         (10)

Like the lovely Philomela, fleeing
 Her hateful prison and seen proudly
 Flying away through trees and grasses,
 Returned once more to freedom and life's joy,
So was I, loosed from the bonds of love,
 Scorning all suffering and the sharp pain
 Of the unbelievable woe reserved
 For whoever loses her soul by loving too much.
I had confidently retrieved (alas, cruel star)
 My trophies from the temple of Cyprian Venus,
 And, proud of their value, I was carrying them away,
When Love suddenly said to me: "I will change
 Your wayward mind"; and he made me a prisoner
 In your power, to renew all my sorrow.

Georgina Masson praises this poem as one of the few in which Tullia "wrote from her heart" (118). Certainly, its first lines celebrate a fantasy of freedom in an unusually exhilarated voice, and it narrates events to a general audience rather than to a specific man until the "your" of the last line.

Yet the sonnet remains grounded in the cultural situation shaping Tullia's ambitions as poet. Her use of "l'alma smarrita" implies repentance, or at least a recognition of the spiritual consequences of passion; thus she hints at the conversion through which she aims for continued support from her patrons. At the same time, she sets up a sliding signifier that potentially promises praise to any male reader. The vagueness of her two loves strategically leaves the identity of both unfixed; by leaving both anonymous, she holds the honor of being her first or second true love open to a variety of men. Third, her image of freedom—and it is hard not to interpret "l'odiata gabbia" as a symbol of the sexual and verbal requirements of courtesanship and courtiership—remains an image of public desirability. Philomela/Tullia's flight is described in visual terms ("in superba vista") that suggest she is still the focus of many eyes, as she hoped to be as a poet.

The sonnet appeals to the multiple audiences Tullia woos throughout her *Rime*, but it also permits a glimpse of a transformed speaker, a free bird-woman singing a melody unheard in the cities and courts of mid-sixteenth-century Italy. Tullia makes no attempt to represent herself as enduringly chaste, the lover of only one man; her narrative of a second enamorment breaks the rules of proper feminine love lyric, as do the many masculine names collected in her text. The balance she establishes between autonomy and dependency in the figure of Philomela might be read as a map of the collection as a whole. Tullia was caught in a grid of economic and cultural structures that determined what she could say, how she could say it, and to whom. But she manipulates those limits in ways that allow her to construct a "vista superba" for herself, a self-representation that assigns her a place among the elite of her day and justifies her claim to the attention of later audiences.

Tullia was more attentive than Pernette to time, to readers to come, and to the durability of her texts. She shared with her male colleagues the habit of seeing literary production as an investment in the future. But both writers recognized that fame, in the present or in the future, required collaboration—that the poet comes into public view through the efforts and echoes of other poets and through alliances with critics. Philip Sidney's Astrophil, speaking to his Stella, spells out the purpose of the compliments exchanged by poets of both sexes in the Renaissance:

> Wit learnes in thee perfection to express,
> Not thou by praise, but praise in thee is raisde:
> It is a praise to praise, when thou art praisde.

> (*Astrophil and Stella*, Sonnet 35)[40]

Women poets expose the processes of reputation-building more clearly than their male interlocutors because, as women, they eroticize the ways that such literary power-broking works. Pernette and Tullia confronted different discursive assignments: the chaste Neoplatonist's devotion to one man, the courtesan's refined compliments to many. But they both demonstrated that a poetic identity is constructed not by an independent, originary voice but through a process of citation and revision of other texts and other poets. By representing their dependency on male models and mentors as a collaboration that proved their merit, Pernette and Tullia used their gender to their advantage.

Pernette's *Rymes* and Tullia's *Rime* demonstrate that literary production, even of "intimate" dialogue, depends on give and take in a public arena. A much more disguised relation to the public world shaped the lyrics of two poets who took up the pastoral tradition of retreat from city and court. In contrast to the openly dialogic texts of these coterie poets, the lyrics of Gaspara Stampa and Mary Wroth raise questions about women poets' claims to be recording purely private feeling in the privacy of woods and meadows. The next chapter analyzes their use of pastoral conventions to inscribe another scene of writing: fidelity to an absent man in the isolation of a country setting.

FOUR

Feminine Pastoral as Heroic Martyrdom

Gaspara Stampa and Mary Wroth

Two women poets who used the pastoral mode to write histories of unrequited love occupied similarly marginal social positions, close to the highest aristocracy of their time but excluded from its inner circles. By birth Gaspara Stampa was a member of the rich mercantile class of Padua. Her father, Bartolomeo Stampa, was a jewel merchant who designed a nobleman's education for his children, Gaspara, Cassandra, and Baldassare: he had them taught Greek and Latin as well as modern languages and music. After her husband's death about 1530, Cecilia Stampa moved the family to Venice, her home city, in order to launch her daughters' careers as musical performers.[1] As *virtuosa* (musician and singer) Gaspara Stampa lacked the privileged status of a noblewoman supported by family wealth; she was an independent entrepreneur, consolidating her career through networks of patronage. She made a name for herself in the *ridotti* (literary salons) of highly placed Venetians such as Domenico Venier and in the Academy of the Dubbiosi, where intellectuals from the Venetian patriciate mixed with poets and scholars from diverse class and geographical origins.[2] It was in the Venier salon that Stampa met a nobleman of the Terraferma (the countryside north of Venice), Collalto di Collaltino, whom she pursued over the course of two years and various separations until their final break in 1550. Stampa acknowledged the class difference between herself and her "lofty count" in her lyrics, yet she persisted in addressing her *Rime* to him. She died at the age of thirty in 1554 before her poems had been published; three years later Collaltino married a woman of his own class. Mary Wroth began higher; she belonged by birth and marriage to the English nobility. She was the daughter of the Welsh heiress Barbara Gamage and of Robert Sidney, made a baron by James I. She was also the niece of Mary Sidney Herbert, the Countess of Pembroke, a translator and poet and the patron of others such as John Donne and George Herbert. In 1604, the younger Mary Sidney's relatives arranged to marry her to Robert Wroth, a substantial landowner and hunting companion of King James, and for the next ten years she was a lady-in-waiting to the queen and a performer, with other court ladies, in spectacles such as Ben Jonson's *Masque of Blackness*.[3] Her relationship to the royal family and to rising poets

such as Jonson set her at the pinnacle of Jacobean political and literary hierarchies. But her husband's death and bankruptcy in 1614, when she was in
her late twenties, and her long-standing affair with her cousin William Herbert, with whom she had two illegitimate children, destroyed her financial
security and resulted in her departure from court.

Both poets wrote pastoral lyrics in the persona of an abandoned lover
taking refuge in rural solitude. In her 311 *Rime*, mostly sonnets, published in
1554 by her sister Cassandra, Stampa analyzes the stages of rarely requited
love and specifies Collaltino di Collalto as its object. The count belonged to a
feudal elite more ancient and more closed than Stampa's Venice. His family,
settled on three estates near Treviso, traced its descent back to the medieval
Longobardi, prided itself on the military valor of its sons, and maintained
feudal notions of autonomy. In fact, the Venetian senate eventually banished
Collaltino for maintaining a private army to be used against his own relatives; he died at the court of the Gonzagas in Mantua.[4] During the two years
of his separations and reunions with Stampa, he was more preoccupied with
chivalrous duty than with her courtship. He spent six months at the court of
Henri II, fought with the French king against the British at Boulogne in 1551,
and was taken prisoner supporting the Sienese in 1552. In 1557 he married
Giulia Torella, a woman who, like him, belonged to the landed nobility.

The difference between his rank and Stampa's is evident in the two portraits juxtaposed in a 1738 edition of the *Rime* edited by Antonio Rambaldo
di Collalto, a descendant of the count (figs. 3 and 4). The portrait of Stampa
combines a set of purely conventional details, not surprisingly, since the
painter whom Antonio di Collalto identifies as the source for the engraving,
Guercino da Cento, was born in 1591, almost forty years after Stampa's
death.[5] Stampa, dressed in a vaguely classical white gown and crowned with
laurel, is depicted above an obviously fictitious coat of arms combining a
lyre, Cupid's bow and arrow, and a Latin motto, "Non est mortale quod
opto" (What I desire is immortal). But for Collaltino's image and attributes,
the engraver could draw upon family portraits (the engraving is taken from a
painting by Titian) and verbal formulas glorifying the noble clan. Collaltino,
blond and bearded, is represented in full battle armor above the actual family crest, which includes the motto "Regum opes aequat animis" (Through
their courage equal to the wealth of kings). He is further identified in a long
epitaph praising his military alliance with Henri II and his patronage of writers: "copiarum Dux, litteratorum Moecenas" (leader of armies, Maecenas to
literati). Stampa, however, rewrites the fact of the count's social superiority
to her in more than two hundred poems in which, as faithful lover, she
claims moral superiority over him.

Mary Wroth's literary output, like Stampa's, was substantial: a long prose
romance, *Urania*, which was printed with a sonnet sequence, *Pamphilia to
Amphilanthus*. Like Stampa, Wroth defines love as a test of fidelity that
women pass better than men. Pamphilia ("the all-loving"), a princess whose
amorous misfortunes are narrated in the romance, loves the unfaithful

Fig. 3. Portrait of Gaspara Stampa from *Rime,* edited by Antonio Rambaldo di Collalto (1738). (By permission of the Houghton Library, Harvard University.)

Fig. 4. Portrait of Collaltino di Collalto from *Rime* (1738). (By permission of the Houghton Library, Harvard University.)

Amphilanthus ("lover of two"), whose return she awaits with exemplary constancy. The Pamphilia/Amphilanthus relationship offers certain parallels to Wroth's liaison with William Herbert, the third earl of Pembroke. Although they both belonged to the same class, gender rules allowed Herbert far greater sexual freedom than Wroth. He was imprisoned for a month in 1601 and banished from court for impregnating Anne Fitton, a court lady, but he refused to marry her; he made a more profitable match in 1604 and continued to form liaisons with women at court, including Wroth. In 1614, they produced a son, the first of two illegitimate children. Such behavior was far from unheard of in the Jacobean court. But Wroth's parents were ashamed enough of the son to send him away from Penshurst (in 1615 the earl wrote to his wife, "it had been to[o] greate a shame he should have stayde in the house"). And a poem to Wroth by Lord Herbert of Cherbury, punning on poets' and infants' feet, proves that she had become the target of "satyrs' " attacks.[6]

After years of battling financial difficulties (Robert Wroth left her with £23,000 in debts) and exile from court, where she was not received after 1614, Wroth published *Urania* in 1621. The book was a *roman à clef*. It deals with the dangers of court life, including the story of Lindamira, a faithful servant to the queen, betrayed by false rumor and banished to the countryside with a jealous husband. It also contains the story of Seralius, a brutal father who threatens his daughter's life to force her into obedience toward her husband. Edward Denny, Baron of Waltham, recognized himself in the figure of the father and attacked Wroth as a slanderer and "hermaphrodite."[7] Other stories of forced marriages and tragic separations in the romance suggest that Wroth was using pastoral fiction to criticize the limits imposed on aristocratic Englishwomen by the family and court politics of the early seventeenth century.[8] Like Stampa, the Pamphilia of Wroth's lyric sequence meditates on her beloved's perfections and prays for his return. But the poems exaggerate the loving woman's isolation. As Josephine Roberts and Elaine Beilin point out, the figure of the man is virtually absent from Wroth's sequence: never named, rarely described, and only occasionally addressed. The main theme of Pamphilia's speeches is her undying loyalty to Amphilanthus throughout their long separations. And, unlike the court and city settings of earlier sonnet sequences by Philip Sidney and Michael Drayton, for example, the site of Pamphilia's self-examination is a country retreat from which characters modeled on the courtiers Wroth actually frequented are significantly absent.[9]

Each poet appeals to a forbidden and elusive lover by representing herself in a pastoral setting in which she repeatedly imagines a sustained erotic relationship with him, as memory or wish. The speaker appears to reject the public world, urban or courtly; she identifies instead with a landscape centered upon the man. Stampa fantasizes leaving Venice to live with the count in the rural peace of Collalto, the hill on which San Salvatore, one of the family's fortified castles, was built; Pamphilia dismisses the courtly pastimes of her companions for the sake of isolated composition of shepherdesses' laments. In an early song (2), she links true love to country surroundings:

> 15 Whether (alass) then shall I goe   Ay mee;
>   When as dispaire all hopes outgoe   Ay mee;
>
>   Iff to the Forest, Cupid hyes,
>   And my poore soule to his lawe ties   Ay mee;
>
>   To the Court? O no. Hee crys fy   Ay mee;
>   Ther no true love you shall espy   Ay mee;
>   Leave that place to faulscest lovers
>   Your true love all truth discovers   Ay mee. . . .
>
>   (P14)[10]

Why do women poets adopt the persona and the discourse of a loving shepherdess? Modern and sixteenth-century theories of pastoral help to identify the reasons that these women poets select abandonment as an occasion for constructing a permissibly powerful poetic sequence. Renato Poggioli argues that the pastoral mode provides a fantasy structure through which the poet resists the political and social constraints of his time: implicitly or explicitly, such poetry includes "a protest against society's power to replace the fruitions with the frustrations of love."[11] The emphasis on the private self in such poetry, Poggioli suggests, is "a symbolic protest" that "acts as a romantic and nostalgic denial of those cultural or material circumstances that condition [the poet's] social status" (167).

Renaissance critics varied in their views of how pastoral was implicated in the milieux it appeared to transcend. In Italy the mode was defined largely as a fantastic one. For example, in the debate over Guarini's tragicomedy *Il pastor fido*, both sides assumed that pastoral bore no relationship to the real world of cities and politics. Giason Denores took this position in 1590 in his attack on Guarini, *Apologia contra l'auttor del Verato*,[12] and although Guarini's defenders accepted changes in the details of pastoral settings to bring them up to date, they defined verisimilitude rather than accurate rendering of contemporary historical realities as the goal of pastoral drama.[13]

In England, however, pastoral was seen as a potentially critical and satirical genre. Philip Sidney remarked in his *Defense of Poesie* that pastoral "sometimes, under the pretty tales of wolves and sheep, can include the whole consideration of wrong-doing and patience."[14] William Webbe, in *A Discourse of English Poetrie* (1586), explained of the shepherd characters used by early writers of eclogues: "under these personnes, as it were in a cloake of simplicitie, they would eyther sette forth the prayses of theyr freendes . . . or enveigh against abuses."[15] In the poems of Stampa and Wroth the abuses inveighed against are committed by men. The pastoral vocabulary legitimates the women's complaints and their desire to break free of the limits imposed on them by their social circumstances. Along these lines, in an instance of life imitating art, the young princess Elizabeth of England, under house arrest at Woodstock before her rise to the throne, used pastoral logic to complain about her banishment and to imagine an escape. Saying she wished she could change places with the milkmaid she heard singing outside her garden, Elizabeth idealized the country girl's freedom in order to re-proach her own enemies. Louis Montrose in his analysis of the incident links the literary mode to a motive of indirect political complaint: "Pastorals that celebrate the ideal of content function to articulate—and thereby perhaps to assuage—*dis*content."[16] Montrose cites Kenneth Burke on the range of inten-tions pastoral humility might conceal: "extending from outright flattery to ironically veiled challenge, . . . the 'reverence' of social privilege" can be "at-tenuated into respect, the respect itself sometimes being qualified until it has moved as far in the direction of disrespect as one might go without unmis-takably showing his hand."[17] Or *her* hand. The pastoral mode provided Stampa and Wroth with a medium for criticizing the sexual politics that sys-tematically deprived women of the power to arrange the social and erotic relations they themselves desired, and it permitted them to articulate and defend their desire to become authors.

A further advantage pastoral offered women poets was its double status as the genre of the humblest form of life and as an elite discourse validated by earlier poets. Sannazaro, for example, who established pastoral norms in Italy with his *Arcadia* (1502), aligned himself with classical poets such as Theocritus and Virgil by imitating their forms and their choice of pastoral as the first step in their careers.[18] Women poets were excluded by gender conventions from composing in publicly oriented genres such as epic, but they could more safely imitate the first stage of the classical poet's evolution, especially since the val-ues attributed to idealized rural life corresponded to the innocent modesty expected of women in early modern Europe. William Empson's definition of pastoral as the "process of putting the complex into the simple"[19] is to the point here: the stress on simplicity made the mode adaptable to definitions of feminine virtue. At the same time, however, the pose of simplicity made op-posite maneuvers possible, as Montrose points out: "In a culture in which pastoral forms have become associated with a refinement of the self beyond the capacity of the multitude—a culture in which the humble pastoral form has acquired a paradoxical prestige—merely to write a pastoral is to make a symbolic claim to membership within society's charmed circle."[20] Like their male contemporaries seeking favor in royal and aristocratic circles, women poets composed pastoral masques (Wroth's *Love's Victorie* is an example) and country house poems (Amelia Lanyer's "To Cookham").[21] In Italy the mem-bers of literary coteries regularly adopted pastoral names in order to glorify their group efforts. For example, Girolamo Muzio in his *Tirrhenia* gave classi-cizing pseudonyms such as Thalia and Titiro to Tullia d'Aragona and her Flor-entine admirers; Stampa eulogized her colleagues in the Accademia dei Dubbiosi as "chiarissimi pastori."[22]

To write in the persona of a shepherdess also freed women poets from the limited roles assigned to the heroines of male-composed pastoral—figures, as Harry Berger points out, who functioned mainly as targets of male pursuit or guarantors of "the male bonding that poetry celebrates."[23] Women poets' appropriation of the pastoral heroine as *speaker* gave them access both to the prestige of bucolic convention and to its veiled critique of social relations. Stampa and Wroth use pastoral conventions to argue that men's public roles belong to an impure, combative realm that disguises masculine callousness as duty and permits injustice to continue unchecked. In contrast, they represent women's fidelity in love as a heroic virtue. Under its surface of simplicity and pathos, feminine pastoral questions masculine power and establishes a vigorous virtue for the woman who writes.

STAMPA'S ANASSILLA: PASTORAL LAMENT AS REPROACH

Stampa's dedicatory epistle to Collaltino, "Allo illustre mio signore," typifies the strategies she uses throughout the poems that follow. She begins with a dedication in which she manages at once to praise the count and to condemn him. She blames him as bad lover and bad reader both:

> Poi che le mie pene amorose, che per amor di V. S. porto scritte in diverse lettere e rime, non han possuto, una per una, non pur far pietosa V. S. verso di me, ma farla né anco cortese di scrivermi una parola, io mi son rissoluta di ragunarle tutte in questo libro, per vedere se tutte insieme lo potranno fare. (79)

> Because my amorous woes, which for love of your Lordship I write out in various letters and poems, have been unable, singly, to make you pitiful toward me or even courteous enough to write me a single word, I have decided to collect them in this book, to see whether, all together, they can succeed.

Her envoi to her "libretto" also reveals the tensions in the collection as a whole. It combines apparent humility with praise for her own devotion: "appreséntati nella più umil forma che saprai, dinanzi al signor nostro, in compagnia della mia candida fede" (present yourself in as humble a way as you can before our lord, accompanied by my pure faith). The fiction of the preface suggests that Stampa addresses her performance as lover and poet to Collaltino, but the sequence as a whole demonstrates that she writes for a larger audience whose sympathy she courts as assiduously as she woos the elusive count.

An important element in Stampa's pastoral strategy is her adoption of the name Anassilla. In her preface she calls the *Rime* "le note delle cure amorose e gravi della sua fidissima ed infelicissima Anassilla" (the record of the grievous loving sorrows of your most faithful and most unhappy Anassilla). Through this pseudonym she associates herself with the pastoral freshness of the count's estates outside Venice. The feudal holdings of the Collalto family were bordered by the river Piave, also called the Anasso after its Latin name (Anaxum). So to call herself Anassilla is to identify herself with Collaltino's property, to link herself to a landscape associated privately with their happiest reunions and publicly with the wealth and tradition of the Collalto clan. In addition, the pseudonym signals Stampa's familiarity with the codes through which Venetian poets identified themselves as members of a group: "Anassilla" was the *nom de plume* she used in the Accademia dei Dubbiosi during the late 1540s.[24] Giorgio Benzone, a friend of Stampa's and possibly the editor of her posthumous *Rime*, used her coterie name in a way that attests to its public currency. His elegaic sonnet introducing her poems opens with the lines: "Ben è d'alta vaghezza il mondo scarco, / poi che spento Anassilla ha morte rea" (The world is totally deprived of noble beauty / now that cruel death has extinguished Anassilla). So while the name suggests the woman's humility toward the count, her wish to have no identity except as a kind of rural water spirit emanating from the lands over which he enjoys seigneurial possession, it also affirms her separate identity as the member of an urban cultural elite. Further, Stampa's use of the name consolidates her identity as a poet: it turns her into an enduring character, much as Tullia d'Aragona's third-person perspective on herself, singing to Cosimo de' Medici "on the banks of the Arno," establishes her as the heroine of a literary future. Through "Anassilla" Stampa adopts in fantasy a Collaltine name she cannot expect to take on through marriage, and she writes herself into literary history as a poet of the Venetian academies.

The *virtuosa's* Venice and the duke's country estate are set up as uneasy rivals in the sequence. Stampa uses the city-country opposition of pastoral in a pair of sonnets that give the convention a local habitation and thereby multiply its contradictions. Sonnet 134 opens with traditional praise of Venice as the seat of republican freedom:[25]

> Queste rive ch'amai sì caldamente,
> rive sovra tutt'altre alme e beate,
> fido albergo di cara libertade,
> nido d'illustre e riposata gente, . . .

> These shores which I used to love so warmly,
> shores sweeter and more blessed than all others,
> faithful dwelling-place of beloved liberty,
> shelter for a famous and confident people, . . .

But Stampa distances herself from the city in favor of Collalto's castle, displacing her status as the citizen of a mercantile city-state into a world of feudal romance. She concedes that such a preference is surprising (as it would in fact have been to Venetians, accustomed to celebrations of the Republic) but she ends with a vision of settled contentment far from the scene of Venetian self-government:

chi 'l crederia? mi son novellamente
sì fattamente fuor del cor andate,
che di passar con lor le mie giornate
mi doglio meco e mi pento sovente.
    E tutti i miei disiri e i miei pensieri
mirano a quel bel colle, ove ora stanza
il mio signor e i suoi due lumi alteri.
    Quivi, per acquetar la desianza,
spenderei tutta seco volontieri
questa vita penosa che m'avanza.

Who would believe it? lately these shores
have so entirely departed from my heart
that spending my days upon them now
brings me only grief and constant regret.
    And all my longing and all my thoughts
turn toward that lovely hill where now abides
my noble lord, with his two proud eyes.
    There in that spot, to satisfy my desire,
willingly I would, alone with him,
live out the rest of my troubled life.

As in many poems, Stampa links the count's land (*quel bel colle*) and the name of the man she loves: Collaltino is Collalto (*colle alto*, "the high hill"). Petrarch and his followers had also played on the multiple meanings of their beloved's names: Laura is simultaneously the woman, the breeze (*l'aura*) that accompanies the poet's memories of her in his country retreat, and the laurel wreath (*lauro*) worn by prize-winning poets. But Stampa's plays on Collalt [in]o take up the count's family name as well as his first name, so that her puns call attention to a group elite. The man is the land he lives on, an aristocrat whose patronymic links him to a noble tradition.

In Sonnet 139, a call to the river Anasso, Stampa works out a triple identification between herself, Collalto as a place, and the people who own it. Her compliment to the entire clan includes a reminder of the praises she has already dedicated to one of its members; indeed, the entire poem suggests that she is breaking down private/public boundaries by seeking love and patronage at the same time. But there is some tension in her adulatory apostrophe to the estate. In her first line she declares that the river is named after her rather than the reverse, a competitive posture that continues throughout the poem and the sequence. Stampa's challenge to the Anasso actually implies a threat to Collalto family unity. She fights the river for the son's attention, attempting to lure him away from the landscape that defines his noble status and separates him from her:

Fiume, che dal mio nome nome prendi,
e bagni i piedi a l'alto colle e vago,
ove nacque il famoso ed alto fago
de le cui fronde alto disio m'accendi,

tu vedi spesso lui, spesso l'intendi,
e talor rendi la sua bella imago
ed a me che d'altr'ombra non m'appago,
così sovente, lassa, lo contendi.

River, which takes your name from mine
and bathes the feet of the high and lovely hill,
site of the famous, lofty beech tree
for whose branches high desire set me afire,
    you often see him, often hear him,
and reflect his lovely image back,
yet with me, who desire no other shade,
you so often, alas, compete for him.

The metaphorical system of the poem subordinates Stampa to the clan she celebrates, yet she opens by claiming the power to name their river. As commemorator of the count's family through the image of the beech, which literalizes the notion of a family tree, and as protector of the Anasso, their territorial border, she serves the Collalti as poet. But she reverses the hierarchy of patron over poet through her witty play with the family name as *il coll'alto*, her *topos*, in the sense of place and verbal formula alike. Yet here, too, a certain resentment darkens Stampa's celebration of the landscape that grounds the clan and the individual man. In line 4 the beech tree represents the man, but in line 11 it hides heaven from her:

Pur, non ostante che la nobil fronde,
ond'io piansi e cantai con più d'un verso,
la tua mercé, sì spesso lo nasconde,
prego 'l ciel ch'altra pioggia o nembo avverso
non turbi, Anasso, mai le tue chiar'onde,
se non quel sol che da quest'occhi verso.

Still, in spite of the way the noble branch
for whom I've wept and sung in many a verse,
thanks to you, so often hides it from me,
I pray to heaven that no rain or threatening cloud
may ever disturb, Anasso, your clear waters,
except this storm of tears I weep forth from my eyes.

She effaces her lower status as urban *virtuosa* to the extent that, like the landscape, she reflects and echoes the count's family name. But the final outburst of tears acknowledges that this fantasized position of inclusion is one that the clan as a whole prevents her from sustaining.

Still, Stampa eulogizes the Collalti persistently. As early as her sixth sonnet, she praises the family as "un sangue illustre, agli alti re vicino" (a distinguished bloodline, ranking with great kings), and in Sonnet 11 she compares Collaltino and his brother Vinciguerra to two branches growing from an "illustrious trunk." Throughout the sequence, she also speaks of her status as a

"vile and abject woman" (8, 148, 150), appearing to accept the difference between her rank and the count's even as she demonstrates her familiarity with
him. For this reason the Anassilla poems, especially when they place the
mournful shepherdess in Collaltine territory, as in Sonnet 139, might seem to
support Empson's view of pastoral as an equalizer of social inequalities, a
mode that suppresses the distance between shepherds, rulers, and poets (and
between men and women) by means of "a stylistic transcending of conflict,"
as Burke puts it.[26] Anassilla would seem to vanish into the Trevisan hills, adding an agreeable feminine *sfumatura* to the patrician landscape and dissolving
the economic and cultural gap that divided Stampa and Collaltino. But the
conclusion of Sonnet 139 disrupts the fantasy of equality: Stampa ends with a
storm of tears, in the sudden turn that structures many of her poems.

As dramatizer of her suffering and composer of her own epitaphs,
Stampa uses pastoral conventions not only to celebrate but to rewrite Collaltino—to rewrite him by condemning him. She also emphasizes her merits as
a technique of negotiating the man's power over her: linking her fidelity as
lover to her persistence as poet, she bargains for a fair return of affection. In
Sonnet 65, for example, the first time she uses her pseudonym in the poems,
she speaks in the character of a detached third-person observer, reminding
the count of his poet-lover's long literary devotion to him. Anassilla as character simultaneously disguises and makes possible the self-praise on which
the poem is built:

> Deh, se vi fu giamai dolce e soave
> la vostra fidelissima Anassilla,
> mentre serrata, sì che nullo aprilla,
> teneste del suo cor, conte, la chiave;
>   leggendo in queste carte il lungo e grave
> pianto, a cui Amor per voi, lassa, sortilla,
> mostrar almen di pietà una scintilla,
> in premio di sua fé, non vi sia grave.

> Alas, if ever you found sweet and tender
> your ever faithful, loving Anassilla,
> while you held the key to her heart, count
> so tightly that no one else could unlock it,
>   as you read in these pages the long, heartfelt lament
> to which, in your favor, Love, alas, destined her,
> may showing at least a glimmer of pity
> in reward for her devotion not burden you too much.

But the deference in that last line—"may it not be too much to ask, let it not
seem a nuisance to you"—is thrown off in the tercets, in which Stampa emphasizes the range and quantity of her lyrics and claims the power to protect
the count from Love's woes. Anasilla's assumption that the count owes her a
return on her devotion brings a new note of demand into the humility that
pastoral decorum assigns the faithful shepherdess:

> Accompagnate almen con un suspiro
> la schiera immensa de' sospiri suoi,
> che mille volte i ciel pietosi udîro.
>   Così sia sempre Amor benigno a voi,
> quanto a lei fu per voi spietato e diro;
> così non sia mai cosa che v'annoi.

> Add at least one sympathetic sigh
> to the immense company of her sighs,
> which the pitying skies have heard a thousand times.
>   In return, may Love be as kind to you
> as through you he was fierce and cruel to her;
> in return, may your life be free of pain.

The sheer number of poems Stampa addresses to the count, begging him to return, to write, or to put an end to her jealous fantasies, suggests her inability to influence him—an apparent powerlessness that gave rise to the Romantic myth of Stampa as a suicide for love.[27] But it is a mistake to read this shepherdess-poet as a powerless victim. In all her poems Stampa invokes audiences beyond the count: personified elements of the pastoral setting, fellow poets, women readers, true lovers, the future in general. Such apostrophes have the effect of turning a group gaze onto the man, often with less than flattering results, and of foregrounding Stampa's activity as a poet. Her scenes of composition, though set in rural privacy, persistently imply a chorus of onlookers beyond the woods of Collalto: she envisions generations of observers who will praise her and blame the count. One of Stampa's goals—eventually, her primary goal—is fame. The female persona claiming such fame introduces further complexities into the pastoral mode.

An early sonnet, 35, turns on the conventional paradox that the soothing effect of country settings intensifies amorous longing: the lovelier the woods, the sharper the pangs of love. Here, too, Stampa invokes Collalto and sets up a bargain with its scenery: if the woods and river soothe her pain, she will pray to nymphs and woodland gods to protect them. The poem moves to a conclusion predictable in pastoral but interestingly nuanced in the case of the woman poet. Stampa represents herself not merely appealing to her surroundings but operating on them as a poet, carving the trees with praises of the landscape. The sylvan poet-sculptor is immortalizing two names: Collalto and Anassilla. Her pastoral inscriptions will commemorate her name as well as the count's:

> e lascerò scolpita in qualche scorza
> la memoria di tanta cortesia,
> quando di lasciar voi mi sarà forza.

> and I will leave, carved here and there in bark,
> the memory of such great courtesy,
> when I am forced to leave you behind.

The effect of many of the *Rime* is exactly this: to record Stampa's virtuosity in ways that leave the count in the dust.

She exploits the critical potential of pastoral by holding the count up for reproach by a public she calls upon as loyalists to her cause. In a madrigal, 236, she concedes that even the count would pity his "misera Anassilla" if he were present to witness her suffering; but since he is not, she appeals to a double audience to acknowledge her superiority as a lover: "Veggano Amore e 'l ciel, che'l tutto vede, / la vostra rotta e la sua salda fede" (May Love and heaven, which sees all things, / See your faith broken and hers faithful still). In 235, she invokes a more secular audience: a world of true lovers, according to whose code Collaltino's indifference is cruel and his poet/shepherdess's constancy is exemplary:

> Conte, dov'è andata
> la fé sì tosto, che m'avete data?
> Che vuol dir che la mia
> è più costante, che non era pria?
> Che vuol dir che, da poi
> che voi partiste, io son sempre con voi?
> Sapete voi quel che dirà la gente,
> dove forza d'Amor punto si sente?
> —O che conte crudele!
> o che donna fedele!

> Count, where is it now,
> the faith you were so quick to promise me?
> What does it mean that mine
> is now more constant than it was before?
> What does it mean that since
> you left, I am always with you in my heart?
> Do you know what people will say
> wherever the power of love is felt?
> "Oh, what a cruel count!
> Oh, what a faithful lady!"

The brevity of the madrigal form and the naïve diction here reinforce the accusation Stampa is making: female innocence betrayed, male arrogance condemned by a *vox populi* of true lovers now and in ages to come. Her audience is no longer the count's rural setting but other lovers and readers summoned as witnesses for the prosecution.

This appeal to a sympathetic audience provides the plot of a sonnet, 151, in which Stampa composes her own epitaph. The first line of the poem is a citation of a sonnet of Petrarch's (*Canzoniere*, 92), in which he mourns the death of Cino da Pistoia, a fellow poet.[28] But Stampa redefines the subject of the lament: she writes the history of her own death in order to accuse Collaltino of murdering her. The elegy assumes a public of supportive women who will be moved to pity by the portrait of the heroine/victim of Love:

> Piangete, donne, e con voi pianga Amore,
> poi che non piange lui, che m'ha ferita
> sì, che l'alma farà tosto partita
> da questo corpo tormentato fuore.

> Weep, ladies, and may Love weep with you,
> since the man does not weep who wounded me
> so deeply that he will soon make the soul depart
> from this my long-suffering body.

Stampa constructs these women not only as witnesses of her fate but record-ers of it, fellow poets:

> E, se mai da pietoso e gentil core
> l'estrema voce altrui fu essaudita,
> dapoi ch'io sarà morta e sepelita,
> scrivete la cagion del mio dolore:
>   "Per amar molto ed esser poco amata
> visse e morì infelice, ed or qui giace
> la più fedel amante che sia stata.

> And if ever a pitiful and noble heart
> granted the final wish of another,
> after I am dead and buried,
> write, ladies, the explanation of my woe:
>   "For loving greatly and being little loved,
> She lived and died unhappy; and here now lies
> the most faithful lover who ever lived.

The last word of the epitaph is reserved for an attack on the count, whose infamy is recorded for eternity:

> Pregale, viator, riposo e pace,
> ed imparar da lei, sì mal trattata,
> a non seguir un cor crudo e fugace."

> Pray, passer-by, she be granted rest and peace,
> and learn from her, so cruelly mistreated,
> never to follow a cruel and flighty heart."

Stampa does not name the count here. Instead, by composing a text that commemorates herself and relegates him to the status of anonymous posses-sor of an inconstant heart, she becomes the scriptor of her own myth rather than the herald of Collaltino as scion of a glorious family.

Stampa also uses pastoral conventions to attack the residual political ide-ology associated with the feudal clans to which Collaltino belonged. In con-trast to Venetian patricians, who carried out demanding political duties in the various councils of the city government, Collaltino's service to the French king typifies the Terraferma nobility's loyalty to an earlier system of international chivalry.[29] He left Venice and Collalto in 1549-50, for example, to fight for Henri II and to represent the Italian nobility at the marriage of Orazio Farnese and Henri's daughter Diane d'Angoulême. Rather than praising such service, Stampa opposes it to rural peace in poems forthrightly critical of noblemen's traditional public roles. In Sonnet 158, a *carpe diem* poem that Croce, astonishingly, labeled as the "hymn of a fallen woman,"[30] she contrasts the short life of military heroism to the pleasures of country love. The poem is less erotic than many male-composed variations on the theme (Marlowe, Ronsard, Muzio), but what is shocking in it is that a woman is pronouncing a negative judgment on the epic world. Such dismissals of epic were frequent among Roman elegists, but Stampa's situation as urban bourgeoise adds historical specificity to her dismissal of heroic ambitions (line 4) and her rejection of military glory (lines 9-11):

> Deh lasciate, signor, le maggior cure
> d'ir procacciando in questa età fiorita
> con fatiche e periglio de la vita
> alti pregi, alti onori, alte venture;
>   e in questi colli, in queste alme e sicure
> valli e campagne, dove Amor n'invita,
> viviamo insieme vita alma e gradita,
> in che 'l sol de' nostri occhi alfin s'oscure.
>   Perché tante fatiche e tanti stenti
> fan la vita più dura, e tanti onori
> restan per morte poi subito spenti.
>   Qui coglieremo a tempo e rose e fiori,
> ed erbe e frutti, e con dolci concenti
> canterem con gli uccelli i nostri amori.

> Alas, my lord, leave off great ambitions
> of going in quest, in this flowering season,
> to endure combats and mortal danger,
> for high rewards, high honor, high adventure;
>   and in these hills, in the sweet safety
> of these valleys and fields, where Love beckons,
> let us share a gentle life of pleasure,
> until the sunlight finally fades from our eyes.
>   For such great struggles and efforts
> only make life harder, and such great honors
> in the face of death suddenly vanish away.
>   Here, timely, we will gather rose blossoms
> and grasses and fruits, and in sweet harmonies
> along with the birds we will sing our love.

The privileging of amorous peace over masculine warfare in this sonnet expands into a depiction of the Golden Age and a diatribe against war in a *capitolo* (an essayistic poem of variable length written in *terza rima*), 242, toward the end of Stampa's *canzoniere*. She specifies the occasion of the

poem, written in June 1551 when Collalto was at war near Bologna: "disio
d'onore / sotto Bologna vi sospinge e sprona" (desire for honor, / beneath
Bologna, goads and spurs you on). But rather than celebrating a victory in
battle, as this opening might lead a reader to expect, the poet invokes a series
of counter-realities in order to condemn war. Her compliment to Collaltino
on his reputation implies that he is as ambitious for gain as for self-sacrifice
(line 21), and she devalues chivalry by centering on an ideal of masculine
behavior in private life instead:

> 19   Felice è quella donna, a cui li dèi
>   han dato amante men illustre in sorte,
>   e men vago di spoglie e di trofei;
>   con qual le sue dimore lunghe e corte
>   trapassa lieta, avendol sempre a lato,
>   fido, costante, valoroso e forte.
>
>   Lucky is the woman to whom the gods
>   have given a lover less fated to fame,
>   and less eager to acquire booty and trophies;
>   with such a man, whether her life is long or short,
>   she lives it joyfully, for he is always at her side,
>   faithful, constant, courageous and strong.

Stampa then moves to a denunciation of the greed and violence of war,
which she contrasts to a happier pastoral past. Many of her themes are conventional (Tibullus, Horace or Virgil might have been models for the invocation of a simpler era),[31] but she revises them to include specifically feminine
concerns—the contentment of shepherdesses as well as shepherds, the fears
of women waiting for news from the front:

> Felice il tempo antico e fortunato,
> quando era il mondo semplice e innocente,
> poco a le guerre, a le rapine usato! . . .
>   Allor le pastorelle inamorate
> avean mai sempre seco i lor pastori,
> dai quai non eran mai abbandonate. . . .
>   Mai poi quegli appetiti ingordi, insani
> di posseder l'altrui robe e l'avere
> da l'antica pietà si fêr lontani.
>   Quindi si cominciâr prima a vedere
> le crude guerre e strepiti de l'armi,
> che fan, misere noi, tanto temere.
>
> Happy was that ancient, blessed time
> when the world was simple and innocent,
> not yet accustomed to wars and robbery!
>   Then all shepherdesses in love
> had their shepherds always with them,
> and they were never abandoned by them. . . .

> But then voracious appetites, wild
> to possess other men's property and goods,
> left ancient piety far behind.
> And so first came into view
> the cruel wars and din of weapons
> which make us, unhappy women, endure such fear.

War for Anassilla is not a field of glory but a rapacious frenzy, against which she invokes a community of women oppressed by the military "splendor" on which clans like the Collalti built their reputation. Stampa's antiheroic reading of military exploits shifts the terms of judgment according to which the count was elevated as "copiarum Dux" in the fulsome caption to his portrait in the Collalto family edition of the *Rime*. No longer dedicating herself to praising the count and his lineage, she questions the validity of a hierarchy that rewards violence on the battlefield rather than *virtù* in love.

Moreover, in poems representing her history as lover and poet, Stampa redistributes the characteristics traditionally ascribed to each sex: the count becomes an inconstant waverer and the woman takes on the virtues of a chivalrous hero. In a late sonnet (198) Stampa declares that her service to Love has taught her strength, persistence, and continence, all of which are attained in Love's court "more than in any other." Croce pointed out this gender reversal in a late study of Stampa. Although his preconceptions led him to describe her poems as merely "spontaneous, as was fitting for a woman," he also remarked, "Through the trials she undergoes for love, she seems to develop self-discipline, to acquire capacities and strengths she lacked at first, and one would say, if a woman were not the issue, that she increases in virility."[32] The woman at issue says exactly this.

The reversal of traditionally gendered qualities occurs especially vividly in the *blason* poems throughout Stampa's collection, in which she shifts from admiration for the count's valor to a critique of his ferocity. Fiora Bassanese remarks astutely, "Collaltino is both idol and sadist" (111). As early as Sonnet 7, a revision of Petrarch's celebration of Laura (*Canzoniere* 248: "Chi vuol veder quantunque pò Natura"), Stampa ends her list of praises with a touch of blame:

> Chi vuol conoscer, donne, il mio signore
> miri un signor di vago e dolce aspetto,
> giovane d'anni e vecchio d'intelletto,
> imagin de la gloria e del valore:
>   di pelo biondo, e di vivo colore,
> di persona alta e spazioso petto,
> e finalmente in ogni opra perfetto,
> fuor ch'un poco (oimè lassa!) empio in amore.

> Ladies, let whoever wants to know my lord
> behold a gentleman with a loving, gentle look,
> young in years and old in wisdom,
> the image itself of glory and valor:

with blond hair and a colorful complexion,
tall in body and broad in the chest,
and, finally, perfect in every action,
except (woe is me!) a little fierce in love.

Typically, she devotes the second part of the poem to a portrait of her own heroism in suffering. In this couple, constancy and strength belong to the woman:

E chi vuol poi conoscer me, rimiri
una donna in effetti ed in sembiante
imagin de la morte e de' martiri,
    un albergo di fé salda e costante,
una, che, perché pianga, arda e sospiri,
non fa pietoso il suo crudel amante.

And then, whoever wants to know me, look again
and you will see a lady in actions and appearance
the image of death and of martyrdom,
    a dwelling-place of fixed and constant faith,
one who, however she weeps, burns, and sighs,
can find no pity in her cruel lover.

In a perceptive study of the rhetoric of this sonnet, Justin Vitiello argues that Stampa draws on the vocabulary of Christian martyrdom in order to emerge the victor, "more human and more heroic than her pitiless lord. . . . In the love-death or martyrdom (whether sacred or profane), the victim gains an awesome strategic advantage."[33] Rather than accepting the position of a slave of love, as Donata Vassalli claims,[34] Stampa insists on her self-sacrifice in order to elevate herself above the count, to rewrite their difference in rank according to a counter-code of amorous piety.

A later poem demonstrates how far Stampa moves into a discourse of shame and blame. Sonnet 174 is a counter-*blason*, a list of the count's misdeeds in which pastoral humility turns into fierce denunciation:

Una inaudita e nova crudeltate,
un esser al fuggir pronto e leggiero,
un andar troppo di sue doti altero,
un tôrre ad altri la sua libertate,
    un vedermi penar senza pietate,
un aver sempre a' miei danni il pensiero,
un rider di mia morte quando pèro,
un aver voglie ognor fredde e gelate,
    un eterno timor di lontananza,
un verno eterno senza primavera,
un non dar giamai cibo a la speranza
    m'han fatto divenir una Chimera,
uno abisso confuso, un mar, ch'avanza
d'onde e tempeste una marina vera.

An unheard of, astonishing cruelty,
a prompt and fickle readiness for flight,
a carriage revealing too much pride in his gifts,
a habit of stealing the freedom of others,
    a pitiless gaze untouched by my suffering,
a mind always bent upon my destruction,
a laugh at my death as I lie perishing,
a persistence in desires as cold as ice,
    an eternal fear of separation,
an endless winter without any spring,
a refusal ever to give food to hope,
    these have transformed me into a Chimera,
a confused abyss, a sea, that outdoes
any real seacoast in breakers and storms.

This poem is one of the best examples in the sequence of how the posture of victimization can be turned into an attack on the victimizer. Stampa turns the melancholy pathos of pastoral into the *meraviglia* of epic—not its glorification of warfare but its effect of surprise and wonder.[35] The Chimera, in Ovid's *Metamorphoses* a fire-breathing female monster that terrorized the countryside of Lycia, was finally killed by Bellerophon.[36] Yet the aspect of the creature emphasized here is not her defeat but her miraculous nature: with the bust of a lion, the body of a goat, and the hindquarters of a dragon, she was an object of awe and terror. Stampa intensifies the wondrous quality of the monster by associating her with a storm-tossed sea, possibly through an aquatic association leading via Charybdis to Scylla, another woman metamorphosed by love. We are a long way from her early identification with the peaceful river Piave/Anasso. The poem is an invitation to an audience beyond Collaltino to marvel at the change in the speaker and the drama of the sonnet: its reversal of *blason* convention, its relentless parallel structure, its unexpected ending. In spite of her apparent paralysis by the count, the woman poet is the active figure in this text.

Frank Warnke cites Rainer Maria Rilke's view of Stampa as typifying the energy of the abandoned woman as poet, whose obsessive love eventually makes the lover himself unnecessary.[37] The hero of Rilke's novel *The Notebooks of Malte Laurids Brigge* mentions Stampa as one of "those powerful examples of women in love, who, even while they called out to him, surpassed the man they loved, . . . who didn't cease until their torment turned into a bitter, icy magnificence." Such women "hurl themselves after the man they have lost, but with their first steps they overtake him, and in front of them is only God."[38] This Romantic celebration of unrequited passion suppresses real power differences between men and women; there is something suspiciously easy in a male poet's imaginary identification with abandoned women. But Rilke is right to recognize the self-sufficiency of the poet of unrequited love. Finally Stampa's subject is not her thralldom to the man but her own triumphant progress through the trials of the erotic relationship and the potential it opens up for her as a poet.

The search for fame exceeding all measure is evident in what Eugenio Donadoni called the "titanic" verse of Sonnet 91.[39] Stampa attacks Collaltino by appropriating military terms in order to exalt her emotional strength over his martial courage:

> Novo e raro miracol di natura,
> ma non novo né raro a quel signore,
> che 'l mondo tutto va chiamando Amore,
> che 'l tutto adopra fuor d'ogni misura:
>   il valor, che degli altri il pregio fura,
> del mio signor, che vince ogni valore,
> è vinto, lassa, sol dal mio dolore,
> dolor, a petto a cui null'altro dura.
>   Quant'ei tutt'altri cavallieri eccede
> in esser bello, nobile e ardito,
> tanto è vinto da me, da la mia fede.
>   Miracol fuor d'amor mai non udito!
> Dolor, che chi nol prova non lo crede!
> Lassa, ch'io sola vinco l'infinito!

> New and rare miracle of nature,
> but neither new nor rare to that high lord
> whom the entire world calls Love,
> whose every act exceeds all measure:
>   my lord's valor, which takes the prize
> from other men and vanquishes all valor,
> (alas) is vanquished only by my suffering,
> suffering that outlives any other heart's pain.
>   As much as he excels all other knights
> in beauty, nobility and daring,
> so much is he conquered by me, by my fidelity.
>   Miracle unheard of apart from love!
> Suffering incredible to those who do not feel it!
> Alas, that I alone surpass the infinite!

The entire poem is built on a strategy of competition: Stampa elevates Collaltino as warrior in order to elevate herself as a figure of miraculous potency. The faithful shepherdess now challenges all comers to a contest in virtù.

Stampa's use of myth contributes further to her heroic self-representation. Besides identifying with the awe-inspiring figure of the Chimera, she rewrites the pathos of Ovidian heroines to emphasize her powers as a poet. In Sonnet 173 she uses the possibilities of wishful fantasy provided by Ovid's tales to invoke the figures of Procne and Philomela as collaborators in an exchange of sympathy and song. The contrast between Stampa's apostrophe to the sisters and Sannazaro's in Eclogue 11 of the Arcadia illustrates the woman poet's sympathetic identification with the victims of Tereus's betrayal. The male poet orders Procne to be quiet; he needs her silence in order to give free rein to his own grief.[40] Stampa, however, aligns herself with the victims of disorderly desire and, by juxtaposing Collaltino's abandonment to Tereus's mistreatment of the sisters, she condemns both men. She refers to the sisters' rape and deception in an accusatory periphrasis that suggests her solidarity with the women:

> Cantate meco, Progne e Filomena,
> anzi piangete il mio grave martìre,
> or che la primavera e 'l suo fiorire
> i miei lamenti e voi, tornando, mena.
>   A voi rinova la memoria e pena
> de l'onta di Tereo e le giust' ire;
> a me l'acerbo e crudo dipartire
> del mio signore morte empia rimena.

> Sing with me, Procne and Philomela,
> rather, weep for my woeful martyrdom,
> now that spring with its flowering days
> brings back, returning, my laments and you.
>   In you spring renews the memory and pain
> of Tereus' shameful act and your just anger;
> to me the bitter, cruel departure
> of my lord brings back pitiless death.

The figures worthy of trust and capable of a generous and enabling exchange are not men but the Ovidian heroine-victims, to whom the woman poet promises an expert elegy:

> Dunque, essendo più fresco il mio dolore,
> aitatemi amiche a disfogarlo,
> ch'io per me non ho tanto entro vigore.
>   E, se piace ad Amor mai di scemarlo,
> io piangerò poi 'l vostro a tutte l'ore
> con quanto stile ed arte potrò farlo.

> So, because my pain is more recent,
> help me, friends, to give vent to it,
> for I lack the inner strength to do so.
>   And if ever Love deigns to abate my woe,
> I will weep for yours every hour of the day,
> with all the style and art I can attain.

This sonnet returns us to the countryside of Anassilla's laments, but it represents her as less isolated than might be expected after her beloved's departure. Stampa assembles a chorus that unites women from the literary past with an assumed audience of women in the future. Displacing Collaltino as the center of attention, she frames the *Rime* not only as a repetition of women's woes in love but as an intervention, an act of resistance to the solo melancholy of pastoral and the near-silence of bird-women unable to construct a discourse of self-affirmation.

Many of the maneuvers I have been analyzing in Stampa's uses of pastoral are drawn together in Sonnet 201. It opens with the outsider's perspective of many of the Anassilla poems: quotation marks surround the reproaches of the abandoned woman, so that a narrative frame encloses the apostrophe to the count. This mode of presentation assigns Anassilla the innocent pathos of a conventional shepherdess, but at the same time it allows Stampa to specify the actual settings that separate lover and beloved and to compose an intimately sarcastic accusation. By assigning the angry speech to a character who is and yet is not herself, Stampa opens the tale of love to readers outside the amorous duo. And by using the imperfect tense to suggest repetition (lines 9-14), she affirms the loyalty of the "pastorella fida" at the same time that she writes herself as agent into the history of romantic representation:

> —E questa quella viva e salda fede,
> che promettevi a la tua pastorella,
> quando, partendo alla stagion novella,
> n'andasti ove 'l gran re gallico siede?
>   O di quanto il sol scalda e quanto vede
> perfido, ingrato in atto ed in favella;
> misera me, che ti divenni ancella
> per riportarne sì scarsa mercede!—
>   Così l'afflitta e misera Anassilla
> lungo i bei lidi d'Adria iva chiamando
> il suo pastor, da cui 'l ciel dipartilla;
>   e l'acque e l'aure, dolce risonando,
> allor che 'l sol più arde e più sfavilla,
> i suoi sospir al ciel givan portando.

> "Is this the living and constant faith
> you often promised to your shepherdess,
> when, departing as the new season arrived,
> you set off for the court of the great French king?
>   Oh, in all the lands the sun warms and beholds,
> most treacherous and ungrateful man, in deeds and words;
> and unhappy me, who became your servant
> for the sake of such a miserly reward!"
>   Thus the heartbroken and wretched Anassilla
> went along the Adriatic shores, calling out
> to her shepherd, from whom heaven took her away,
>   and the waves and the breezes, sweetly resounding,
> at the hour when the sun sparkles most brightly,
> moved here and there, lifting her plaints to the sky.

Like the character of Anassilla, the seaside description in this sonnet typifies the complexity of Stampa's sequence. The marine setting appears to conform to previous texts; Anasilla's shores recall Sannazaro's *Piscatory Eclogues*. But Stampa's text is far more heterogeneous than her predecessor's. The echoing waves and breezes fail to harmonize the diverse positions and tones the sonnet includes: the anger at the count, the complaint of unrewarded service, the class and gender disparities between the elite man's self-display at the French court and the woman's complaint sung in Venice. I have been arguing that Stampa, as bourgeois *virtuosa*, manipulated pastoral convention in order to articulate a critique of the amatory conventions and the social hierarchies of her time. However attractive the romantic feudalism of the Veneto might have seemed, it was finally not a code that belonged to her. She expanded the eclogue from a vehicle for memory and lament into a mixed mode in which class critique and self-promotion outweigh the apparent humility of the pastoral speaker. By constructing Anassilla both as faithful shepherdess and female hero, Stampa built up a poetic text that escaped old inheritances—of land and literary convention—and redistributed the social and literary "properties" of Renaissance culture.

MARY WROTH'S PAMPHILIA: RENUNCIATION AS MERIT

Mary Wroth's sonnet sequence is less obviously "titanic" than Stampa's. She refrains from direct attacks on the inconstant man and makes no claims about the immensity of her powers as poet. But Pamphilia, too, turns the humiliating position of the abandoned woman into proof of her heroic constancy. In the eighty-three sonnets and twenty songs included in the revised edition of *Pamphilia to Amphilanthus*, the speaker's self-deprecation shades into dazzling asceticism, through which she demonstrates her superiority to the shallowness of court amours and the triviality of the lyrics in which they are encoded. Wroth's male predecessors and contemporaries wrote love poetry as an exercise in courtly eloquence and as displaced complaint about political frustration: Wyatt, Spenser, Sidney.[41] Her grafting of pastoral songs with sonnets, likewise, was inflected by her position as a female courtier out of favor with her monarchs.

The poems suggest that Wroth's motives in constructing Pamphilia's character were complex. As an idealized alter ego, the pastoral princess proves her loyalty to Amphilanthus in what may have been a rhetorical move designed to win back the affection of an actual lover, the erring Earl of Pembroke. Josephine Roberts argues that Wroth intended Herbert to recognize himself as the model for Amphilanthus; she assigned one of the earl's poems to Amphilanthus in the unpublished second part of *Urania*, in which the hero recites Herbert's "Had I loved butt att that rate" as his own composition.[42] More publicly, Pamphilia's high moral seriousness may have been intended to restore Wroth's reputation at court and to remind her former associates of her power to judge them. Her contemporaries recognized that her romance was satirically barbed. John Chamberlain reported court opinion that Wroth "takes great libertie or rather license to traduce whom she pleases," and Sir Aston Cokayne, in his poem "A Remedy for Love," commented, "The Lady *Wrothes Urania* is repleat / With elegancies, but too full of heat."[43] So the pastoral mode in which many of the songs are written serves several purposes for Wroth: it permits veiled references to court vice at the same time that it affirms Pamphilia's innocence. And pastoral stages her exile as a test situation, a trial through which she proves her purity and courage. Pamphilia's country solitude is represented not as the retreat of a wealthy aristocrat but as a fortress from which Wroth banishes sensual love, thus demonstrating her moral rather than class merit to the courtly judges who have banished her.

The first song in *Pamphilia to Amphilanthus* combines many of the themes of the sequence and typifies its resolute melancholy. It begins with a reversed pathetic fallacy. The abandoned shepherdess invokes the patterns of the natural world in order to assert their irrelevance to her inner landscape:

> The spring now come att last
> To trees, fields, to flowers,
> And medowes makes to tast
> His pride, while sad showers
> Which from mine eyes do flow
> Makes knowne with cruell paines
> Cold winter yett remaines
> Noe signe of spring wee know.
> (P7)

Like Stampa, Wroth compares the male beloved to a sun: he is a "blessed star" (Sonnet 25) with eyes brighter than "Sunns faire light" (Song 6). But he is also a sun from whose warmth the speaker is excluded:

> The Sunn which to the Earth
> Gives heate, light and pleasure,
> Joyes in spring, hateth dearth,
> Plenty makes his treasure.
> His heat to mee is colde,
> His light all darknes is
> Since I am bar'd of bliss
> I heate nor light beeholde.

Again like Stampa, Wroth delays any explanation of who is speaking until the end of the poem. Only after the unmediated "I" has established her misery does she identify the character lamenting it. The third-person perspective clarified in the third stanza produces an effect of objectivity that legitimates the shepherdess-poet's complaint:

> A sheapherdess thus sayd
> Who was with griefe oprest
> For truest love beetraid

> Bard her from quiett rest
> And weeping thus sayd she
> My end aprocheth neere
> Now willow must I weare
> My fortune soe will bee. . . .

Wroth's allusion to the willow draws on popular culture; the folk songs of her day linked the river-bank tree to the death of a young woman. But the poem is also a highly formalized, self-consciously literary performance. Like Anassilla, this shepherdess constructs a scene of writing through which she blames the faithless man and praises herself:

> The barck my booke shall bee
>   Wher dayly I will wright
> This tale of haples mee
>   True slave to fortunes spight;
> The roote shall bee my bed
>   Wher nightly I will lye,
>   Wayling inconstancy
> Since all true love is dead.

Like Stampa, Wroth composes her own epitaph and addresses it to an ideal reader, a true lover capable of understanding and preserving the woman's complaint:

> And thes lines I will leave
>   If some such lover come
> Who may them right conseave,
>   And place them on my tombe:
> She who still constant lov'd
>   Now dead with cruell care
>   Kil'd with unkind dispaire,
> And change, her end heere prov'd.

The parallel between Stampa's sonnets 35 and 151 and this song provides striking evidence that pastoral conventions of solitary complaint and posthumous recognition had particular resonance for women poets.[44] Stampa and Wroth *were* solitary as love poets: they wrote as exceptional women rather than as members of a group. Symptomatically, their alter egos engage in frustrated monologues rather than coterie dialogues. But Wroth, unlike Stampa, hesitates to claim fame outright in the present tense of her sequence. The expectation that a sympathetic reading is likely only after a lovelorn shepherdess has died of grief has sources not only in European lyric tradition but also in Wroth's conflict with an English milieu in which writing at all could lead to the accusation that she was a "Hermaphrodite."

Given such constraints, it is understandable that she uses the landscape of pastoral to write in an unimpeachably "correct" vein. The fourteenth song of the sequence is a good example of the didactic potential of pastoral. By setting up an analogy between the regularity of the seasons and the inconstancy of her lover, the singer implies that there is something unnatural, even perverse, in the short-lived affection of less faithful lovers. The persistence of the refrain reinforces the exemplary self-portrait of the shepherdess:

> The spring time of my first loving
> Finds yett noe winter of removing
> Nor frosts to make my hopes decrease
> Butt with the sommer still increase.
>
> The trees may teach us loves remaining
> Who suffer chang with little paining
> Though winter make theyr leaves decrease
> Yett with the sommer they increase. . . .
>
> Those that doe love butt for a season
> Doe faulcefy both love, and reason,
> For reason wills if love decrease
> Itt like the sommer should increase.
>
> Though love some times may bee mistaken
> The truth yett ought nott to bee shaken,
> Or though the heate awhile decrease
> Itt with the sommer may increase.
>
> (P73)

The poem ends by repeating its first stanza. This is a double strategy. By focusing again on Pamphilia's perfection, the final lines offer a model for Amphilanthus, while, less didactically and more pleasurably, they guarantee him a warm welcome if he returns:

> And since the spring time of my loving
> Found never winter of removing
> Nor frosts to make my hopes decrease
> [It] Shall as the sommer still increase.

The song locates the natural cycle in a forested countryside to justify a subtle attack on the man and to hint at an erotic promise.

More typically, however, Wroth's nature poems fixate on tragic seasons and landscapes: winter and night. She locates Pamphilia in relentlessly bleak settings, deprived of light, comfort and companions. The places in which Pamphilia waits in vain go unidentified; there is no reference to a city, a court, or an ancestral estate. Other people are invoked only to be dismissed as distractions from Pamphilia's project of winning Amphilanthus back by proving how intensely she is willing to suffer for him. Wroth's exile from court is figured in the sequence partly through her frequent apostrophes to allegorical figures rather than human beings. Pamphilia addresses mythological figures and personified abstractions such as Venus and Jealousy far more often than she speaks to her distant beloved or to the dimly sketched courtiers she occasionally mentions. Like a knight proving his mettle through a solitary vigil or a hermit purifying herself in a cave, Pamphilia embraces her exile. The sequence represents her virtue as *virtù*: she sacrifices the sunshine of social life to the dark night of the true lover's ascesis.

But night also had a specific historical connotation in Wroth's poetry. Her first public triumph at court was her appearance as one of twelve Ethiopians led by Queen Anne in Jonson's *Masque of Blackness* in 1605: she played the role of Baryte, representing gravity and balance, and she carried an emblem, an urn twined with vines, representing the fruitfulness of earth. She performed again as one of the "daughters of Niger" in Jonson's *Masque of Beauty*.[45] So Pamphilia's references to black visions would also have been received as reminders of Wroth's past glories at Whitehall. Both the quality of darkness and the sphere she carried in the masque were mentioned as her emblems in poems later written to her by Ben Jonson, George Chapman, and George Wither.[46] The pastoral fiction of *Pamphilia to Amphilanthus* recalls its author's earlier relation to darkness as a theme of self-display in court pageantry but relocates it in a setting of rural privacy.

Sonnet 19 typifies the nocturnal and hibernal mood of the sequence. Pamphilia implies that only spirits less elevated than hers are comforted by daylight. She invokes the fading trees of autumn as a chorus of worthier alter egos:

> Come darkest night, beecoming sorrow best;
>   Light; leave thy light; fitt for a lightsome soule;
>   Darknes doth truly sute with mee oprest
>   Whom absence power doth from mirthe controle.
> The very trees with hanging heads condole
>   Sweet sommers parting, and of leaves distrest
>   In dying coulers make a griefe-full role;
>   Soe much (alas) to sorrow are they prest.
>
>   (P22)

In the tercets, the autumnal imagery is unexpectedly gendered. The summer mourned for by the natural landscape is represented not as a departing male lover but as a feminine figure, a royal presence surrounded by unnamed subordinates, and the conclusion leaves the identity of what is longed for unclear: we are told only that Pamphilia lacks the sight of what she desires. Might the withered hopes attributed to the fallen leaves be hopes for a restoration of royal favor, imagined through the convention of an appeal to the queen for amorous favor?

> Thus of dead leaves her farewell carpett's made:
>   Theyr fall, theyr branches, all theyr mournings prove;
>   With leavles, naked bodies, whose huese vade
>   From hopefull greene, to wither in theyr love,
> If trees, and leaves for absence, mourners bee
> Noe mervaile that I grieve, who like want see.

Many of the most forceful poems in the sequence establish Night as a
feminine figure with whom Pamphilia identifies and through whom she can
prove her merit. In Sonnet 12, she makes the identification explicit:

> My thoughts are sad; her face as sad doth seeme;
> My paines are long; Her houers taedious are:
> My griefe is great, and endles is my care:
> Her face, her force, and all of woes esteeme.
>
> (P13)

Sonnet 15 opens similarly. Wroth directs far-reaching compliments to Night:
she compares the sober dignity of her outer appearance to her moral clarity
and purifying effect. And Pamphilia/Wroth takes on both qualities through
her earlier framing of Night as a mirror image of herself:

> Truly poore Night thou wellcome art to mee:
> I love thee better in this sad attire
> Then that which raiseth some mens phant'sies higher
> Like painted outsid[e]s which foule inward bee;
> I love thy grave, and saddest lookes to see,
> Which seems my soule, and dying hart intire,
> Like to the ashes of some happy fire
> That flam'd in joy, butt quench'd in miserie. . . .
>
> (P17)

In fact, the speaker's speeches to Night construct the most sustained relationship imagined in the sequence. Unlike Amphilanthus, Night can be
counted on for regular appearances and sustaining company. Sonnet 15 ends
with the implication that Night has lenitive power in the political as well as
the psychic world. She is represented as the mediator of daytime justice,
promising relief not only to lovers but, as the generality of "to uss" and "all
ill" in line 11 suggests, to other categories of the oppressed as well:

> I love thy count'nance, and thy sober pace
> Which evenly goes, and as of loving grace
> To uss, and mee among the rest oprest
> Gives quiet, peace to my poore self alone,
> And freely grants day leave when thou art gone
> To give cleere light to see all ill redrest.

This poem, too, raises the possibility that Night is a figure for Queen
Anne, through whom Wroth imagines regaining court approval. If the
link is there, it is made via a complex intermeshing of symbolic convention and social ambition: the poet offers her pastoral isolation as evidence of her purified values, which distinguish her from her peers at
court. Wroth rewrites the exile of a woman accused of adultery as the
precondition for the ending of that exile, just as Pamphilia's willingness

to suffer for unrequited love demonstrates that she deserves to have her love requited.

Pamphilia affirms her identification with Night by dismissing daytime revelry as foreign to her system of merit through renunciation. In Sonnet 9, for example, she distances herself from an audience enjoying ordinary pleasures: "Bee you all pleas'd? your pleasures grieve nott mee: / Doe you delight? I envy nott your joy: / Have you content? contentment with you bee." More heroically than the merely "contented," she welcomes grief's challenge because it proves that her love is constant enough not to quail at rejection: "Lett sad misfortune, haples mee destroy." In the marital and po-litical metaphors of her final lines, she rewrites despair at Amphilanthus's indifference into a position she herself has chosen:

> Joyes are beereav'd, harmes doe only tarry;
>   Dispaire takes place, disdaine hath gott the hand;
>   Yett firme love holds my sences in such band
>   As since dispis'ed, I with sorrow marry;
> Then if with griefe I now must coupled bee
> Sorrow I'le wed: Dispaire thus governs mee.
>
>   (P10)

In other poems, too, Pamphilia sets her private meditations against the "poore vanities" of court and country-house entertainments as proof of her dedication to higher things. In Sonnet 23, she names five pastimes as foils to her solitary self-control:

> When every one to pleasing pastime hies
>   Some hunt, some hauke, some play, while some delight
>   In sweet discourse, and musique showes joys might
>   Yet I my thoughts doe farr above thes[e] prise. . . .
> When others hunt, my thoughts I have in chase;
>   If hauke, my mind att wished end doth fly,
>   Discourse, I with my spiritt tauke, and cry
>   While others, musique choose as greatest grace.
> O God, say I, can thes fond pleasures move?
> Or musique bee butt in sweet thoughts of love?
>
>   (P26)

Pamphilia's declaration of independence, like those of her uncle Philip Sid-ney, also a writer of love poetry while he was exiled from court, requires that she invoke and enumerate exactly the activities she rejects;[47] she demon-strates her familiarity with the public world because such familiarity proves that she knows what she is sacrificing for love. Like the melancholic young men of Jacobean poetry and portraits, she turns her back on trivial pursuits.[48] She accuses courtly lovers of lacking sincerity in Sonnet 40, another poem that recalls Sidney's *Astrophil and Stella*. Like Astrophil, Pamphilia con-demns lovers' posturing to affirm her own honesty:

Itt is nott love which you poore fooles do deeme
  That doth apeare by fond, and outward showes
  Of kissing, toying, or by swearings glose,
  O noe thes are farr off from loves esteeme; . . .
Tis nott a showe of sighes, or teares can prove
  Who loves indeed which blasts of fained love
  Increase, or dy as favors from them slide; . . .

(P46)

But rather than invoking a virile plain style as antidote, as Sidney did, she invokes the discretion required of court ladies. Hidden emotions and secret glances are most genuine, eyes speak more truthfully than mouths at court:

Butt in the soule true love in safety lies
  Guarded by faith which to desart [deserted] heart still hies.
  And yett kinde lookes doe many blessings hide.

Wroth's focus on mistreatment and banishment as challenges to constancy also produces a late song (11) in which she works out a cross-class, cross-gendered identification between a lovelorn shepherd and the princess Pamphilia. Both figures share the constancy of the ideal lover, but the bitter conclusion of the poem suggests that neither will be rewarded for it:

Love as well can make abiding
  In a faythfull sheapheards brest
As in Princese whose thoughts sliding
  Like swift rivers never rest. . . .

Constancy his chiefe delighting
  Strives to fle[e] from phant'sies strang; . . .

This a sheapheard once confessed
  Who lov'd well butt was nott lov'd
Though with scorne, and griefe opressed
  Could nott yet to change bee mov'd
But him self hee thus contented
  While in love hee was accurst:
This hard hap hee nott repented
  Since best lovers speed the wurst.

(P60)

The posture of stoic resignation breaks down in other poems, however, in which Pamphilia resists her "hard hap." Pastoral humility gives way to scenes of public spectacle, including ghastly images of feminine suffering. The political vocabulary of such poems, I suspect, is more than metaphorical conceit. The loss Pamphilia complains of is not only the loss of love but the loss of just estimation, of prestige in a world of power and self-display from which she claims to have exiled herself rather than to have been exiled against her will. But this is not self-punishment for trangressions of sexual codes;[49] Wroth's self-abasement encodes a demand for better treatment. Sonnet 13, addressed to Amphilanthus, typifies her rhetoric of submission. She appeals to the man as though he were a warrior tyrant needing to be recalled to the *noblesse oblige* of kings:

> Deare fammish nott what you your self gave food;
>> Destroy nott what your glory is to save;
>> Kill nott that soule to which you spiritt gave;
>> In pitty, nott disdaine your triumph stood;
> An easy thing itt is to shed the blood
>> Of one, who att your will, yeelds to the grave;
>> Butt more you may true worthe by mercy crave
>> When you preserve, nott spoyle, butt nurrish good; . . .
>
> (P15)

The meekness with which she frames her final request for a look from his eyes makes a refusal seem inhuman. Pamphilia asks for so little: a glance, as brief as he likes. Yet this willingness to accept rejection is also a way of managing it. Again Pamphilia rewrites a catastrophe she cannot control as a condition she accepts, in fact, one she proposes:

> Your sight is all the food I doe desire;
>> Then sacrifies mee nott in hidden fire,
>> Or stop the breath which did your prayses move:
> Think butt how easy t'is a sight to give;
>> Nay ev'n deserte; since by itt I doe live,
>> I butt Camaelion-like would live, and love.

This argument is typical of the structure of Wroth's sonnets. It opens with an entreaty but shifts gradually into a celebration of the speaker's miraculous capacity to feed on frustration, as the chameleon lives on air.

Pamphilia's refusal of comfort leads her to reject the traditional claim of love poets that composing verses relieves their anguish. Unlike Petrarch and his followers, this poet does not write "per sfogare la mente" (to relieve her mind). Pamphilia opens Sonnet 8 by saying, "I seeke for some smale ease by lines," but she concludes that poems only "Increase the paine; griefe is nott cur'd by art." In Sonnet 39 she rejects the pleasure of composition as mere vanity: "Nor can I as those pleasant wits injoy / My owne fram'd words, which I account the dross / Of purer thoughts." But this is false modesty; the poems prove not only her constancy but also the virtuosity with which she uses rhetorical devices to demonstrate her worth. Her metaphors, her appeals to her readers, and the framework ordering the poems all contribute to her self-representation as the survivor of unrelenting psychic trials.

One of the most startling metaphors Wroth employs is the rack, the stretching device used to extort confessions. It first appears in Sonnet 36, in which Pamphilia speaks to her heart as the only witness of a love that must be kept secret. Wroth establishes a public scene framed by the prying eyes traditionally associated with court life. "What torments hast thou suffered," Pamphilia says to her heart: "thou tortur'd wert with racks which longing beares / Pinch'd with desires which yett but wishing reares" (P41). A heart stretched on a rack is a bizarre and frightening conceit, not entirely diminished by the aphoristic final couplet, which Pamphilia addresses to a wider audience to praise her strength in contrast to the pretense of lesser lovers: "For know more passion in my hart doth move / Then in a million that make show of love."

The political dimension of the metaphor is extended in a much bleaker later poem, Sonnet 4 of the second series in the sequence, which narrates Pamphilia's struggle against jealousy. Here the rack concretizes the vulnerability of the lover by paralleling it to the terror of a political prisoner. Wroth uses the vocabulary of torture not to describe one experience in terms belonging to a totally different realm; rather than writing a metaphysical conceit, she breaks down the opposition between unrequited love as a private dilemma and the pursuit of favor as a public one. Her figures for constraint correspond to her real social entrapment: she links the rack to solitary confinement and represents Pamphilia's search for "favor" as frustrated by male authorities—suspicion and jealousy, personified as jailers:

> I ame by care sufficiently distrest,
> > Noe rack can strech my hart more, nor a way
> > Can I find out for least content to lay
> > One happy foote of joye, one step that's blest; . . .
> > > > (P66)

The scene of imprisonment is concretized further by the figure of Jealousy, identified as a go-between for Suspicion. The entire episode recalls Webster's treatment of the imprisonment of the Duchess of Malfi. Wroth, likewise, constructs a scene that contrasts Pamphilia's innocence to the brutality of her guards, and she appeals for sympathy in the stunned wonder of Pamphilia's comment on her entrapment:

> Butt to my end thou fly'st with greedy eye,
> > Seeking to bring griefe by bace jealousie,
> > O in how strang a cage ame I kept in?

The woman's dependency on the capricious man is described in a language of "favor" equally relevant to a courtier's dependency upon a royal patron. Pamphilia discovers no solution; she can only guess at and adapt to the unpredictable moods of power:

> Noe little sign of favor can I prove
> > Butt must be way'de, and turnd to wronging love,
> > And with each humor must my state begin.

It is a long way from Wroth's pastoral songs to this sonnet of incarceration, but they are interconnected: her pastoral songs reverse the hostile public arenas invoked in her sonnets by means of an idealized counterrepresentation of the humiliations she faced as a debt-ridden widow retired from court.[50] Yet she does not despair of influencing the world from which she is excluded; she lays claim to public support by making a spectacle of her suffering. In Sonnet 42 she stages her mistreatment as a theatrical scene, soliciting the sympathy of witnesses she imagines as the audience in a playhouse. The poem opens with an eerie scene of dismemberment as Pamphilia points to the excision of her heart:

> If ever love had force in humaine brest?
>   If ever hee could move in pensive hart?
>   Or if that hee such powre could butt impart
>   To breed those flames whose heat brings joys unrest.
> Then looke on mee; I ame to thes adrest,
>   I, ame the soule that feeles the greatest smart;
>   I, ame that hartles trunk of harts depart
>   And I, that one, by love, and griefe oprest.
>
>   (P48)

In the tercets, Wroth directs the gaze of her audience away from the cut-up body of Pamphilia to the blind figure of Love, who, like Amphilanthus, ignores her appeals. She sets up only one possible response for her observers: the pitiful response the god and the man withhold from her. Pamphilia declaims the poem in the posture of a tragic heroine, but she is also an orator using public space to denounce injustice:

> Non[e] ever felt the truth of loves great miss
>   Of eyes, till I deprived was of bliss;
>   For had hee seene, hee must have pitty show'd:
> I should nott have bin made this stage of woe
>   Wher sad disasters have theyr open showe
>   O noe, more pitty hee had sure beestow'd.

Pamphilia's performances as solitary shepherdess equally position her as public sign. In either mode, the woman calls upon the gaze of the outer world for her own ends.

The introspective scene of the pastoral songs is further transformed into a public pageant in Wroth's corona, "A crowne" of fourteen sonnets "dedicated to Love." She represents the process of comprehending love through an architectural conceit: the novice travels through a maze. The first and final lines of the sequence—the same, as the rules of the form require—establish fearful curiosity as the condition of the female lover: "In this strang labourinth how shall I turne?" Elaine Beilin argues that the corona maps out a progress from earthly to divine love,[51] but its setting and vocabulary also suggest that its fantasy of fulfillment is a courtier's fantasy, and not an entirely happy one. The speaker's quest is set in the court of Love, where reason is advisor and Love "ruler must / Bee of the state which crowne hee long hath worne." Pamphilia reaches her goal by rejecting lust, represented by Venus, and approaching Venus's son, the "lord commander of all harts," to whom she offers herself and her poems in the language of an oath of feudal fealty: "I offer to your trust / This crowne, my self, and all that I have more, / Except my hart which you bestow'd before" (Sonnet 13). The final sonnet introduces the theme of jealousy again, but this time the term seems to include the envy of fellow courtiers: Pamphilia sees "curst jealousie" returning as an enemy to her and to the king. Her final vow is to defend the ruler as well as herself against Love's "enimies." In Wroth's allegorical scheme, constancy is both an emotional and a political virtue.

Several of Wroth's readers consider the corona the high point of *Pamphilia and Amphilanthus*.[52] The fourteen sonnets are certainly a technical tour de force, and the ingenuity of the allegory is impressive. But the corona is also revealingly contradictory. In its early sonnets Pamphilia uses Platonic and Christian discourses to sermonize. She urges fellow lovers to accept Love as their "Tuter" (5, 6), to direct their "phant'sies" nowhere "Butt wher they may returne with honors grace" (8), and to agree that lust "ought like monster borne / Bee from the court of Love, and reason torn" (9, 10). Yet Wroth fulfills the corona's requirement for an identical opening and closing line in a verse that calls Pamphilia's knowledge of true love into question. If she has really had a revelation of love's "glory and might" (11), how is it that the final sonnet leaves her in the same fearful perplexity with which she entered the "labourinth"? One explanation for the inconsistency is the public ambition Wroth hoped to satisfy by writing and publishing her poems. I have been arguing that an expiatory motive shapes the sequence. This is the motive Pamphilia declares in the final sonnet of *Pamphilia to Amphilanthus*: she renounces love poetry as the "discource of Venus," appropriate only to "young beeginers." In the "crowne of Sonetts," too, Wroth's paean to pure love offers proof that she has reformed. But if her intention was to regain her position at court, she knew how risky such attempts were. Love's labyrinth may well be a figure for the anxiety of courtiers in their quest for favor. Wroth's nets and bridles, her techniques for attracting and controlling the readers and rulers of her Jacobean milieu, are Pamphilia's pastoral innocence and her stern advice on how to serve a king of love, how to "bee in his brave court a glorious light" (corona 3, 4).

A late song sums up Wroth's balancing act between propitiatory charm and reproachful lament. In the third song following the corona, a farewell to winter, Ovid's Philomela appears as harbinger of spring and as a figure for Pamphilia herself. The first two stanzas celebrate the new season and fantasize a permanent end to the loss of love:

Come merry spring delight us
For winter long did spite us
In pleasure still persever
Thy beauties ending never,
  Spring, and growe
  Lasting soe
With joyes increasing ever;

Lett colde from hence be banisht,
Till hopes from mee bee vanisht,
But bless thy dainties growing
In fullnes freely flowing
  Sweet birds sing
  For the spring
All mirthe is now beestowing; . . .

(P93)

But the final stanza introduces Philomel and complicates the sweetness of the bird-woman's song with complaints about her past and present condition. Rather than imagining an exchange of poetry with the mythological heroines, as Stampa does, or encouraging Philomel to "take some gladnesse" because her pain is lessening while his increases, as Philip Sidney had done (*Certain Sonnets*, 4), Wroth insists on the permanent ambivalence in the nightingale's song, on the darkness underlying its cheerfulness. The last line focuses on a violation that no springtime renewal can efface. Rather, it suggests that the pained sweetness of the song must be heard as an accurate rendering of the singer's catastrophic past:

Philomeale in this arbour
Makes now her loving harbour
Yett of her state complaining
Her notes in mildnes straining
  Which though sweet
  Yett doe meete
Her former luckles payning.

This song condenses Wroth's uses of pastoral into a densely signifying lyric. The first two stanzas match each other and the tradition exemplarily. The witty variation in line length, the formulaic shorthand that abridges the seasons into the growth/cold opposition, the alliteration on "s" that links the short lines all typify the formal pleasures of pastoral—to reverse Empson's formula, its predictable complication of the simple. This is what Wroth's readers expected from a pastoral song and what she gives them in the figure of Pamphilia as shepherdess. But a shock is produced by the shift from the merry voice welcoming spring to the third-person narrator telling us with those two insistent "yetts" to listen to the dissonance in Philomela's song. Wroth's sequence does not resolve the problems of frustrated desire and banishment from a once friendly court any more than Philomel's metamorphosis into a nightingale frees her from the memories that make her into a perpetual reminder of her rape and loss of human status. But the swallow's song in the myth and the noblewoman's poetry in 1621 both appropriate available languages to win a hearing for the woman's complaint.

Wroth's sequence registers restrictions on feminine speech more than Stampa's: its anger is more repressed, its voices are more restrained. Differences in class and culture helped to produce this contrast. Stampa's more outspoken and self-acclaiming style corresponds to her economic independence as *virtuosa* and her practice at being heard in the academies of Venice; Wroth, writing in Protestant England and facing censure from the Stuart court, confronted stricter demands for proper feminine speech and deference to authority. But like Philomela, both poets turn what might appear to be a masochistic dwelling on loss into resistance: to silence, to rejection, to the subject position assigned to women in masculine lyric conventions. The sheer size of their collections—by far the longest analyzed in this study—suggests that their exclusion from the inner circles of ducal and courtly milieux intensified their ambitions. Their banishment from inaccessible paradises drove them toward sustained labor in the new field of feminine pastoral.

Stampa's and Wroth's books contrast in other ways as well to those of two poets who published from more coherent social positions. Louise Labé and Veronica Franco also lived and wrote on the margins of aristocratic culture, but each belonged to a clearly defined class: Labé was the wife of a wealthy Lyonnais ropemaker, Franco was a prosperous Venetian courtesan. Resolutely urban, they rarely use pastoral conventions; instead of lament and reproach, they adopt strategies of seduction and comic irony; and they transform the complaint of the solitary woman into a defense of women as a group. Yet the tension between conciliation and challenge in Stampa's loving denunciations and Wroth's ascetic dramas is also at work in the poems of Labé and Franco. The class and ideological systems negotiated by the Venetian *virtuosa* and the Jacobean courtier posed similar problems for the ropemaker's wife and the mistress of Venice's millionaires.

FIVE

Eros Equalized

Literary Cross-Dressing and the Defense of Women in Louise Labé and Veronica Franco

In 1612, Marie de Gournay published a defense of women, *L'Egalité des hommes et des femmes*, in which she pointed to differences among women as proof that nurture rather than nature determines feminine abilities: "Se trouve-t-il plus de différence des hommes à elles que d'elles à elles-mesmes, selon l'institution qu'elles ont prinse, selon qu'elles sont eslevées en ville ou en village, ou selon les Nations?"[1] (Can there be more difference between men and women than between women themselves, according to the education they have received, where they have been brought up, in village or city, or in what nation?) She specifies one telling difference: the intellectual successes of French and English women are greater than those of Italian women because Italians keep their wives "shut up in the dungeons" of their houses while English and French women enjoy a free "commerce du monde." Her term has several connotations: economic exchange, contact with diverse social milieux, open conversation. De Gournay pinpoints the cultural exposure essential to women writers anywhere, a kind of freedom, as her *ville/village* opposition suggests, less available in the country or a small town than in a full-fledged city. Lyon and Venice, centers of international capitalism famous for their "commerce du monde," were the sites of publication of two extraordinary women's texts, Louise Labé's *Euvres* and Veronica Franco's *Rime*. How did living in these cities affect their female citizens as poets?

LOUISE LABÉ: THE ROPEMAKER'S WIFE, THE HUMANISTS' HEROINE

Lyon was a city of Italians: bankers who lent the French kings money to support their wars (the Florentine Tommaso Gadagni, for example, settled in Lyon as the major banker to François I)[2] and publishers whose books rivaled those of Aldus Manutius in Venice.[3] Lyon's Italian current ran throughout Louise Labé's life. She wrote the first sonnet of her twenty-four in Italian; she published her *Euvres* in 1555 with a printer, Jean de Tournes, whose engraver and press designer had learned new techniques during a long stay in Venice;[4] and in 1565 she dictated her will at the house of an Italian lawyer-financier, Thomas Fortini.

155

In addition, Lyon had a special royal permission (*franchise*) to hold independent fairs up to four times a year, a mercantile advantage that helped it to become the commercial center of Europe throughout the early 1500s. The city also enjoyed relative autonomy from the Parisian court and from the theological control of the Sorbonne. The absence of a fixed court hierarchy, combined with the dominance of wealthy artisans and moneymen in local government, seems to have made Lyon a place in which class boundaries were more fluid than elsewhere in France.[5] Louise Labé's father, for example, began as a fairly modest ropemaker, but by the time of his death in 1552, he was a substantial citizen, living on revenues from property and asked to sit on municipal councils and administer local charities.[6] Karine Berriot observes that while the ropemaker himself never sought the literary polish that his daughter displayed (he died illiterate), it was a common practice among men of his class to train and display their wives and daughters as possessors of cultural luxuries previously reserved for the aristocracy: "the powerful merchants of Lyon delegated to selected women of their rank the task of converting cash into prestige-value."[7]

Labé's visibility as a conspicuously cultured *bourgeoise* brought her into contact with a variety of highly placed Lyonnais and travelers. She was celebrated by the humanists' circle, the *Sodalitatum Lugdunense*, composed of local scholar-poets such as Maurice Scève and his friend Pontus de Tyard, visiting court officials such as the poet Clément Marot, and occasional members such as the scholar Henri Etienne and the Parisian lawyer Guillaume Aubert.[8] But she attracted hostility as well, for example, from a disgruntled nobleman of the region, probably because she had not included him in her mixed gatherings of aristocrats, humanists, and merchants. Philibert de Vienne, in his *Philosophe de cour* (1547), gave her the backhanded compliment of reporting that her admirers found her at least not as greedy for cash as Laïs, the fabled courtesan of Corinth.[9] Her contacts with elites native to the city or visiting it also made her the target of a scurrilous poem, published in 1557, two years after her *Euvres*. The "Chanson nouvelle de la Belle Cordière de Lyon" is narrated by a voyager who claims that the ropemaker's wife went to bed with him and then with a lawyer, a tax collector, a shoemaker, a miller, and a rich Florentine.[10] The song rewrites Labé's upward mobility as promiscuous hubris. For one thing, the term "la cordière" (the ropemaker's wife) effaces her status as independent poet who used the last name neither of her father, Pierre Charly, nor of her husband Ennemond Perrin, but of her father's first wife, Guillemette. Guillemette had previously been married to Humbert dit Labé ("called Labé," after a piece of property he owned, sometimes spelled "L'Abbé"). When Pierre Charly married her, he acquired that property and took the name of her first husband. To call Louise "the ropemaker's wife," as the song does, is to insist on her membership in an artisan family, to replace her in her clan rather than in her literary coterie. And to represent her relations with men of different professions as based entirely on the desire for money is to rewrite her "commerce du monde" as mere sexual accessibility.

The religious climate in Lyon and beyond also produced hostile responses to Labé. Natalie Davis sums up the varying judgments Labé's Protestant and Catholic contemporaries made of her as follows:

> the public and independent identity of Louise Labé was based on behavior that was unacceptable in a modest and brave Reformed woman. The books Louise read and wrote were lascivious; her salons an impure gathering of the sexes; and her literary feminism impudent. She was talked of in Geneva as a lewd female who had corrupted the wife of a Lyon surgeon, persuading her to abandon her Christian husband for the sake of pleasure. . . . A Catholic deacon in Lyon, Guillaume Paradin, himself a humanist and a literary man, thought Louise virtuous, angelic of face, and with an understanding superior to her sex. Calvin said she was a strumpet.[11]

Such accusations as were officially recorded against Labé now seem to have been concocted mainly as ammunition in battles between men—by historians in Lyon as well as ecclesiastics abroad.[12] Her display of learning and her gatherings of high-ranking as well as highly educated men made her vulnerable to gossip on the part of Lyonnais who resented her transgression of social boundaries.

One form this resentment took was an interpretation of Labé as a man-woman: her crossing of class lines seems to have been displaced into an equally taboo crossing of gender barriers. In her autobiographical third elegy she recounts that her early training in "carrying the lance and spurring a superb horse into sudden turns" might have made the onlooker take her for Ariosto's Bradamante or Marfisa (lines 47–44). Her brother François, a noted fencer and horseman, may have trained her, and she may have performed in a Lyonnais tournament imitating the siege of Perpignan for Henri II before his victory there. But Labé herself does not mention Perpignan in her elegy. Rather, she frames her military self-portrait with representations of herself as properly feminine: a skilled needlewoman and the obedient servant of Venus, once Love distracted her from loving only "Mars and knowledge." It was her male contemporaries who laid the stress on her manly qualities. Guillaume Aubert initiated the myth that she had fought at the actual battle of Perpignan;[13] Antoine du Verdier remarked in his memoirs that her admirers called her "la capitaine Loys."[14] Calvin, in a letter attacking the Catholic churchman Gabriel de Saconay, named Labé as one of the prostitutes who wore men's clothes to the prelate's sexual orgies, proof that he was able to "metamorphize women into men."[15] And François Billon in *Le Fort inexpugnable de l'honneur du sexe femenin*, blaming men for speaking scandal of women, reinforced Labé's masculine reputation. Using the tendency to link Cleopatra with "la belle Cordière de Lyon" as an example of masculine libels of women,[16] Billon protested that such accusations overlooked Labé's virtues and concealed men's responsibility for feminine vice. But he himself repeated the assumption that a woman who excels in activities unusual for her sex thereby becomes a man: "to the extent that the masculine sex today is lascivious or vicious in other ways, this ropemaker's wife can certainly be called a Man, all the more because she is expert in every honorable virile activity, especially in Arms, and even in Letters." The social unconscious that takes a woman's public activity as evidence of sexual rule-breaking and interprets both as masculine brings about a curious transformation: it turns a woman who represents herself as a highly sexual female into a man.

Yet an accomplished woman could also be admired in Lyon. Secular poems suggest that Labé's status as a Lyonnaise poet was a source of admiration to humanist residents and visitors, who aligned her with the city's free mercantile spirit and glamorous prosperity. In the twenty-four poems published at the end of her *Euvres*, for example, she is frequently celebrated in a setting defined by the two rivers of Lyon, the Rhône and the Saône. Guillaume Aubert's ode elevates the city by linking it to classical myth. He addresses Labé as the daughter of Venus, conceived on the hill named after her mother (Lyon's Mont Fourvière, legend had it, had once been called Forum Veneris), and praises the poet as "la Ninfe Lionnoize."[17] Less fantastically, the scholar Jacques Peletier du Mans composed an ode naming Labé as the leading attraction of the city, which he describes by narrating a walk through its pearl and silk markets and its printing houses.[18] At the end of the poem, Peletier presents Labé as the last and best of the city's attractions, a guarantee that "the flight of winged Fame" will follow both. Jean de Tournes extended the identification of the woman with the city by framing her *Euvres* with the tripartite name "Louize Labé Lionnoize," which he set on the title page and at the end of her final sonnet. By doing so, he advertised woman, city, and his own profession there simultaneously.

To what extent does this identification as *bourgeoise*, literally a city dweller rather than a landed noblewoman, enter into the writing of Labé herself? Recent critics have interpreted her texts as challenges to the cultural privileges of the aristocracy. Enzo Giudici, for example, links her use of vernacular French to the rivalry between Lyon, the progressive merchant capital, and Paris, the court center, and to the feminism of the early sixteenth century:

> To write in French and not in Latin meant breaking the bonds of authority, revolting against the tyranny of the past and recognizing only the laws of nature and spontaneity; it meant . . . affirming the liberty and autonomy of the individual personality. And these were exactly the demands, goals and characteristics of feminism, which helps to understand the fundamental unity of the two currents. . . . It explains the peculiar and long-lasting union, remarkable throughout the entire Renaissance, between the debate over the French language and the debate over women.[19]

Karine Berriot extends this argument throughout *Louise Labé: La Belle Rebelle et le François nouveau*. She interprets poems in praise of Labé as acknowledgments of "the prestige of literature as a consecration of the ascendancy of a new bourgeoisie, formed from the middling classes of artisans and business-

men, and at the same time the new status of French as the official legal language, that is, the language of the nation" (14). She takes Labé's prose
dialogue *Le Débat de Folie et d'Amour* as an example: a deliberate populariza-
tion that transforms the Erasmian dialogue in Latin into colloquial French and
into an implicit defense of artisans and laborers. Folly opposes Venus's rejection of any but the most cultivated souls as proper lovers; even "les gens de
labeur" are capable of being improved by love.[20] Berriot argues further that in
her sonnets Labé appropriates and transforms aristocratic conventions into an
"amorous discourse that ennobles, in the literal sense, the prosaic universe of
the merchant class and legitimates it at the same time" (71).

Labé's preface to her *Euvres*, a famous manifesto of early modern feminism, supports the view that she wrote to legitimate her class. She dedicated
her book to Clémence de Bourges, the daughter of a nobleman of Lyon, in
terms that simultaneously underline the nobility of her dedicatee and insist on
their shared citizenship: "A M. C. D. B. L," that is, "A *Mademoiselle* Clémence
de Bourges, *Lyonnaise*" (41, emphasis mine).[21] In this epistle Labé attacks gender rather than class inequality; female learning will stimulate men, she says,
to imitate women "for fear of being ashamed to see themselves surpassed by
those to whom they have always claimed to be superior in almost every way"
(42). Yet to argue against one hierarchy was to argue against others that inter-
sected with it. Even though Labé's defense of women's education applies to
the female sex as a whole rather than to women of particular classes, her
phrasing echoes bourgeois conduct books. She dismisses aristocratic luxury in
a phrase that recalls Bruto: the woman who succeeds in writing down her
ideas can "adorn herself with them rather than with necklace chains, rings
and sumptuous gowns, which become ours only through use." She argues
that learning is an ideal investment, not more sublime but more solid than
worldly goods: "But the honor that knowledge brings us will be entirely our
own and cannot be stolen from us either through the cleverness of thieves, the
strength of our enemies or the passage of time." Her prediction that women's
examples will stimulate men to put "more effort and study into worthy sciences" emphasizes acquired skill over inherited virtue in a vocabulary of energetic self-improvement, and bourgeois self-esteem is clear in her warning to
Pernette that the inherited "favors of fortune" should not distract her from the
honor earned by "those who pursue the arts and sciences." Literary production for Labé is not the offhand verbal elegance of a courtier or queen but the
result of serious effort to acquire "the goods" of the intellect. Giudici comments, "Louise's manifesto is . . . the program of the bourgeoisie, the society
that henceforth, against the monopoly of the castle and the convent, was to
revalorize culture."[22]

The desire for equality leads Labé to a new kind of erotic imagination
in her love poems: a focus on the pleasures of mutuality, even identity,
between the lovers. For one thing, she addresses her sonnets to a fellow
poet whom she treats as an equal rather than a mentor. A related tendency
in the sonnets is a certain reflexivity, an ironic play with and against the

conventions of love poetry. As in her intercutting of popular and learned registers in the *Débat*, Labé occasionally adopts a humorous detachment from the hallowed Petrarchism and courtly Neoplatonism of her contemporaries. Her adaptation of elite discourse is inflected by the interests and language of her own groups—including her sex. Throughout her poems she transforms traditional troubadour and stilnovist calls to ladies as the audience for love poetry into appeals to a concrete historical audience of women readers in Lyon.

The biographical question of who Labé's lover was is a vexed one; critics have suggested figures as various as Henri II, Clément Marot, and Maurice Scève.[23] One more reasonable possibility is Olivier de Magny, a nobleman born in Cahors and educated in Paris, who spent some time in Lyon in 1554 on his way to Rome as a companion to French churchmen. Whatever his actual relationship to Labé was, his poems make it clear that he wanted to make some sort of capital out of his acquaintance with her. He composed two of the eulogies included at the end of her *Euvres*, mentioned her by name in several of his early poems (*Les Souspirs*, 1556), and addressed a sneering ode to her husband, calling Ennemond "Sire Aymon" in a mocking echo of the name of a hero of chivalrous romances (*Odes amoureuses*, 1559).[24] In this ode, Magny confirms the suspicion of Labé's critics that she was trying to rise above her station, although he does so at the expense of the husband rather than the wife. He contrasts the elegance of his musically and verbally talented "madame parfaicte" to the prosaic disorder of "Sire Aymon's" narrow workshop and greasy apron. The open contempt registered in this poem is permitted by Magny's position at the top of a class hierarchy corresponding to the gender hierarchy whereby men possessed much greater sexual freedom than women. This masculine privilege is unapologetically invoked in another of Magny's odes, "D'Aymer en plusieurs lieux" (Loving in many places):

> Pource qu'en ceste Amour diversement escripte
> Je parle ore avec Anne, ore avec Marguerite,
> Magdaleine, et Loyse, on me pourrait blasmer
> D'aymer en trop de lieux pour me faire bien aymer. . . .
> [Mais] La Nature m'a faict, et la Nature est belle
> Pour la diversité que nous voions en elle: . . .
> 37 Aymons donques par tout, et ces sottes constances
> Chassons de noz amours et de noz alliances,
> Aymant quand on nous ayme, et nous gardant tousjours
> La liberté d'entrer en nouvelles amours.[25]

> Because in this Love book, composed of variety,
> I speak now with Anne and now with Marguerite,
> With Madeleine and Louise, I might be accused
> Of loving too many to be loved in return. . . .
> But Nature produced me, and Nature is beautiful
> For the variety that we perceive in her. . . .

> So let us love everywhere, and banish foolish faith
> From our intrigues and from our unions,
> Let's love when we're loved, and always maintain
> The freedom to enter new love affairs.

In contrast, as the sexual restraint demanded of women would lead one to expect, Labé's elegies and sonnets focus on a single beloved.

But the two poets are not always so different. In Sonnet 55 of *Les Sous-pirs*, a collection Magny published in Paris in 1556, the year after Labé's *Euvres* were published in Lyon, he uses exactly the same description of a disdainful brown-eyed beloved as appears in the quatrains of Labé's Sonnet 2: "O beaux yeux bruns, ô regards destournez" (Oh, beautiful brown eyes, oh, glances turned aside).[26] Whatever the actual relations between Labé and Magny may have been, an intertextual link is established by these two lyrics: they open with an identical description of the beloved, interspersed with an identical narration of the lover's suffering. This parallel suggests that the nobleman saw something to gain from publicizing his dialogue with a bourgeois woman whose literary ambitions were more like his than their class difference might predict. Amorous rivalry similarly structures Labé's contributions to this dialogue. She often represents herself in thralldom to love, but she also challenges the beloved man: she calls him out and criticizes him as lover and poet both. Yet in her most experimental poems, often radical revisions of classical texts, she imagines an erotic ideal neither of dominance nor of submission but of difference-dissolving, gender-blurring unity. Even as Labé attacks the privileges her beloved enjoys, in the fiction of the sequence she fantasizes that they can rise to a new level of equality in the form of a shared identity.

Labé's Sonnet 10 establishes a first similarity between lover and beloved: like her, the man is a poet. She represents him wearing a laurel crown and surrounded by an admiring crowd, possibly as the hero of a ceremony of poetic laureation:

> Quand j'aperçoy ton blond chef couronné
> D'un laurier verd, faire un Lut si bien pleindre,
> Que tu pourrois à te suivre contreindre
> Arbres et rocs: quand je te vois orné,
> Et de vertus dix mile environné,
> Au chef d'honneur plus haut que nul ateindre,
> Et des plus hauts les louenges esteindre: . . .

> When I see your blond head crowned
> With green laurel, making a lute weep so well
> That you could force trees and rocks
> To follow you; when I see you, decorated,
> And encircled by ten thousand merits,
> Attaining a peak of honor higher than any other,
> And surpassing the praises given the highest men: . . .

A sense of awed distance from the hero might be seen in this opening description, which attributes the combined powers of Orpheus and Amphion to the lover. But elsewhere in her poems, Labé consistently claims for herself the qualities that she attributes to the man here. In Sonnet 23 she announces indirectly that she is blond like him by citing his description of her "tresse dorée" (golden tresses). In Sonnet 12, "Lut, compagnon de ma calamité," she describes herself as playing the same instrument he does, so sweetly that she, too, brings about metamorphoses: "En mes ennuis me plaire suis contreinte, / Et d'un dous mal douce fin esperer" (In the midst of my woe, I am forced to feel pleasure / And to hope for a sweet end to a sweet pain.) Most important, she claims renown equal to his in her second Elégie, addressed to him as a traveler in Italy. Labé declares that she surpasses any rival because of her international reputation for eloquence, one of the qualities for which the male poet is being celebrated in Sonnet 10:[27]

> 55 Si say je bien que t'amie nouvelle
>   A peine aura le renom estre telle,
>   Soit en beauté, vertu, grace et faconde,
>   Comme plusieurs gens savans par le monde
>   M'ont fait à tort, ce croy je, estre estimee. . . .
> 61 Non seulement en France suis flatee,
>   Et beaucoup plus, que ne veus, exaltee.
>   La terre aussi que Calpe et Pyrenee
>   Avec la mer tiennent environnee,
>   Du large Rhin les roulantes areines,
>   Le beau païs auquel or'te promeines,
>   Ont entendu (tu me l'as fait à croire)
>   Que gens d'esprit me donne quelque gloire.
>
> Yet I know well that your new love
> Can hardly have the reputation I do
> For beauty, skill, grace or eloquence,
> For which learned men throughout the world
> Have—though I think wrongly—made me famous. . . .
> I am praised not in France alone,
> And exalted, far more than I want to be.
> The land that Gibraltar and the Pyrenees
> And the sea all together surround,
> The sandy banks of the broad Rhine,
> And the lovely country you travel in now,
> All have heard (you've convinced me of it)
> That men of discernment attest to my fame.

In Sonnet 10, as well, the basic strategy is the woman poet's assumption that her fame will win the male poet's love. The "nom" (famous name, renown) she offers her beloved is *her* name. Her reputation in the circles they both inhabit will add to his:

Lors dit mon coeur en soy passionnée:
Tant de vertus qui te font estre aymé,
Qui de chacun te font estre estimé,
Ne te pourroient aussi bien faire aymer?
Et ajoutant à ta vertu louable
Ce nom encor de m'estre pitoyable,
De mon amour doucement t'enflamer?

Then my passionate heart says secretly,
"So many merits which make you beloved,
Which win esteem from every man,
Could they not make you love, as well?
And, adding to your praiseworthy merit
The further fame of being pitiful to me,
Of gently catching fire from my love?"

This is certainly one of the most worldly invitations to love in women's lyric. The woman poet woos the man by offering him a share of her own visibility, bartering social for erotic esteem.[28] As poet, she assumes an androgynous identity of interests between herself and the poet she loves: the public gaze that attracts her to him in the scene of his laureation should attract him to her in the scene of her admirers on both sides of the Alps.

In other sonnets, Labé imagines not so much a shared spotlight as a shifting competition between the lovers. Her plays with the *topos* of the lover's glance link woman and man in a process of power reversals. For example, in Sonnet 3, she describes her own eyes in conventional Petrarchan hyperbole as the "springs and fountains of a thousand rivers" wept for her beloved, whom she describes as a more than human figure: "O cruautez, ô durtez inhumaines, / Piteus regars des celestes lumières" (Oh, cruelty, oh, inhuman hardheartedness, / Pitiful glances from heavenly eyes). Although both lovers are equally larger than life, the man holds the upper hand. But in Sonnet 6, Labé turns her opening celebration of the man's return into a triumph for the loving woman. Her description of the man as Flora's gift, the rose used in classical and medieval poetry as the symbol for a desirable maiden, brings about a change in gender and visual perspective. Labé assigns the power of the gaze to the goddess Aurora:

Deus ou trois fois bienheureus le retour
De ce cler Astre, et plus heureus encore
Ce que son oeil de regarder honore.
Que celle là recevroit un bon jour,
Qu'elle pourroit se vanter d'un bon tour
Qui baiseroit le plus beau don de Flore,
Le mieus sentant que jamais vid Aurore,
Et y feroit sur ses levres sejour!

Twice or thrice blessed the return
Of this bright star, and more blessed still

> Whatever his eye honors with a look.
> What a wonderful day that woman would see,
> What great good fortune she could claim,
> She who could kiss Flora's loveliest gift,
> The most fragrant flower Aurora ever saw,
> And rest a long time upon his lips!

The poem ends with an aggressive statement of the speaker's power to fascinate the man through her look. A note of vengeful pleasure surfaces at the end of the sonnet when Labé replaces the masculine with the feminine gaze totally, making herself the victor in the ocular contest:

> C'est à moy seule à qui ce bien est dù,
> Pour tant de pleurs et tant de tems perdu:
> Mais le voyant, tant lui feray de feste,
> Tant emploiray de mes yeux le pouvoir,
> Pour dessus lui plus de credit avoir,
> Qu'en peu de temps feray grande conqueste.

> To me alone this reward is due,
> In return for my tears and so much wasted time.
> But when I saw him, I'd greet him with such joy,
> I'd use the power of my eyes so well
> To win from him what I am owed,
> That in no time I'd conquer him completely.

This quality of daring, Labé's confident, even defiant posture, signals the sexual and social challenge that the bourgeois woman poet is aiming at the dilettante nobleman. She takes a stance as equal match for the man and for Amour as god.[29]

Yet her challenges coexist with an equalizing attempt to dissolve differences between lover and beloved. Two of her sonnets narrate a reversal through which she loses her autonomy: this man's love is dangerously contagious. In 16, she tells how her consolation of her lover for a love she did not share led unexpectedly to his conquest of her. Sonnet 20 tells the same tale: once she began to pity the man, "autant que luy aymay ardentement" (I began to love as passionately as he). The I/you, he/she reversal is enacted in a more immediate way in the eight lines published by both Labé and Olivier de Magny. The confusion of subject and object thematized in the parallel passages has caught the attention of Françoise Charpentier and François Rigolot, who recognize that questions of priority (who wrote the lines first?) are less interesting than the implications of the parallel. Charpentier points out "the willed lack of distinction" between the body of the speaker and of the person spoken to; Rigolot interprets the "deliberate confusion" in the lines as a dramatization of the "interior chaos" shared by both lovers.[30] Labé's lines in Sonnet 2 differ from Magny's only in her use of the modernized spelling promoted by her humanist associate Jacques Peletier du Mans:

O beaus yeus bruns, ô regars destournez,
O chaus soupirs, ô larmes espandues,
O noires nuits vainement atendues,
O jours luisans vainement retournez:
O tristes pleins, ô desirs obstinez,
O tems perdu, ô peines despendues,
O mile morts en mile rets tendues,
O pires maus contre moy destinez.

Oh, beautiful brown eyes, oh, glances turned away,
Oh, hot sighs, oh, tears spilled forth,
Oh, dark nights, awaited in vain,
Oh, shining days, returned to no avail,
Oh, sad laments, oh, stubborn desires,
Oh, time lost, oh, wasted suffering,
Oh, thousand deaths hidden in a thousand nets,
Oh, worst misfortunes, fated to my undoing.

As Rigolot asks, whose sighs are these, who is shedding tears, which of the lovers is waiting for night (23)? Labé resolves the confusion to some extent in her tercets, in which she names her lover's beauty and musicality as causes for the effects she feels. These are still effects of blissful confusion, however, as affirmed by her amused comment that his charms exceed what she needs to be overwhelmed: "Tant de flambeaus pour ardre une femmelle!" (So many torches to ignite a mere female!). Magny intensifies the blurring of internal and external states in the last lines of his poem by calling on additional inner and outer audiences as witnesses to his distraction: "O vous mes yeux, . . . / O dieux, ô cieux et personnes humaines" (Oh, you, my eyes, / Oh, gods, oh, heavens and other human beings). Intertextually, the status of the lines as shared property dissolves boundaries between inner and outer world, female and male lover, first and second author, owner/imitator of the quatrains.[31] In contrast to poems in which Pernette du Guillet corrects Scève by differentiating her version of Neoplatonic love from his, the parallel established between the sonnets of Labé and Magny effaces sexual and textual difference.

In Sonnet 13 Labé elaborates the same mutuality in a sustained fantasy of permanent, blissful union. She reworks two Ovidian subtexts, tales of couples unified into one being: Salmacis and Hermaphroditus, Baucis and Philemon. In Book Four of the *Metamorphoses* Ovid tells the story of the nymph Salmacis, whose determined pursuit of a resistant boy, Hermaphroditus, finally melds her permanently into him, in a mixture no longer male and female but both at once:

73   . . . mixta duorum
      corpora iunguntur faciesque inducitur illis
      una; velut siquis conducat cortice, ramos
      crescendo iungi pariterque adolescere cernit,

sic, ubi conplexu coierunt membra tenaci,
nec duo sunt sed forma duplex, nec femina dici
nec puer ut possit, nec utrumque et utrumque videtur.

. . . mixed together, their two bodies join, and their two faces
become one; as branches are grafted onto the trunk of a tree,
she encircles the youth, so that their limbs blend in a tight
embrace; they are not two but a double body, nor can they be
said to be woman or boy, for they seem neither yet both.

In Ovid's narrative of this commingling, Hermaphroditus laments the effem-
inacy the transformation imposes upon him, and two similes attribute a sinister violence to Salmacis: she is like a snake caught by an eagle, winding her
body around his head and lashing his wings with her tail, and she entraps
him like an octopus seizing an enemy at the bottom of the sea. But Ovid also
compares the nymph to ivy vines weaving themselves around tall tree
trunks (365: "ut solent hederae longos intexere truncos"), and Labé sets this
lighter and gentler image at the center of her sonnet. Her poem may also
allude to the calm permanence and long-lasting honor earned by Baucis and
Philemon, unified into a double-trunked tree as a reward for their hospitality
to the gods (8, 718–19): "ostendit adhuc Thyneius illic / incola de gemino
vicinos corpore truncos" (in Thrace even now / the native in the fields
points out two trunks that form a twinned body).

Both of Ovid's narratives shift from the simple past to the historical present, concrete tenses that make the tales vivid and produce an effect of aston-
ishment. Labé's poem is set in a wishful conditional, yet her fantasy of
tranquil union nonetheless achieves an effect of alluring immediacy. The
narrative movement of Sonnet 13 cannily familiarizes the erotic union it represents: what is initially set up as an impossible wish is made aurally and
tactilely concrete through imagined dialogue and parallel actions (the man's
embrace, the woman's). Labé also dissolves the body/mind opposition implicit in Neoplatonism's noncorporeal ideal. In her last lines, lips and spirit
meet in an embrace represented as spiritual and physical at the same time:

Oh si j'estois en ce beau sein ravie
De celui là pour lequel vois mourant:
Si avec lui vivre le demeurant
De mes cours jours ne m'empeschoit envie:
Si m'acollant me disoit, chere Amie,
Contentons nous l'un l'autre, s'asseurant
Que ja tempeste, Euripe, ne Courant
Ne nous pourra desjoindre en notre vie:
Si de mes bras le tenant acollé,
Comme du Lierre est l'arbre encercelé,
La mort venoit, de mon aise envieuse:
Lors que souef plus il me baiseroit,
Et mon esprit sur ses levres fuiroit,
Bien je mourrois, plus que vivante, heureuse.

Oh, if I were caught up in the lovely breast
Of that man, for whom I live in death;
If I could live the rest of my short days
With him, unhindered by Envy;
If, putting his arms around my neck, he said,
"Dear love, let us fulfill one another,
Certain that no tempest, sea or current
Can ever separate us while we live";
If, holding him in my embrace,
Just as by ivy a tree is encircled,
Death came, envious of my pleasure,
At the moment he kissed me most sweetly,
And my soul breathed its last upon his lips,
Willingly I would die, more than alive: in bliss.

Labé is not, finally, a poet of unrequited love. Like Pernette du Guillet, she imagines and demands happiness. In this sonnet she defines it as the attainment of a permanent condition of self in and as the other, a pre- (or post-) gendered fusion with the beloved.[32]

Rhetorically, Labé's poem transforms the loss of distinct sex in Ovid's myth of Hermaphroditus into a cross-gendered triumph for the woman speaker. The woman poet ventriloquizes the man: she invents the speech she wants to hear from him (ll. 6–8). And in the simile of the ivy-twined tree, where the source-text provides a female/male pairing (Ovid's *hederae* are feminine, his *troncos* masculine), Labé's French makes both the tree and the ivy twining around it masculine. The active role of the woman embracing the man (l. 9) sets up the expectation that the tree simile of line 10 refers to the woman speaking rather than the man who embraces her; because the adverbial clause beginning with "comme" (as) appears to modify the subject of the verb in the preceding line, the woman appears to be embraced by, as well as embracing, the tree-man. The inversion of subject and verb in line 10 also makes the ivy encircling the tree seem to refer to man and woman alike, in spite of the masculine form of the adjective ("encercelé"). Rigolot, analyzing Labé's *Débat* and elegies, points to a deliberate "scrambling" of grammatical gender as the poet's technique for marking her poems as antitraditional because written by a woman.[33] In this sonnet, a similar gender ambiguity is established, but one that positions Labé as masculine. To the extent that the woman poet verbalizes sexual desire in her poems, she adopts the position of a masculine speaker—not because, as psychoanalysis has assumed, active sexual desire is essentially masculine, but because lyric tradition had it so. In 1550 in France the poet imagining sexual pleasure and convincing his partner to share it was conventionally a man. In order to elaborate her own fantasy of erotic bliss as a shared subjectivity that breaks down masculine/feminine hierarchies, Labé reconstructs an Ovidian simile in which encircling and encircled lover become identical—under a masculine sign.[34]

She draws on classical sources again for her famous Sonnet 18, "Baise m'encor, rebaise moy et baise," another poem in which masculine literary tradition and the woman poet's fantasy of erotic identity meet in an interplay that disturbs gender expectations. Not surprisingly, the poem ends by foregrounding Labé's awareness of the way in which she is disrupting social, sexual, and lyric convention: she apologizes to her lover for the "folly" she has imagined. The metacritical consciousness in this poem has much in common with other poems in which she takes an ironic distance from the credentials she is displaying as a poet. Her first sonnet, "Non havria Ulysse o qualunqu'altro mai," written in Italian and in the Petrarchan vocabulary of sweet suffering in love, demonstrates her competence in imitating her male predecessor, as does the relentless oxymoron of Sonnet 8: "Je vis, je meurs; je me brule et me noye" (I live, I die; I burn and I drown).[35] Yet Labé preserves a certain detachment from these familiar patterns. In the *Débat*, she makes Mercury an amused critic of Petrarchan opposites: "Avoir le coeur separé de soymesme, estre meintenant en paix, ores en guerre. . . . bruler de loin, geler de pres. . . . ne sont ce tous signes d'un homme aliené de son bon entendement?" (98: To have one's heart separated from oneself, to be now at peace, now at war, to burn at a distance and freeze up close, aren't these all signs of a man alienated from sanity?). Robert Greene in his popular translation/adaptation of the *Débat* (London, 1584) takes Labé's parody of oxymoron a step further by naming her target outright:

> It is not also unknowne unto you how many sundrie passions do perplexe the poore passionate Lovers, all which proceede of Follie: as to have ones heart separated from himself, to be now in peace and then in warre, . . . blushing one while and looking pale another, fraught whollie with feare, hope and shame, seeking that carefully which he seemeth to flee, and yet doubtfully dreading not to finde it, . . . to burne in colde and freeze in heate, to be crossed altogether with contraries, which be signes not onely of follie, but of phrensie.[36]

Labé scrutinizes the Petrarchan *blason* she mocks more systematically than oxymoron. She produces a short *blason* in Sonnet 2: "O ris, ô front, cheveus, bras, mains et doits: / O lut pleintif, viole, archet et vois" (Oh, laugh, oh, forehead, hair, arms, hands and fingers, / Oh, plaintive lute, viol, bow and voice). But the brevity of the list suggests limited enthusiasm for such naming of the beloved's parts. In Sonnet 21 she submits the genre to a probing theoretical interrogation. A detailed ideal of feminine beauty had been elaborated by Petrarch and poets imitating him: golden hair, eyes like stars, teeth like pearls, skin as white as lilies, cheeks as red as roses.[37] But no equivalent set of desiderata for a beloved man had been established by women poets. Labé's sonnet explores this lack in a series of questions to which the answers are absent because women poets have been absent from the construction of traditions of *descriptio*:[38]

Quelle grandeur rend l'homme venerable?
Quelle grosseur? quel poil? quelle couleur?
Qui est des yeus le plus emmieleur?
Qui fait plus tot une playe incurable?

What height makes a man worthy of admiration?
What breadth? what kind of hair? what complexion?
Whose eyes are most sweetly alluring?
Who gives most quickly love's incurable scar?

These first lines point out a negative space in poetic convention. They also invite readers of the female sex (perhaps men as well) to fill the vacuum, to fantasize the perfect man as if for the first time. Labé begins to do so herself in her second quatrain, in which she proposes musical skill (mirroring her own as she has remarked on it in earlier sonnets) as one element of masculine desirability. Yet her questions about musicality, the result of artful training, are followed by a demand for artless charm:

Quel chant est plus à l'homme convenable?
Qui plus penetre en chantant sa douleur?
Qui un dous lut fait encore meilleur?
Quel naturel est le plus amiable?

What kind of singing best suits a man?
Who penetrates most deeply by singing his pain?
Who improves upon even a well-tuned lute?
What inborn manner makes a man most lovable?

This turnabout, the value imputed to the "naturel," is explained by the rest of the sonnet, in which Labé rejects the possibility of defining an objective standard of beauty. True love, she declares, is irrational, unable and unwilling to justify its choices. Thus she raises feminine subjectivity above the objective standards claimed in the male-composed *blason*:

Je ne voudrois le dire assurément,
Ayant Amour forcé mon jugement:
Mais je say bien et de tant je m'assure,
Que tout le beau que lon pourroit choisir,
Et que tout l'art qui ayde la Nature,
Ne me sauroient acroitre mon desir.

I would not want to say for certain,
For love has influenced my judgment.
But I know and am certain of this much, at least:
That all the beauty that one could choose
And all the art that embellishes Nature
Would never be able to increase my desire.

Labé rejects the *blason* again in a sharp final attack on the politics of lovers' language. In Sonnet 23, reproaching the man for his long absence,

she catechizes him on his use of hyperbolic praise unaccompanied by proof
of devotion. Like her mockery of his vow to die before he stops loving her,
her citation of his conventional compliments is bitterly parodic:[39]

> Las! que me sert, que si parfaitement
> Louas jadis et ma tresse dorée,
> Et de mes yeus la beauté comparee
> A deus Soleils, dont Amour finement
> Tira les trets causez de ton tourment?
> Ou estes vous, pleurs de peu de duree?
> Et Mort par qui devoit estre honoree
> Ta ferme amour et iteré serment?

> Alas, what good does it do me now
> That you once praised so perfectly my golden hair
> And the beauty of my eyes, which you compared
> To two suns, from which Love subtly
> Shot the arrows that caused your woe?
> Where are you, tears that lasted so briefly,
> And Death, which was supposed to guarantee
> Your faithful love and oft-repeated vows?

Exemplarily, the woman poet pulls back from such exaggerations herself.
The sonnet shifts suddenly from attack to apology as Labé withdraws her
accusation by explaining that, in contrast to the man's praises and promises,
she has erred in her outburst by being too truthful. Yet she retains control of
the situation by setting up a form of blackmail based on the innocence of her
declared expectations: attributing true faith to her beloved after all, she holds
her fire. The last word of the poem, her invocation of his "martyrdom," a
staple of Petrarchan vocabulary, pulls him back into the code from which he
has strayed:

> Donques c'estoit le but de ta malice
> De m'asservir sous ombre de service?
> Pardonne moy, Ami, à cette fois,
> Estant outree et de despit et d'ire:
> Mais je m'assur', quelque part que tu sois,
> Qu'autant que moy tu soufres de martire.

> So it was your malicious intent
> To enslave me by pretended loyalty?
> Pardon me, my love, this once,
> For I've been maddened by spite and rage.
> But I am certain, wherever you may be,
> As much as I, you suffer martyrdom.

Labé writes this poem to criticize amorous convention, but not to jettison it
entirely. Her conclusion affirms that she and her beloved are in the discourse

together. What she demands (or wishes) again is mutuality: that his behavior correspond to his oaths and to hers.

These strategies for drawing her beloved into a shared identity also motivate her kiss sonnet, a text in which she is hyper-conscious of the risk in her poetic performance. In Sonnet 18, she challenges the man to an erotic contest, which she ends with a disclaimer similar to the one in Sonnet 23, a comment on her own "excess" that first rejects and then affirms it. Like her sonnet on the eternal embrace, this one begins with a revision of Roman poetry, in this case Catullus's Song 5, "Vivamus, mea Lesbia, atque amemus," in which the poet invites his mistress to an exchange of kisses, hyperbolically numbered in the hundreds and thousands: "Da mi basia mille, deinde centum, / Dein mille altera, dein secunda centum, / deinde usque altera mille, deinde centum" (Give me a thousand kisses, then a hundred, / Then another thousand, then a hundred, / Yet another thousand, then a hundred).[40] Labé's first move is to rewrite the poem downward, to reduce its vast numbers through a sort of comic deflation: for Catullus's first thousand and hundred kisses, she substitutes a mere five. Yet her opening loses nothing in intensity. For one thing, it has new resonance as a female takeover of the *basium*, or kiss poem, traditionally spoken by a man.[41] Her direct command and her promise to reciprocate, even to outdo her male lover, typify her posture as amorous and poetic rival:

> Baise m'encor, rebaise moy et baise:
> Donne m'en un de tes plus savoureus,
> Donne m'en un de tes plus amoureus:
> Je t'en rendray quatre plus chaus que braise.

> Kiss me once more, kiss me again and kiss me:
> Give me one of your tastiest kisses,
> Give me one of your most loving ones:
> I'll return you four, hotter than coals.

As the poem continues, in present and future tenses more confident than the wishful conditional of "Oh si j'estois en ce beau sein ravie," Labé celebrates the lovers' closeness and the woman's power simultaneously. She appropriates but dramatically feminizes the seductive and philosophical authority of her male predecessors: from a maternal-sounding soother of pain she becomes an expert in kissing, an inviter to shared pleasure (repeating the appeal voiced by the male lover in 18: "Contentons nous l'un l'autre") and a theorist of Neoplatonic union in the formulaic couplet of her ninth and tenth lines:[42]

> Las, te pleins tu? ça que ce mal j'apaise,
> En t'en donnant dix autres doucereus.
> Ainsi meslans nos baisers tant heureus
> Jouissons nous l'un de l'autre à notre aise.
> Lors double vie a chacun en suivra.
> Chacun en soy et son ami vivra.

> Alas, are you unhappy? here, let me cure the hurt
> By giving you ten more kisses, sweet ones.
> So, mixing our joyful kisses together,
> Let us delight in each other at our ease.
> Then a double life will come to each of us,
> Each will live in himself and in his lover.

But this slowly built up representation of reciprocal bliss is abruptly interrupted by the poet's apparent recognition that she has gone too far. Labé suddenly acknowledges another audience, not her lover but Love, to whom she apologizes for the "madness" of her fantasy:

> Permets m'Amour penser quelque folie:
> Tousjours suis mal, vivant discrettement,
> Et ne me puis donner contentement,
> Si hors de moy ne fay quelque saillie.

> Allow me, Love, to think such madness,
> I suffer constantly, living alone,   .
> And I can find no happiness for myself
> Unless I make a leap beyond myself.

What is it that Labé is apologizing for here? The outspoken eroticism of the poem? "Discrettement," as Rigolot points out, had two meanings in the sixteenth century: "separately" (the lover is separated from the beloved) but also "discreetly," in the sense of wisely, reasonably, prudently. Does Labé's folly lie in speaking so indiscreetly of physical love, that is, so much more frankly than a woman was expected to do? In making this imagined seduction public? Is she apologizing for the presumption in her intercutting of Catullus with Plato, for her insistence that carnal and spiritual love can coexist, even reinforce each other? For the forwardness of her invitation to the man? Probably all of these. But her final lines temper the apology. Indeed, they almost withdraw it: Labé implies that such madness is a necessity to her. The sexual and military connotations of her final word, "saillie" (the mounting of a female animal by a male, a sudden attack designed to break a siege), suggest that she is not about to give up "folie," not about to accept the chastity and self-containment assigned to the sixteenth-century woman. Peggy Kamuf suggests that the sonnet's "folly" consists in the breaking down of distinction between speaking lover and addressed beloved. Labé's Amour works by obliterating subject/object oppositions: "Love . . . names a place of thinking that cannot be identified *with* or *in* a person, falling as it does between the Poet and her addressee, a 'je' and a 'tu,' joining them in a name which is neither the one nor the other because it is both one and the other."[43] As in Labé's other poems of fantasized fulfillment, the separate, properly bounded self is represented as a hindrance to delight. Only by moving beyond the borders of individual subjectivity and the limits of class and gender decorum can the woman poet affirm love as liberating bliss.

Affirm it she does, however, most anxiously to an audience of women, the female citizens of Lyon. Her appeals to her city sisters are complex, an effort to produce feminist solidarity rather than a celebration of it. When Labé invokes a public that judges her positively, it is made up of men: the "gens savans" and "gens d'esprit" of her second elegy, for example, named along with "tant d'hommes" and "maints grans Signeurs" who also admire her. Fame comes from men, blame from women: when she considers the possibility of censure for her life and works, she has women in mind. Her call to her sex "to raise their minds a bit above their distaffs and spindles and bestir themselves to make the world understand that if we are not made to command, at least we are worthy companions, both in the private and the public spheres, to those who govern and are obeyed" (*Epistre dédicatoire*, 42) challenges the restriction of women to the private household, a constraint that predisposed some of them to criticize any other woman's entry into the public sphere. Labé's mistrust is a symptom of what Maïté Albistur and Daniel Armogathe call the "elitist feminism" of early modern Europe, practiced by women who defined themselves as exceptions because they lacked the mass movement that would have made a group identification possible.[44] Mistrust of women was strongly marked in two earlier writers, the Brescian Laura Cereta and the Veronese Isotta Nogarola, who wrote that the women of their cities were their fiercest critics: Cereta attacked her female enemies for their envy and impudence, while Nogarola complained to a humanist man that the women of Verona were making her life impossible with their mockery.[45] But Labé destabilizes the judge's role assigned to women by making sustained efforts to bring her women readers over to her side. One effect of her acknowledgment that there might be something to blame in her conduct and her book may have been to stir up interest in readers of both sexes: by inviting women to sympathize with her, she implicitly invites men to eavesdrop on a scene of feminine confession. But she directs her rhetoric mainly toward short-circuiting women's disapproval, often by redirecting arguments embedded in men's poetry to remind her *lectrices* of the vulnerability all women share.

In her first elegy, she asks her female audience to read her account of her suffering open-mindedly. She bases this appeal on a logic of double solidarity. Because her women readers are as exposed as she is to love's dangers and society's blame, she promises them the tolerant reading she herself wants; and because their pain in love is likely to turn them into singer-poets like her, she offers herself as a literary model:

> 43 . . . Dames, qui [mes maux] lirez,
> De mes regrets avec moy soupirez.
> Possible, un jour je feray le semblable,
> Et ayderay votre voix pitoyable
> A vos travaus et peines raconter,
> Au tems perdu vainement lamenter.

Ladies, who will read my woes,
Sigh with me over my regrets.
Some day I may do the same for you,
And help your voice, worthy of pity,
To recount your struggles and pain,
To lament your lost and wasted days.

Her appeal becomes more calculating as she goes on: pragmatism rather than purity is the basis of her warning that the stricter a woman's chastity is, the greater her downfall will be. She also shifts the terms by which such a fall is measured by linking susceptibility to passion with elevated rank. Love as king demands greatest obedience from his most highly placed subjects:

Quelque rigueur qui loge en votre coeur,
Amour s'en peut un jour rendre vainqueur.
Et plus aurez lui esté ennemies,
Pis vous fera, vous sentant asservies.
N'estimez point que lon doive blamer
Celles qu'a fait Cupidon inflamer.
Autres que nous, nonobstant leur hautesse,
Ont enduré l'amoureuse rudesse:
Leur coeur hautein, leur beauté, leur lignage,
Ne les ont su preserver du servage
De dur Amour.

Whatever strictness is fixed in your heart,
Some day Love can conquer it entirely.
And the more hostile to him you've been,
The worse he'll treat you once he knows you're his slave.
Do not believe that we ought to condemn
Women whom Cupid has set aflame.
Others than we, however high ranking,
Have had to endure rough treatment as lovers.
Their high hearts, their beauty, their noble descent
Failed to protect them from being enslaved
To merciless Love.

Labé's example is no less than Semiramis, the queen of Assyria. In her re-writing *in bono* of a figure more often emphasized as an epitome of vice, for example, in Boccaccio's *De claris mulieribus*,[46] Labé identifies with the Assyrian queen, who became a military heroine because she disguised herself as a man—her son Ninus—to fight her people's enemies in her husband's place. But Semiramis was also represented as sexually insatiable, willing to commit incest with her son and to make laws allowing equal sexual liberty to her subjects. Labé suppresses this aspect of the legend by leaving the object of the queen's love unspecified. Instead she invokes the queen as alter ego: estranged from her "virile courage," deprived of the helmet that once covered her blond hair, leaving her "furious coursers" behind, to languish on an amorous couch.

From this improving revision of a classical heroine, Labé moves to a satiric strategy familiar from men's poetry: she uses the portrait of the grotesque old woman from the *carpe diem* tradition to ward off the high-minded chastity she fears in her women readers. An obvious point of comparison is Ronsard's sonnet to Hélène (II, 24), in which he presents her with his fantasy of her as "une vieille accroupie" (a hunched old woman), regretting the love and fame she might have enjoyed if she had not resisted him. His conclusion typifies *carpe diem* strategy in the hands of male poets: "Vivez, si m'en croyez, n'attendez à demain: / Cueillez dès aujourd'huy les roses de la vie" (Live, if you believe me, don't wait for tomorrow, / Starting today, pick the roses of life).[47] Labé makes her potentially disapproving woman reader the target of her portrait of the "povre vieille," ridiculous in powder and wig, who fails to be loved in her old age because she has "blamed Love" in her youth:

99 Alors de fard et eau continuelle
   Elle essayoit se faire venir belle,
   Voulant chasser le ridé labourage,
   Que l'aage avoit gravé sur son visage. . . .
   Et plus estoit à son gré bien fardee,
   De son Ami moins estoit regardee.

   Then with powder and repeated perfume
   She tried to make herself beautiful,
   Hoping to smoothe the wrinkled furrows
   That age had engraved upon her face. . . .
   But the more she thought she was well made up,
   The less her beloved wanted to look at her.

Thus Labé puts a technique of masculine seduction to a new use. In her text the question posed by male poets ("Do you want to be punished for your prudish resistance to me by a hideous and lonely old age?") is re-posed by a woman as "Do you want to be punished for your prudish reading of me by a hideous and lonely old age?" In a cannily cross-gendered appropriation of men's lyric, she dismantles the surveillance of women by women, one way in which patriarchal control of her sex was maintained. Her plea for a sympathetic reception adds a new politics of gender to traditional manipulations of women readers.

In her third elegy, Labé employs another tactic for winning women over: she adopts the viewpoint of religious sermon and social satire to argue that envy and scandal-mongering are worse sins than passion. The poem opens with an echo of the first elegy, but it is less apologetic; Labé challenges the assumption that her theme, young love, should be judged as harshly as mature sin:

> Quand vous lirez, ô Dames Lionnoises,
> Ces miens escrits pleins d'amoureuses noises,
> Quand mes regrets, ennuis, despits et larmes
> M'orrez chanter en pitoyable carmes,
> Ne veuillez pas condamner ma simplesse,
> Et jeune erreur de ma fole jeunesse,
> Si c'est erreur: mais qui dessous les Cieus
> Se peut vanter de n'estre vicieus?

> When you come to read, ladies of Lyon,
> These writings of mine, full of lover's complaints,
> When you hear my regrets, sorrows, anger and tears
> Sung in *chansons* deserving your pity,
> Do not, I beg you, condemn my naïveté
> Or the youthful straying of my wild youth—
> If straying is what it is. But who under heaven
> Can truthfully claim to be free of vice?

As the second thought of line 7 implies, Labé argues that love is a virtue compared to the antisocial vices she goes on to list: envy, the sowing of discord, avarice, slander. Lying, deceiving, and abusing others, she claims, has always repelled her as much as speaking evil of them (ll. 25–26). By denying that she is guilty of the sins that women readers will commit by denouncing her, she turns the tables on female moralists again. The history of her detractors suggests that she would have been wise to aim such arguments at the men of her city as well, but her persistent attention to women readers shows her conviction that safety lay in courting positive responses from them.

As in her poems to the man, however, Labé finally abandons her challenging mode for an appeal to shared feeling. In her twenty-fourth sonnet, a farewell to the women of her city, she expiates the history of passion narrated in the sonnets by emphasizing the misery that has accompanied it:

> Ne reprenez, Dames, si j'ay aymé:
> Si j'ay senti mile torches ardentes,
> Mile travaus, mile douleurs mordentes: . . .
> Las que mon nom n'en soit par vous blamé.
> Si j'ay failli, les peines sont presentes.

> Do not reproach me, Ladies, for having loved,
> For having felt a thousand burning torches,
> A thousand griefs, a thousand biting pains. . . .
> Alas, may my name not be condemned by you.
> If I have fallen, I suffer for it now.

But this apparent confession of guilt quickly shifts to a defense and to the offer of an excuse her critics may need themselves:

> Mais estimez qu'Amour, à point nommé,
> Sans votre ardeur d'un Vulcan excuser,

> Sans la beauté d'Adonis acuser,
> Pourra, s'il veut, plus vous rendre amoureuses:

> But realize that Love, when the time is right,
> Without giving you a Vulcan as excuse,
> Or justifying your ardor with Adonis' beauty,
> Can make you fall more deeply in love.

Her final tercet, too, asserts the equality of all women as potential victims of love. Consequently, she ends with a warning to her sex to be not more virtuous but more careful than she has been:

> En ayant moins que moy d'ocasion,
> Et plus d'estrange et forte passion.
> Et gardez vous d'estre plus malheureuses.

> Though you have less reason for it than I,
> And a more transforming and violent passion.
> So beware of being more unhappy still.

The entire poem constructs a shared female condition, breaking down the division between confessing lover and judging audience. Any love poetry, as the texts of these eight poets show, aims for a public. But in Labé's apostrophes to a female readership, she deliberately de-privatizes the voice of the woman in love. "Any of you could be me," she says. "So read me as you would be read."

Throughout her *Euvres* Labé interweaves the two approaches she combines in this final poem: challenge and conciliation. With her women readers and with the man, she invents an alliance, working to create a circle of empathetic equality where it does not yet exist. I have been arguing that Labé was a radically antihierarchical and utopian poet, though not a revolutionary one. But in 1790 a battalion of the National Guard of Lyon represented her, precisely, as a revolutionary heroine. The dialectic between the demand for equality and the wish for unity that I have analyzed in her poems is translated wonderfully into visual terms in the Lyonnais battalion's banner, which the *Almanach de Lyon* describes and explains as follows:

Louise Charly, the wife of a ropemaker, wrote in 1550 a poem on liberty. Her beauty and learning produced the following emblem. The Belle Cordière is dressed simply, seated on a lion: a garland of flowers falls from her left shoulder to her right side; in her right hand she holds a pike interwoven with lilies and capped with the hat of William Tell, the restorer of Helvetian liberty; on this pike is also fitted a scroll with this motto on it: "Belle Cordière, Charly, you predicted our destiny, / For to break our chains you first flew free." On the other side of the scroll is engraved: "Belle Cordière, your hope was not in vain." On William Tell's hat the tricolor is displayed. In her left hand, Louise Labé holds her poem on French liberty, resting on a globe of the earth. The lion rests one paw on the book of the Constitution; . . . on one side is an olive tree, a sign of peace, on the other a laurel, the sign of fame; books are piled at her feet, designating her knowledge.[48]

Like the Guardsmen's flag, Labé's poem on liberty has been lost. But the emblems of freedom, power, and fame assembled in this representation of the woman poet provide a brilliant guide to her *Euvres*. The nickname that signals her membership in a class contesting the privileges of the aristocracy, her wielding of previously masculine costume and weapons to preserve liberty, the olive and the laurel as signs of aspiration to new social alliances and literary fame, and the books that mark her as a cultivated reader are as revealing about the woman poet as about the city that figured her as its heroine.

VERONICA FRANCO: THE SATIRIST'S RIVAL, THE CHAMPION OF WOMEN

Venice, a commercial city as eager to advertise its independent and progressive identity as Lyon, offered cultural openings to women in one category of its population: the courtesans who occupied a position of ambitious marginality in the "Most Serene Republic." While married women of the upper class were, as Marie de Gournay remarked, strictly cloistered in the patrician households of the city,[49] Venetian courtesans were famous throughout Europe for the splendor of their dress and their polished conversation. Historians of prostitution have estimated that as many as one out of ten inhabitants of Venice earned a living through sex,[50] partly because of the high number of foreign travelers (merchants, bankers, ambassadors, sailors of various ranks, tourists) in the city, partly because a strict system of property preservation required the sons of patrician families to marry late or not at all. A Venetian diarist of the early sixteenth century, Marin Sanudo, estimated that there were 11,654 prostitutes in the city out of a total population of about 150,000, a staggering figure but one that recent historians find plausible.[51] Highly placed courtesans, supported by one or two wealthy clients at a time and living a life of splendid luxury, were obviously much rarer than ordinary prostitutes. A catalogue of the "principal courtesans" published in the city in 1565 lists 215;[52] Montaigne in his *Journal de voyage en Italie* (he was in Venice in the winter of 1580) estimated that there were 150 of them, "spending as much on their households and clothing as princesses do."[53]

Glamorous prosperity distinguished the *cortigiana onesta* (honored courtesan)—or, as she was less reverently termed by the lawmakers of the city, the *meretrice sumptuosa* (luxury prostitute)—from lesser courtesans (*la cortigiana di lume*), the poorly paid *meretrice*, and the abject *puttana* (whore).[54] The Venetian Senate and the special committee it appointed to oversee public morality alternately tolerated and harassed all four classes of women. The city profited from the taxes and fines prostitutes paid, but from the 1530s on, officials regularly issued decrees intended to protect the fortunes of male citizens against their demands.[55] These laws included sumptuary codes forbidding any *meretrice* to dress in the silks, brocades, lace, gold embroidery, and pearls reserved for aristocratic women. Prostitutes were also prohibited from living along the Grand Canal, where they competed with nobles for valuable property, and from attending church on important holidays, where they distracted the attention of the pious from religious ceremonies.[56] By 1570 the city council found the number and effrontery of *meretrici* so overwhelming that it banished them from the city, although this, like most anti-prostitution laws, was never effectively enforced.

The wording of many of the laws suggests that what was most objected to in the *cortigiana onesta* was the difficulty of distinguishing her from women with higher social status. A case in point is the lament published by the Senate in 1543 as a preface to an early sumptuary law: "The number of prostitutes in our city has grown excessively, and abandoning all modesty and shame, they go out in public, in streets, churches and other places, so well dressed and adorned that they are often confused with women of the nobility and citizenry, not only by foreigners but by natives, as well."[57] Montaigne was not alone; many visitors described *cortigiane oneste* as rivaling princesses in their costumes and palaces. Moreover, they compared their speech favorably to that of noblewomen, less accustomed to any "commerce du monde."[58] Montaigne remarked that courtesans charged a special fee for conversation alone, which could be separated from "la negociacion entière"; Thomas Coryat in his travel book *Coryats Crudities* (1611) warned fellow Englishmen, "thou wilt find the Venetian Courtezan . . . a most elegant discourser; . . . she will assay thy constancy with her Rhetoricall tongue."[59]

This cultivated eloquence was the symbolic capital, the special luxury offered by the *cortigiana onesta* to clients capable of paying her immense fees.[60] She studied music, she read, and she wrote. Such efforts were mocked by satirists. But self-cultivation as a means to a profitable "commerce du monde" paid off: courtesans constituted a distinct class of independent entrepreneurs. After two decades or so of more or less steady relationships with wealthy men of various classes, Roman courtesans hoped to retire to the countryside outside Rome in country villas attached to *vigne*, pleasure gardens where they could continue to entertain into their old age. Franco, typifying Venetian success, died in the city at the palazzo of the Morosini, a distinguished patrician clan, leaving money and gifts of jewels to her sons (two of whom she recommended to the care of Andrea Tron, a patrician who was presumably their father) and her servants.[61] The chances of achieving such prosperity were much less certain than the likelihood of inheriting solid property through a patrician or bourgeois father or husband, however, which explains why many courtesans came from artisanal or declassé families. Veronica Franco's father, Francesco Franco, was a *cittadino*, a member of the class of merchants and professional men who, though denied participation in the highest levels of government, were regularly appointed to its salaried bureaucracy and assigned special rights in trading and in diplomacy;[62] the Franco family had a coat of arms.[63] But by the 1560s, Franco's mother was listed in the Venetian *Catalogo* as a courtesan and as her daughter's go-between. Franco was twenty at the time the *Catalogo* was published, but by her thirties, she had risen into associating with the old patriciate of Venice in coteries that admitted members on the basis of wit and learning rather than social status. In Venice, these literary salons were called *ridotti*; a particularly influential one was the Accademia della Fama, headed in the 1550s by Domenico Venier. Ruled by neither court nor church, the Venetian academy appears to have offered a new and open space for humanist intellectuals, including women.[64]

Franco displayed her links with Venier's circle in a variety of ways. Her *Rime* (1575) are presented as a group-composed text. Of twenty-five *capitoli*, variable-length poems written in *terza rima*, eighteen are hers; seven are written by an "incerto autore" (unnamed writer). The first *capitolo* is attributed to Marco Venier, although his name was torn out of one of the three surviving copies of the collection[65]—perhaps a sign of the Venier family's ambivalence toward having their names officially linked to Franco's. She also called on members of the academy such as Domenico and Marco Venier and Celio Magno to contribute to a collection of poems in memory of Estor Martinengo, a nobleman of the Terraferma, which she dedicated to his brother Francesco (1575). Her poems of praise appear in various places: an anthology assembled in honor of the Paduan official Giuseppe Spinelli, the *Canzoniere* of the Paduan poet Bartolomeo Zacco, Muzio Manfredi's *Tragedy of Semiramis*. But it is especially in her *Rime* and her *Lettere familiari* (1580) that she can be seen constructing the reputation of an honored woman of letters. Like Louise Labé, Franco links her fame to the admiration she receives from illustrious men. Her text resembles Labé's in other ways, too: in her frank diction, in her self-confident and occasionally defiant tone, in her ironic detachment from literary convention, and in a defense of female freedom against moral censure that aligns both poets with the feminism of their time. Franco's claim to equality with her interlocutors is more sexually explicit than Labé's because she is advertising her stock in trade. But like Labé, she appropriates male-derived genres and rhetorics in critical and liberatory ways.

The poems and letters Franco dedicated to famous men typify her ability to turn a compliment into a self-portrait attesting to her own virtuosity. One of her most stellar addressees was the French prince Henri de Valois, who spent ten days in Venice in 1574 on his way home to be crowned Henri III of France. She called attention to the honor his visit brought her in two sonnets published along with a dedicatory epistle in her *Lettere* six years later. In the poems she draws on classical mythology and the visual arts to publicize her admiration of the king—and his for her. As Henri left, she gave him a small enamel portrait of herself, an image she takes as the pretext for both poems. The first sonnet compares the king to Jove, disguised for one of his visits to mortals, a compliment that implies that she is a Semele (or a Danaë or another of the mythological heroines painted by

Venetians using courtesans as models). Franco builds the poem around the paradox of immensity enclosed in a small space, in order to point out the class-crossing novelty of the king's presence in her house and the contrast between her full bodily presence and the portrait that records it in miniature. The sonnet moves from praise for the king to praise for the courtesan, who shines in his reflected glory and turns the focus at the end of the poem onto the enamel image of herself:

> Come talor dal ciel sotto umil tetto
> Giove tra noi qua giù benigno scende,
> e perché occhio terren dall'alt'oggetto
> non resti vinto, umana forma prende:
>   così venne al mio povero ricetto,
> senza pompa real ch'abbaglia e splende,
> dal fato Enrico a tal dominio eletto,
> ch'un sol mondo nol cape e nol comprende.
>   Benché sì sconosciuto, anc'al mio core
> tal raggio impresse del divin suo merto,
> che 'n me s'estinse il natural vigore.
>   Di ch'ei di tanto'affetto non incerto,
> l'imagin mia di smalto e di colore
> prese al partir con grato animo aperto.
>
>   (353)

> As when from the heavens to a lowly roof
> Jove, benign, descends to us here below,
> and to avoid blinding earthly eyes
> with such a lofty sight, he takes human shape:
>   so to my humble dwelling came Henri,
> without regal show, which blinds and dazzles,
> Henri, chosen by fate for such an empire
> that one world alone cannot contain it.
>   And though I did not recognize him, into my heart
> He shone such a ray of his divine power
> ´ that my inborn strength was overcome.
>   So, not doubting the depth of my affection,
> he took my image, in enamel and paint,
> away with him in a gracious, openhearted spirit.

The poem is quintessentially Venetian in the unabashed grandiosity of its praise: its use of classical myth to glorify the present and its salute to Henri as ruler of another ocean empire. Yet however Franco elevates the king, her public narrative of his visit has a leveling effect: this prodigy, after all, came to her in the body of a man in sexual need and left as the recipient of her portrait. Whatever the king's power over her, she retains the power to give presents—and to reveal his visit to her reading public.

Her second sonnet opens with a gift-giving formula, through which, since the gift is a representation of herself, her generosity and her beauty become the subject of the poem. She implies, in fact, that the miniature does not do justice to her living, breathing devotion:

> Prendi, re per virtù sommo et perfetto,
> quel che la mano a porgerti si stende:
> questo scolpito e colorato aspetto,
> in cui 'l mio vivo e natural s'intende.

> Take, oh, king, sum of virtue and perfection,
> what my hand reaches out to offer you:
> this carved and colored version of myself,
> in which my living, real self is represented.

In the tercets, she balances the king's public triumphs with her efforts to do him justice poetically by inviting him into an exchange of gazes through which she sets the portrait alongside the poem she has just completed in his honor. Franco's emphasis on her desire to praise the king in words goes hand in hand with her emphasis on herself as a woman poet. I read the final image to which she refers not only as the miniature but as this poem itself, a more truthful (though certainly not less artificial) portrait of who she is:

> E come 'l tuo immortal divin valore,
> in armi e in pace a mille prove esperto,
> m'empìo l'alma di nobile stupore,
>   così 'l desio, di donna in cor sofferto,
> d'alzarti sopra 'l ciel dal mondo fore,
> mira in quel mio sembiante espresso e certo.

> And just as your undying, godlike valor,
> proved a thousand times in war and in peace,
> filled my soul with high astonishment,
>   See the desire, felt in a woman's heart,
> to raise you above the earth and beyond the skies
> expressed and affirmed in this image that resembles me.

Both poems set up an implicit contest between the painter and the poet. The portrait freezes and diminishes the woman, but she eternalizes the king and expands him to more than life size through her laudatory apostrophes. Franco outdoes the miniaturist by demonstrating the verbal expertise with which she can serve Henri.

Her relationships with artists were more often collaborative than competitive, however. In her final *capitolo*, 25, she allies herself with artists by praising Marcantonio della Torre as the patron of the painters and sculptors who have decorated his country villa. She also links herself specifically to Jacopo Tintoretto in a letter (21) thanking him for the full-size portrait he has recently completed of her. As in her sonnets to Prince Henri, her compliments reflect as much on her as on Tintoretto. She names him explicitly in the first sentence of her letter, atypically (most of her letters leave the addressee unnamed) but understandably: by writing to one of the most distinguished painters of the city, she demonstrates her familiarity with a protégé of the Venetian cultural elite. The painting has not been identified, but Lynne Lawner conjectures that it might have been Tintoretto's *Flora*, now in the Prado, or one of several paintings from his workshop that resemble it.[66] Lawner's argument is less than conclusive, but she makes an interesting point about the formulaic quality of the Floras painted by Tintoretto and his followers: they used classical mythology to produce these paintings "in series, as commodity items" (101). Throughout her *Rime*, Franco, too, draws on classical conventions of representation to produce herself as a commodity item. But she does so in an intricately rhetorical way that sets her apart from the silent models in the canvases of Tintoretto and his followers. Her elegant compliments to the painter position her as the subject of a literary self-portrait she herself composes.

The Tintoretto text reproduces the strategy of Franco's sonnets to Henri III: she praises the painter to the skies in return for the evidence of her desirability that his portrait communicates to her public. She begins by invoking the debate between the ancients and the moderns, siding with the moderns against those who argue that recent times have produced no equals to Apelles, Zeuxis, or Praxiteles. Her long sentence reaches its climax with a dazzling compliment to Tintoretto: "Io ho sentito dire a galantuomini non poco versati nell'antichità, et di quest'arte intendentissimi, che sono stati ne' nostri tempi, e sono oggidì, pittori e scultori i quali non solo pareggiare ma anco preporre se deono agli antichi, come sono stati Michelangelo, Rafaello, Tiziano et altri, e ora sète voi"[67] (I have heard gentlemen deeply versed in antiquity and most expert in these arts say that in our era and even today, there have been painters and sculptors who must be ackowledged not only to equal but to surpass the ancients, as Michelangelo, Raphael, Titian and others have done, and as you do today). This is a strategy of glory by association. Franco links herself to the gentleman connoisseurs, presumably members of the Venier academy, at the same time that she links Tintoretto with the master painters of central Italy and with his great Venetian predecessor. She goes on to say that the painting combines magical accuracy with irresistible seductiveness, a compliment that works in the same way as Catherine des Roches's compliment to Sincero as portraitist of Charite. The woman subsumes the man's pictorial skill as homage to her own merit: "Vi prometto che, quando ho veduto il mio ritratto, opera della vostra divina mano, io sono stato un pezzo in forse se ei fosse pittura o pur fantasima innanzi a me comparita per diabolico inganno, non mica per farmi innamorare di me stessa, come avvenne a Narcisso, perché, Iddio grazia, non mi tengo si bella che io tema di avere a smaniare delle proprie bellezze, ma per alcun altro fin, che so io?" (35) (I swear to you that when I saw my portrait, the work of your godlike hand, I hestitated a moment, wondering whether it was a painting or rather a hallucination appearing before me through some trickery of the devil, not, certainly, to make me fall in love with myself, as happened to Narcissus, for, thank God, I don't think myself so lovely that I fear going insane over my own beauty, but if it has some other purpose, what do I know of it?). Franco's final pose of uncertainty belies her purposes: to guarantee the truthfulness of the painting and to raise the possibility that other viewers might be less able than she is to resist its invitation. She also asserts her modesty toward her own beauty, as she does toward her writing in the final sentence of the letter. Nature, knowing she has been outdone by the painter, will deny all men the ability to record his genius: "E io, certa di non riuscire a tanta impresa, pongo giù la penna" (And I, certain not to succeed in such a great undertaking, lay down my pen). But if Franco has not done justice to Tintoretto, she has certainly done justice to herself in this intricate encomium.

Humility, however, is only one of Franco's strategies. She is also capable of extremely challenging texts. Like all courtesans, she was vulnerable to attacks by satirists; such poems, often aimed at their clients as well, were hung from the statue of a hunchback, "Il Gòbbo," in a public square near San Marco with the intention of embarrassing the man and reducing the woman to the status of common whore, a threat to reputation and income both.[68] Franco faced a severe attack of this kind in a trio of defamatory poems written by Maffio Venier, a distant cousin of Marco's: two *canzoni* in dialect, one accusing her of venality and another of hideous ugliness, and a sonnet playing on the name "Veronica," used by one of her admirers as a compliment but parodied by Maffio in the phrase "ver unica puttana" (a true whore, one of a kind).[69] Tita Rosenthal has argued that Franco's belief that Marco rather than Maffio Venier was her attacker governs the exchange of poems in her *Rime*, beginning with a pair of *capitoli* establishing a dialogue between Marco Venier and Franco.[70] To publicize her alliances with the Venetian patriciate, the *cortigiana onesta* sets a patrician's love poem at the beginning of her collection. Venier uses the vocabulary of Greek and Roman mythology to compose compliments all the more titillating for their circumlocutions. He concedes the courtesan's skill as a poet but, in his own interest, emphasizes her skill as a lover:

> 151   A Febo è degno che si sodisfaccia
> dal vostro ingegno; ma da la beltate
> a Venere non meno si compiaccia:
>   le tante da lei grazie a voi donate
> spender devete in buon uso, sì come
> di quelle, che vi diede Apollo, fate:
>   con queste eternerete il vostro nome,
> non men che con gli inchiostri; e lento e infermo
> farete il tempo, et le sue forze dome.

> It's proper that Phoebus should be pleased
> by your genius; but let your beauty to Venus
> be no less delightful. The many graces

that she has bestowed on you
you should put to good use, as you do
with those that Apollo has given you.
    Through her gifts you'll make your name eternal,
no less than with ink; and you'll slow down
and weaken time, and master its power.

Like Labé's reference to the "many great lords" who court her, Venier's compliments prove Franco's desirability. In *Capitolo* 2, the first of her poems in *Le Rime*, she also takes Venier's text as an occasion to advertise her sexual talents and her code of honor as courtesan. She begins with a challenge: he must prove to her that his affection is real. "Fatti, non favole," she demands: deeds, not declarations. On that condition, she will prove to him that his flattering estimate of her erotic skill is justified:

> 37   dagli effetti, signor, fate stimarvi,
>   con questi in prova venite, s'anch'io
>   il mio amor con effetti ho da mostrarvi. . . .
> 46   Aperto il cor vi mostrerò nel petto,
>   allor che 'l vostro non mi celerete,
>   e sarà di piacervi il mio diletto;
>   e s'a Febo sì grata mi tenete,
>   per lo compor, ne l'opere amorose
>   grata a Venere più mi troverete.
>   Certe proprietati in me nascose
>   vi scovrirò d'infinita dolcezza,
>   che prosa o verso altrui mai non espose.
>
>   Impress me, Signor, with your actions,
>   bring them to the proof, if you expect
>   me to show my love to you in actions. . . .
>   I will show you my heart, open in my breast,
>   as long as you don't hide yours from me,
>   and pleasing you will be my delight;
>   and if you think I'm cherished by Phoebus
>   for the works I compose, in the work of love
>   you'll find me far more cherished by Venus.
>   Certain capacities hidden within me,
>   Infinitely sweet, I'll reveal to you,
>   which prose or verse never showed a man.

This forthright acknowledgment of her profession, Alvise Zorzi suggests, is the reason that so many of Franco's later critics either attacked her for her sins or tried against all evidence to deny that she was a courtesan.[71] Her witty braggadoccio certainly runs counter to the repentance and conversion attributed to her by writers who tried to make her into a figure acceptable to Counter-Reformation morality. Yet she ends by declaring her high standards of conduct. Contrary to the accusations constantly made by satirists (includ-

ing Maffio Venier) and moralists, the *cortigiana onesta* insists that she lives
not for gain but for honest rapports with clients whom she can respect:

> 94   E però quel, che da voi cerco adesso,
>   non è che con argento over con oro
>   il vostro amor voi mi facciate espresso;
>   perchè si disconvien troppo al decoro
>   di chi non sia più che venal, far patto
>   con uom gentil per trarne anco un tesoro.
>   Di mia profession non è tal atto.
>
> But what I seek from you right now,
> is not that with silver or with gold
> you express your love to me,
>   for it is totally improper for anyone
> who is not merely venal to make a pact
> with a gentleman to extract a treasure from him.
>   This is not an act suited to my profession.

Instead, she writes, she wants Venier to put himself at her service by producing "opre" (efforts in general, but also literary works) according to her expectations. Perhaps Franco was asking Venier to contribute to the memorial
volume she was assembling for Estor Martinengo (she makes this request in
two of her letters, 32 and 39); perhaps she wanted further *capitoli* through
which she could publicize his attraction to her. Perhaps, as Tita Rosenthal
argues, she was testing Venier because she suspected him of being the author of poems insulting her for her venality.

In any case, this first poem establishes her skill in erotic dialogue. Like
Guazzo's lady of Casale, she simultaneously holds the man off and leads
him on. In a witty parrying of Venier's flirtatious classicism, she returns to
his Apollo/Venus opposition but breaks down the separation he has established by representing the god and the goddess as a couple making love in
mortal fashion. "Modi," as she uses it in line 164, probably means not simply "methods" but sexual positions, as illustrated, for example, by the engraver Marcantonio Raimondi:[72]

> 160   Febo, che serve a l'amorosa dea,
>   e in dolce guiderdon da lei ottiene
>   quel che via più, che l'esser dio, il bea,
>   a rivelar nel mio pensier ne viene
> 164   quei modi, che con lui Venere adopra,
>   mentre in soavi abbracciamenti il tiene;
>   ond'io instrutta a questi so dar opra
>   sì ben nel letto, che d'Apollo a l'arte
>   questa ne va d'assai spazio di sopra,
>   e 'l mio cantar e 'l mio scriver in carte
>   s'oblia da chi mi prova in quella guisa,
>   ch'a' suoi seguaci Venere comparte.

Phoebus, when he serves the goddess of love
and as a sweet reward receives from her
what blesses him far more than being a god,
    comes into my mind to reveal to me
the positions that Venus adopts with him
when she holds him in her sweet embraces;
    expertly instructed, I know so well
how to use them in bed that Apollo's art
is vastly exceeded by this one,
    and my singing and writing on paper
are both forgotten by the man who tries me
in the guise Venus shares with her followers.

Franco cuts through Venier's hellenizing euphemism with a breathtakingly direct promise and a down-to-earth simile that reverses traditional male/female roles in sex much as she is reversing them in this discourse of seduction:

S'avete del mio amor l'alma conquisa,
procurate d'avermi in dolce modo,
via più che la mia penna non divisa.
    Il valor vostro è quel tenace nodo
che me vi può tirar nel grembo, unita
via più ch'affisso in fermo legno chiodo:

If your soul is truly conquered by love for me,
find a way to have me in this manner,
far sweeter than anything my pen devises.
    Your virtue is the firmly tied knot
that can draw me to your lap, joined to you
more tightly than a nail in hard wood.

Franco then retreats to a more restrained vocabulary, however. She returns to the courtly language of her earlier request for proof of devotion and describes Venier's reward in a discreetly periphrastic formula:

178   . . . farvi signor vi può de la mia vita,
che tanto amar mostrate, la virtute
che 'n voi per gran miracolo s'addita.
    Fate che sian da me di lei vedute
quell'opre ch'io desio, chè poi saranno
le mie dolcezze a pien da voi godute;
    e le vostre da me si goderanno
per quello ch'un amor mutuo comporte,
dove i diletti senza noia s'hanno.

What can make you lord of my life,
is virtue, which you seem to love so,
which so miraculously shows forth in you.

> Bring it about that I see you complete
> the works I desire; for then it is certain
> you'll enjoy in full the pleasures I offer;
>   and I, too, will revel in those you provide,
> in the manner permitted by mutual love,
> when lovers share delight without hindrance.

The form of Franco's *capitolo*, almost two hundred lines long and working out its persuasion through a twisting, repetitive course, is very different from the short sonnet in which Labé challenges her lover to prove the truth of his vows (Sonnet 23). Yet the order of events in both textual performances is similar: a challenge to the man, a recantation, a return to a more conventional vocabulary of desire. In both cases, the woman poet makes her reciprocation of the lover's desires conditional on his demonstration that he is more than a rhetorician, that his sincerity matches his eloquence. I share the contemporary critical consensus that it is ahistorical to pose questions about the "sincerity" of Petrarchan and Neoplatonic poetry: its male practitioners wrote mainly to demonstrate their competence in fashionable courtly discourses rather than to confess private feeling.[73] Yet women poets obviously mistrust the self-serving use of these rhetorics; they ask for something more. Franco's *capitolo* suggests that she wants an end to the power relations whereby the discourses of seduction, like the cash that pays for it, belong to men alone. A deep suspicion of the facility with which masculine rhetoric can be deployed marks both these poets. They respond to it not simply by imitating the languages of courtship but by challenging their partners to prove that their texts have some grounding beyond verbal etiquette.

Franco's suspicion of the clichés of masculine discourse extends to an ironic treatment of them in her own poems and to outright critique of their misuse in men's. The plot and perspective of *Capitolo* 8 suggest her detachment as a courtesan from the emotional extremes traditionally represented as a lover's condition. The poem is written as a response to a man who has declared his love; Franco begins by announcing in familiar Petrarchan metaphors that she loves someone else. But she localizes her state by punning on her own name at the end of her second line:

> Ben vorrei fosse, come dite voi,
> ch'io vivessi d'Amor libera e franca,
> non còlta al laccio, o punta ai dardi suoi.

> I wish indeed it were true, as you say,
> that I live free and exempt from Love,
> not caught in his snares or pierced by his darts.

A long narrative of unrequited loves follows. Franco explains that she cannot return the love this man offers her because she loves another man; he loves another woman; this woman rejects her suitor in the same way that Franco rejects hers. To recount all this amorous suffering she adopts a high Ovidian and Petrarchan vein: misery petrifies her into a Niobe-like rock, her interlocutor at least has the relief of pouring forth his woes: "parlando meco disfogate il vostro duol" (by speaking to me you give vent to your grief). But when a further complication presents itself as a possibility—that her would-be lover is rejecting another woman in the same way that her beloved rejects her—the love plot multiplies into comedy. Franco pinpoints the crazy symmetry of the situation and displaces her own amusement onto the figure of Love:

> 70   Fors'ancor voi del vostro amor conquisa
> altra donna sprezzate, e con la mente
> dal piacerle v'andate ognor divisa;
>   e, s'a lei sète ingrato e sconoscente,
> in suo giusto giudicio Amor decide
> ch'un'altra sì vi scempia e vi tormente.
>   Fors'anco Amor del comun pianto ride,
> e, per far lagrimar più sempre il mondo,
> l'altrui desir discompagna e divide;
>   e, mentre che di ciò si fa giocondo,
> de le lagrime nostre il largo mar
> sempre più si fa cupo e più profondo.

>   Perhaps, too, you disdain another woman
> conquered by love for you, and leave
> any intention of pleasing her far behind;
>   and since you are cold and ungrateful to her,
> Love, in his just wisdom, decides
> that another woman should scorn and torment you.
>   Perhaps, indeed, Love laughs at our common plight,
> and to make the world weep even more,
> he divides the desires of others as well;
>   and while he waxes merry over it all,
> the vast sea of all our tears
> goes on turning darker and deeper still.

Franco's humor here is crucially determined by her profession: Love's laughter undercuts the hyperbole of the sea of tears just as the practiced courtesan sees through the protestations of storm-tossed lovers. As past performer in many erotic scenes, she can play three roles at once: the unrequited lover, the sympathetic listener, and the ironic stage manager of the entire comedy. As objective commentator on all five star-crossed lovers, moreover, she manages to turn aside the demands of her suitor in an ingeniously amusing way.

She is less tactful with another suitor, against whom her defense takes the form of severe literary criticism. In *Capitolo* 11, the "incerto autore" elaborates a conceit based on her presence in Verona, which he asks her to leave to join him in Venice:

Invero una tu sei, Verona bella,
poi che la mia Veronica gentile
con l'unica bellezza sua t'abbella.
   Quella, a cui non fu mai pari o simìle,
d'Adria ninfa leggiadra, or col bel viso
t'apporta a mezzo 'l verno un lieto aprile.

Truly, you are one of a kind, lovely Verona,
since my graceful, gracious Veronica
beautifies you with her unique beauty.
   She, who's never had equal or peer,
the pretty nymph of the Adriatic, now with her lovely face
brings a joyful April to your midwinter.

The anonymous author (possibly the Veronese count Marcantonio della Torre, whose country estate Franco celebrates in her final *capitolo*) showers extravagant pastoral praises on the "nymph," whom he represents as a sun capable of bringing summer to the entire city, "a high and unheard-of miracle of goodness." In *Capitolo* 12 Franco counters with an appeal to civic pride and verisimilitude: why does this man praise Veron[ic]a when he could praise Venice, a higher subject about which he could tell the truth without flattery?

9 . . . lodar quel ch'al giudicio ancor poi vale:
   lodar d'Adria il felice almo ricetto,
   che, benché sia terreno, ha forma vera
   di cielo in terra a Dio caro e diletto.
      Questa materia del vostro ingegno era,
   e non gir poetando vanamente,
   obliando la via del ver primiera.
      Senza discorrer poeticamente,
   senza usar l'iperbolica figura,
   ch'è pur troppo bugiarda apertamente,
      si poteva impiegar la vostra cura
   in lodando Vinegia, singolare
   meraviglia e stupor de la natura.

. . . praise what is valued more by good judgment,
   praise the blessed, kindly refuge of the Adriatic,
   which, although earthly, truly has the form
   of heaven on earth, beloved and cherished by God.
      This was a topic worthy of your genius,
   rather than wandering off in vain poetizing,
   forgetting the path of primal truth.
      Without running on in the manner of poets,
   without using hyperbolic comparisons,
   which are all too clearly lies,
      you could have put your effort
   into praising Venice, the singular
   marvel and real wonder of nature.

Franco's correction of her poet's excessive compliments goes deep. Not only does she firmly rewrite his opening by replacing "the pretty nymph of the Adriatic" with "the blessed, kindly refuge of the Adriatic"; she also exposes his attribution of false wonders to ephemeral beauty by implying that he knows as well as she does that such praises should be reserved for the "gracious birthplace" they share. Like Labé, Franco mocks the falsity of male-composed praise for the lady. But she puts a political discourse in its place: a sustained verse celebration of the myth of Venice, the "royal virgin who dominates the sea, inviolate," (22–23), a city miraculously founded by God as a center for "his faith, oppressed elsewhere" (40–42), the shore chosen as the site of all earthly delights (43–45). To demonstrate her detachment from the follies of erotic poetry, she enters into the tradition of praise for Venice, a long-standing discourse constructed in the Middle Ages, amplified by Petrarch in letters praising its government and ceremonies throughout the 1350s,[74] and a staple of contemporary poetry—including Maffio Venier's 1576 *canzone* praying for the city's recovery from the plague.[75] Franco invokes the myth to signal her solidarity with the Venetian elite whose interests it served and to position herself as teacher/critic, a role officially closed to her but that she could claim in the debate opened by the unsuspecting poet of Verona.

Franco meets an interlocutor on more equal ground in a poem in which she again breaks down the boundaries separating private and public discourses: in *Capitolo* 13, she challenges a treacherous lover to a duel. (Rosenthal argues that her addressee was probably Marco Venier, whom she suspected of writing Maffio's attacks.) The entire poem hilariously recontextualizes the vocabulary of chivalry. The battlefield Franco finally reveals she has in mind is her own bed, to which she invites the man in a long shared joke in which she displays her sexual and verbal skills simultaneously. She opens by calling attention to her grasp of dueling terminology, first by pretending she is unsure of it and then by dismissing its rules. In fact, she is thoroughly in control of both the jargon and the man, for whom she sets up a surprise by delaying throughout thirty lines her explanation of the kind of battle she has in mind:

> Non più parole: ai fatti, in campo, a l'armi,
> ch'io voglio, risoluta di morire,
> da sì grave molestia liberarmi.
>   Non so se 'l mio "cartel" si debba dire,
> in quanto do risposta provocata;
> ma perchè in rissa de' nomi venire?
>   Se vuoi, da te mi chiamo disfidata;
> e, se non, ti disfido; o in ogni via
> la prendo, ed ogni occasion m'è grata.

> No more words: to deeds, to the battlefield, to arms!
> for, resolved to die, I want
> to free myself from such maddening vexation.

Should I call this a challenge? I don't know,
since I am responding to a provocation;
but why should we duel about words?
    If you want, I'll say you've challenged me;
if not, I challenge you. In either case
I accept, and I welcome any chance to fight.

The rest of the poem follows from Franco's offer that the man choose the place and weapons. Like Venus dressed in Mars's armor, the courtesan takes over the rites and accoutrements of masculinity. She encourages her opponent in a sustained *double entendre* to bring his sturdiest sword, assumes they will confront each other "nude of any armor," and, playing on the death/ orgasm ambiguity, imagines them dying spectacularly together at the same moment: "teco morrei d'egual colpo ferita" (I would die with you, struck down by the same blow). As frankly erotic as Labé's *basium*, Franco's poem ends with a similar withdrawal: she concedes that she has been merely fantasizing. But like Labé she returns to another version of her desire, a wish for revenge and for her own separate "death":

86   O mie vane speranze, onde la sorte
      crudel a pianger più sempre m'invita!
        Ma pur sostienti, cor sicuro e forte,
      e con l'ultimo strazio di quell'empio
      vendica mille tue con la sua morte;
        poi, con quel ferro ancor tronca il tuo scempio.

      Oh, vain hopes of mine, over which
      cruel fate, as always, calls me to weep!
        But hold up, my heart, be true and strong,
      and with the final destruction of this wicked man
      avenge your thousand deaths with his one.
        Then, with the same blade, end your own torment.

Franco's verbal game here corresponds to a sartorial inversion practiced by courtesans in her city: cross-dressing. Such female transvestism was recorded in several Venetian representations of courtesans. One example is an anonymous engraving, about 1590, of a sort of soft-porn paper doll whose long courtesan's skirt, cut away, reveals that she is dressed in men's underclothes and tights, which jar comically with the high clogs (*pianelle*) she wears to increase her height (fig. 5).[76] The Senate condemned women's use of men's clothing, claiming that it was intended to lead young men into exceptional vice;[77] the satirist Aretino, always ready to invert social proprieties, wrote to a courtesan named la Zufolina that he relished her appearance in boy's clothes as much as her wit.[78] Lawner suggests that courtesans cross-dressed to be mobile and to participate in the many forms of masking and disguise in the city. But the link between transvestism and verbal wit in Aretino's letter is a better clue to what Franco does in this poem: she surprises, amuses, and titillates her interlocutor by putting on a male discourse at the same time that she insists on her female sexuality. Wearing the dueler's verbal costume is funny, an irreverent carnivalization of the knightly code; and the disguise, meant to be seen through, intensifies her erotic appeal.

Franco uses this vocabulary less playfully for public self-defense. In one of her letters, 47, she invites a man (possibly Marco Venier, after she discovered that Maffio, not he, was her attacker) to a practice session in the terminology of knightly challenge, which she hopes will help her to compose a counterattack: "I beg your Lordship, as a master of the art, to teach me some surprise stroke, and even to take your sword in hand—not one with a cutting edge, but one for sport—and use it against me in a skillful match . . . in the language best suited to you" (65–66). The same request is the subject of

Fig. 5. Illustration of a paper-doll courtesan wearing masculine undergarments. (Pietro Bertelli's *Diversarium Nationum Habitus*, 1592, by permission of the Folger Shakespeare Library.)

her *Capitolo* 23, in which she asks for advice on how to phrase a challenge properly:

> 10   vengo a voi per consiglio, a cui son note
>   le forme del duello e de l'onore,
>   per cui s'uccide il mondo et si percuote.
>   A voi, che guerrier sète di valore,
>   e ch'oltre a l'esser de la guerra esperto,
>   vostra mercede, mi portate amore.
>
>   I come to you for counsel, you who know
>   the rituals of dueling and of honor,
>   by which men kill and wound each other.
>   To you, who are a courageous warrior,
>   and who, besides being expert in war,
>   all thanks to you, feel love for me.

The gist of this *capitolo* is Franco's claim to injured innocence. She represents herself as responding to intolerable provocation from a cowardly man, a claim that shows she already understands one use of chivalrous vocabulary: to construct an ennobling justification for intended violence.

In her self-defense (*Capitolo* 16), she finds other uses as well for the for-malized vocabulary of dueling. For one thing, the poem establishes a much more elevated register of discourse than the abusive dialect of Maffio Venier; she maintains a hyper-correct formality intended to demonstrate that what-ever her opponent's actual social status may be, she outclasses him linguisti-cally. Further, the code of noblemen's duels corresponds to the courteous language courtesans used with their clients and expected in return: both are forms of social control. Franco accuses Maffio Vener of infringing the code in several ways: he fights with "insidious rather than open weapons," unwor-thy of a "cavalier"; he attacks women, who are no match for him; he strikes an unarmed opponent. Her countermoves are exemplarily courteous. She reminds him of the "great sweetness" women bring to men who know how to respond to graceful gentility ("gentilezza"), implying that he is too coarse for such pleasures; she explains with exaggerated politeness that by calling her "unica" with insulting intent, he has simply revealed his ignorance be-cause the word has a positive connotation (any dictionary will tell him that it describes a woman "whose reputation is glorious, who surpasses all others in beauty, valor and virtue"); and her precise use of chivalrous terms con-trasts to the imprecision she attributes to him, as in her formal challenge: "di provocarvi a rissa in campo ardisco, / con cor non poco a la vendetta ac-ceso" (56–7: I dare to challenge you to a duel on the battlefield, / with a heart inflamed with desire for just vengeance). Franco's motive is to shame her detractor with the dignity of her takeover of knightly speech.

But the energy this *tenzone* (poetic debate) sustains for over two hundred lines comes mainly from its gender-bending aggression. Franco claims to equal the man on his own terms. Her ruling metaphor, that speech is a weapon and that her arsenal of languages matches his, positions her not as a virtuous victim but as a virtuoso amazon. Her invitation to debate translates the *vanto* (the self-aggrandizing posture) of the knightly challenger into a claim to literary and critical omnipotence. Knowing that Maffio was capable of writing not only in Venetian dialect but in the pure Tuscan defended by Bembo and the Latin used by scholars, she uses the convention whereby the challenger offers his opponent the choice of weapons to insist on her equal linguistic competence:

> 112   La spada, che 'n man vostra rade e fora,
>   de la lingua volgar veneziana,
>   s'a voi piacer usar, piace a me ancora:
>   e, se volete entrar ne la toscana,
>   scegliete voi la seria o la burlesca,
>   chè l'una e l'altra è a me facile e piana.
>   Io ho veduto in lingua selvaghesca
>   certa fattura vostra molto bella,
>   simile a la maniera pedantesca:
>   se voi volete usar o questa o quella,
>   ed aventar, come ne l'altre fate,
>   di queste in biasmo nostro le quadrella,
>   qual di lor più vi piace, e voi pigliate,
>   chè di tutte ad un modo io mi contento,
>   avendole perciò tutte imparate.

> The sword that strikes and pierces in your hand—
> the common Venetian tongue—
> if you want to use it, I want to, too;
>   and if you want to enter into Tuscan,
> choose yourself its learned or comic form,
> for both alike are smooth and easy for me.
>   I've seen, in a rustic language,
> certain writings of yours, very lovely,
> as is your more learned mode.
>   If you want to use one or the other,
> as in your other attacks, to fan
> the fires of our contest of insults,
>   take up whichever pleases you best,
> for I will accept any one equally,
> having learned them all for this occasion.

Like Labé, Franco makes no pretense of aristocratic *sprezzatura*: she admits the hard work that guarantees her opponent's defeat. There is perhaps a deliberate misunderstanding in her *sfida*: given that Venier's insulting dialect was the "weapon" that prompted her to respond, it was unlikely that he would engage her in a Bembist or Latin polemic. Her challenge nonetheless demonstrates to her readers that she deserves the "glorious reputation" of a woman of letters, which she claims by rewriting her attacker's text.

Franco's defense of women in this poem threatens several axioms about gender difference. Christine de Pisan had argued that women were mentally more agile than men because they had to be; Franco states categorically that they can also be more agile physically. Moreover, she breaks down the stereotype according to which courage is an attribute of all men. Valor varies in the male sex, no essential link exists between physical and mental strength, and only women's underestimation of their capacities has kept them from using their power:

> 64   Quando armate ed esperte ancor siam noi,
>   render buon conto a ciascun uom potemo,
>   chè mani e piedi e core avem qual voi;
>   e, se ben molli e delicate semo,
>   ancor tal uom, ch'è delicato, è forte;
>   e tal, ruvido ed aspro, è d'ardir scemo.
>   Di ciò non se ne son le donne accorte;
>   che, se si risolvessero di farlo,
>   con voi pugnar porìan fino a la morte.
>
> When we women, too, are armed and trained,
> we'll be able to stand up to any man,
> for we have hands and feet and hearts like yours;
>   and although we may be soft and delicate,
> some men who are delicate are also strong;
> and others, though rude and rough, are cowards.
>   Women have not yet realized this,
> for if they once resolved to do it,
> they could fight to the death with any of you.

Franco may have derived some of her feminist positions from a current of late sixteenth-century thought in defenses of women by her compatriots Lucrezia Marinelli and Moderata Fonte,[79] and some of her arguments appear in earlier texts such as Cornelius Agrippa's *De nobilitate et praecellentia foeminei sexus* (1509).[80] Like Labé, Franco presents herself not as an exceptional woman but as a typical one, able to provide an example to others because she shares their situation. She adopts the traditionally masculine role of defender of women by pointing to Venier as their common enemy:

> 73   E per farvi veder che 'l vero parlo,
>   tra tante donne incominciar voglio io,
>   porgendo essempio a lor di seguitarlo.
>   A voi, che contra tutte sète rio,
>   con qual'armi volete in man mi volgo,
>   con speme d'atterrarvi e con desio;
>   e le donne a difender tutte tolgo
>   contra di voi, che di lor sète schivo,
>   sì ch'a ragion io sola non mi dolgo.

> And to convince you that I speak the truth,
> among many women I want to go first,
> leaving others an example to follow.
>   To you, who are so savage toward us all,
> I turn with whatever weapons you want,
> with the hope and will to throw you to the ground;
>   and I undertake to defend all women
> against you, who are so scornful of them
> that with reason I'm not alone to complain.

All in all, Franco rejects the structural oppositions of sixteenth-century gender ideology. She represents herself as a woman who is sexually active outside marriage, but she refuses guilt; she defends herself against a man's misogyny by claiming to have more virtues, including masculine ones, than he does. Her claim to equality with men, like her assumption of the role of a leader of women, collapses the division between private and public spheres, especially the assignment of chastity to women and courage to men. Franco's appropriation of masculine discourses and her solidarity with women recall the Lyonnais *bourgeoise* who drew similar confidence from her membership in a self-made rising class.

Yet the defiance in Franco's challenge to Maffio Venier was an exceptional response to an exceptional danger. In another defense of women, *Capitolo* 24, she works out a more conciliatory rhetoric in the interests of courtesans in particular. A language of tact and flattery was required of Venetian men as well, particularly patricians seeking election to the governing bodies of the city. As Robert Finlay points out, "A politics of ceremony and simulation had to be learned if a patrician were to be successful in his term of office."[81] To reform a man who has insulted and tried to beat a fellow courtesan, Franco formulates an appeal in exquisitely courteous language, which she teaches him to imitate. Attacks on courtesans were common and violent enough to have produced the expression "dare la sfregia," to give the scar. If a courtesan's go-between or *ruffiano* (pimp) was not there to protect her physically, she had only her verbal powers to depend on. Franco exemplifies the diplomacy required under such circumstances by conceding that what she has heard about this man may not be true (an implicit reproach for his readiness to believe the worst of his mistress) and sets herself up as a model of proper behavior between the sexes:

> 19   basta che mi tegniate per amica,
>   come infatti vi son, sì che in giovarvi
>   non sarei scarsa d'opra o di fatica.
>   Ed or ch'io mi conduco a ragionarvi
>   di quanto intenderete, a quel m'accosto,
>   che dè' chi fa profession d'amarvi.
>
>   Only consider me your friend,
>   as indeed I am, so that I would spare

no effort or trouble to do you good.
   So now I undertake to speak with you
so that you will understand, from my example,
how someone who claims to love you should behave.

The gist of her argument is another defense of women, but this time she emphasizes their voluntary "vassalage" to men for the sake of keeping peace between the sexes and procreating the human race. Her claims for women's intellectual and moral superiority focus on the flexibility and tolerance that their attacker lacks:

55   Povero sesso, con fortuna ria
       sempre prodotto, perch'ognor soggetto
       e senza libertà sempre si stia!
          Né però di noi fu certo il difetto,
       che, se ben come l'uom non sem forzute,
       come l'uom mente avemo ed intelletto.
          Né in forza corporal sta la virtute,
       ma nel vigor de l'alma e de l'ingegno,
       da cui tutte le cose son sapute:
          e certa son che in ciò loco men degno
       non han le donne, ma d'esser maggiori
       degli uomini dato hanno più d'un segno.
          Ma, se di voi si reputiam minori,
       fors'è perchè in modestia ed in sapere
       di voi siamo più facili e migliori.

       Unlucky sex, which fickle fortune
       leads here and there, for you are always subject
       to others, and always deprived of liberty!
          But this weakness is certainly not our fault,
       for if we are not as muscular as men,
       like men, we have a soul and intellect.
          And virtue does not consist in strength of body,
       but in liveliness of soul and mind,
       through which all things are known;
          and I know that in this trait women have
       no lesser status, but have shown signs—
       more than one—of being greater than men.
          If we are reputed to be lesser,
       perhaps it's because our modesty and wisdom
       are more yielding and deeper than yours.

In contrast to the dominating irrationality of "l'uom tiranno e fello" (the tyrannical and fierce male), Franco invokes the reasoned behavior of more enlightened men. Society shows us, she says, that civilized men revere women; she advises her interlocutor to follow the example of his own sex as well as hers. She adds tactically that if a man who has offended a woman genuinely repents, he will be forgiven, showing this man how to expiate his attack on her fellow courtesan:

148   Ma, poi che non può adietro ritornarle,
         con dolci modi a l'offese ripara,
         e, quanto può, si sforza d'annullarle;
            ritorna ancor l'amata al doppio cara
         nel rifar de la pace; e, per turbarsi,
         più d'ogni parte l'alma si rischiara.

         But since he cannot take back his misdeeds,
         he uses sweet manners to repair the offense,
         and, as far as he can, he tries to undo them;
            then his loved one returns, twice dearer
         to him as they make peace; and for all the turmoil,
         finally both their spirits are cleared.

Franco does not order the recipient of the poem to follow this example; rather, she makes the outcome look enticing and offers it as a choice. Her indirect persuasion typifies the conciliatory aspect of the courtesan's rhetoric. She asserts the virtues and rights of her sex within a strategic framework built not on direct physical or social power but on rules of courtesy upon which her and her fellow courtesans' safety depends. But Franco also responded to the necessity of protecting herself against unpredictable men by acquiring exceptional mastery of literary and political languages, of aggressive argument as well as seductive logic. All of her poems position her in direct relation to her readers.

One term for such directness in Italian is *franchezza*, a word with two connotations: frankness and freedom. Franco had no illusions about the life of a courtesan, as her letter (22) to a woman who wanted to turn her daughter into one proves: she warns her of the misery of sexual "servitude," of the need to "eat with the mouth of another, sleep with the eyes of another, move according to another's will" (38). Yet even here she is "franca" in both senses of the word: direct, certainly (she adds that the daughter lacks beauty, the basic equipment for the profession), and also free, in the sense that she is able to analyze the world she lives in, to assess another woman's chances for success in it, to write in a persuasive way to a fellow citizen. In French, *franchise* has the same meanings as *franchezza*: freedom and frankness. It is not surprising to discover that one of Labé's most sympathetic modern critics, Fernand Zamaron, entitled his study *Louise Labé, dame de la franchise.*[82]

I have interpreted the frankest speeches of these poets as a consequence of the relative autonomy available to them in the societies they inhabited. The ropemaker's daughter and the courtesan wrote with a sense of the social and literary boundaries they were transgressing, but they persistently wrote past them. They claimed the same right to fame as their male contemporaries and they appropriated old and new arguments to defend women as members of the same sex. More intimately and perhaps more surprisingly, their love poems demonstrate the interdependence of social and sexual equality in the demands and fantasies of women's writing in their time. Women throughout Europe used the conventions of love lyric as a screen and channel for various desires: for intellectual freedom, for social recognition, for spiritual self-determination. But Labé and Franco wrote about sexual pleasure as sexual pleasure. Economic and cultural mobility in Lyon and Venice can hardly account for this new feminine eroticism in its entirety. But the openness of both cultures certainly made possible what their conservative moralists were trying to prevent: outspoken women celebrating their sexual and rhetorical power simultaneously. The enfranchised cities of Lyon and Venice certainly contributed to Labé's and Franco's oppositional feminism and their challenging reinscription of sixteenth-century languages of love.

Notes

INTRODUCTION

1. Christine Gledhill, "Pleasurable Negotiations," in *Female Spectators: Looking at Film and Television*, ed. E. Deidre Pribram (London: Verso, 1988), 67.

2. For Gramsci's own remarks on hegemony, see Antonio Gramsci, *The Modern Prince and Other Writings*, trans. Louis Marx (New York: International Publishers, 1957), 135–88, esp. 186–87.

3. Stuart Hall, "Encoding/Decoding," in *Culture, Media, Language*, ed. Stuart Hall, Dorothy Hobson, Andrew Lowe, and Paul Willis (London: Hutchinson, 1980), 136. Further remarks on viewer positions quoted in my text come from this article.

4. Thomas M. Greene, *The Light in Troy: Imitation and Discovery in Renaissance Poetry* (New Haven: Yale University Press, 1982), 38.

5. For a now-classic analysis of the gendered power relations implicit in the Petrarchan *blason*, see Nancy J. Vickers, "Diana Described: Scattered Woman and Scattered Rhyme," in *Writing and Sexual Difference*, ed. Elizabeth Abel (Chicago: University of Chicago Press, 1982). See the extension of this analysis to male/male rivalry in her " 'The blazon of sweet beauty's best': Shakespeare's *Lucrece*," in *Shakespeare and the Question of Theory*, ed. Patricia Parker and Geoffrey Hartman (London and New York: Methuen, 1985) and also Pat Parker's "Rhetorics of Property: Exploration, Inventory, Blazon" in *Literary Fat Ladies: Rhetoric, Gender, Property* (London and New York: Methuen, 1987).

6. The title of Stephen Greenblatt's recent book, *Shakespearean Negotiations: The Circulation of Social Energy in Renaissance England* (Berkeley: University of California Press, 1988), signals widespread interest in negotiation as a model. Greenblatt's focus is not Marxist, however. He defines the Elizabethan stage as a structural crossroads, a site of diverse cultural forms, rather than using negotiation as a conceptual framework to analyze countermoves within and against reigning ideology. Instead he argues, in free-market terms, that the fantasy status attributed to the theater by Shakespeare's audience gave that theater "an unusually broad license to conduct its negotiations and exchanges with surrounding institutions, authorities, discourses, and practices" (18–19). He goes on to a very interesting statement, using terms apparently similar to Hall's and Gledhill's, but he uses them to describe the relative free play available in a privileged cultural space: "the circulation of social energy by and through the stage was not part of a single, totalizing system. Rather it was partial, fragmentary, conflictual; elements were crossed, torn apart, recombined, set against each other; particular social practices were magnified by the stage, others diminished, exalted, evacuated" (19). I see the usefulness of negotiation, rather, as the basis for an analysis of deliberate strategies that human agents direct against repressive cultural systems. For Greenblatt's "stage," I read "women's textual practice," with all the differences that entails.

7. Claudine Hermann, *Les Voleuses de langue* (Paris: des femmes, 1976).

8. Showalter first used the term "gynocritics" in "Toward a Feminist Poetics," in *Women's Writing and Writing about Women*, ed. Mary Jacobus (London: Croom Helm, 1979). She defines the concept further in "Feminist Criticism in the Wilderness," *Critical Inquiry* 8 (Winter 1981): 202ff.

9. Early comments on these changes include Alice Clark, *Working Life of Women in the Seventeenth Century* (London: Routledge, 1919; rpt. 1982) and Joan Kelly-Gadol, "Did Women Have a Renaissance?" in *Becoming Visible: Women in European History*, ed. Renate Bridenthal and Claudia Koonz (Boston: Houghton Mifflin, 1977). See, for more recent work, Part V of *Women and Work in Preindustrial Europe*, ed. Barbara Hanawalt (Bloomington: Indiana University Press, 1986).

10. Myra Jehlen, "Archimedes and the Paradox of Feminist Criticism," in *The Signs*

Reader, ed. Elizabeth Abel and Emily K. Abel (Chicago: University of Chicago Press, 1983), 69–96.

11. See, for the political dimensions of the medieval lyric that contributed to Renaissance love poetry, Georges Duby, *The Chivalrous Society*, trans. Cynthia Postan (London: Edward Arnold, 1977); for Neoplatonism as a class code, José Giudici, "De l'amour courtois à l'amour sacré: la condition de la femme dans l'oeuvre de B. Castiglione," in *Images de la femme dans la littérature italienne de la Renaissance*, ed. André Rochon (Paris: Sorbonne Nouvelle, 1980); for Petrarchism, Louis Adrian Montrose, "Celebration and Insinuation: Sir Philip Sidney and the Motives of Elizabethan Courtship," *Renaissance Drama*, n.s. 8 (1977); Arthur Marotti, " 'Love is not Love': Elizabethan Sonnet Sequences and the Social Order," *ELH* 49 (1982); and Ann Jones and Peter Stallybrass, "The Politics of *Astrophil and Stella*," *SEL* 24 (1984).

12. For an extremely interesting study of linkages between sonnets and portrait miniatures in Elizabethan England, see Patricia Fumerton, " 'Secret' Arts: Elizabethan Miniatures and Sonnets," *Representations* 15 (Summer 1986).

13. For editorial misrepresentations in Italy, see my chapters on Tullia d'Aragona and Gaspara Stampa; Fiora Bassanese is excellent on critical misreadings of Stampa in *Gaspara Stampa* (Boston: Twayne, 1982), 32–34. For a study of Labé's reception, see Ann R. Jones and Nancy J. Vickers, "Canon, Rule and the Restoration Renaissance," *Yale French Studies*, no. 75 (Autumn 1988), esp. 23.

14. Judith Newton, "Making—and Remaking—History: Another Look at 'Patriarchy,' " in *Feminist Issues in Literary Scholarship*, ed. Shari Benstock (Bloomington: Indiana University Press, 1987), 125.

1. THE MIRROR, THE DISTAFF, THE PEN

1. Ruth Kelso, *Doctrine for the Lady of the Renaissance* (Urbana: University of Illinois Press, 1965; rpt. 1978), 25, 32.

2. Virginia Woolf, *A Room of One's Own* (New York: Harcourt, Brace, 1929), 60. Woolf's perception is expanded in many directions by Luce Irigaray in her brilliant discussion of how philosophical and psychoanalytic discourses have positioned women as the lesser others of men's self-representations: *Speculum de l'autre femme* (Paris: Minuit, 1974), trans. as *Speculum of the Other Woman* by Gillian Gill (Ithaca: Cornell University Press, 1985).

3. Luce Guillerm, Jean-Pierre Guillerm, Laurence Hordoir, Marie-Françoise Piéjus, eds., *Le Miroir des femmes, 1: Moralistes et polémistes au XVIe siècle* (Presses universitaires de Lille, 1983), 10.

4. For a typical anti-aristocratic view, see Richard Brathwaite's *The English Gentlewoman* (London, 1631). For attacks on citizens' wives, see Linda Woodbridge, *Women and the English Renaissance: Literature and the Nature of Womankind, 1540–1620* (Urbana: University of Illinois Press, 1984), 173–76, and Katharine Rogers, *The Troublesome Helpmate: A History of Misogyny in Literature* (Seattle: University of Washington Press, 1966), 125–27 . A hilarious satire of Puritan women occurs in Thomas Middleton's *A Chaste Maid in Cheapside*, 3:ii. For an analysis of the political uses of "wild Irishwomen," see Peter Stallybrass, " 'An enclosure of all the best people in the world': Nationalism and Imperialism in Late Sixteenth-Century England," in *Patriotism: Ideology and Myth in the Making of English National Identity*, ed. Raphael Samuel (London: Routledge and Kegan Paul, 1989).

5. The classic essay arguing that attention to gender requires a reevaluation of periodization is Joan Kelly-Gadol's "Did Women Have a Renaissance?" in *Becoming Visible: Women in European History*, ed. Renate Bridenthal and Claudia Koonz (Boston: Houghton Mifflin, 1977). The argument is expanded in the introduction to *Rewriting the Renaissance: The Discourses of Sexual Difference in Early Modern Europe*, ed.

Margaret Ferguson, Maureen Quilligan, and Nancy Vickers (Chicago: University of Chicago Press, 1986). For increasing constraints on women in England, see Lisa Jardine, *Still Harping on Women: Women and Drama in the Age of Shakespeare* (Totowa, N.J.: Barnes and Noble, 1983), especially chaps. 2, 3, and 5 . See also Susan Cahn, *The Industry of Devotion: The Transformation of Women's Work in England, 1500–1660* (New York: Columbia University Press, 1987).

6. For Protestant family theory, see Christopher Hill, *Society and Puritanism in Pre-Revolutionary England* (Manchester: Panther, 1969), chap. 13; Lawrence Stone, *The Family, Sex and Marriage in England, 1500–1800* (New York: Harper and Row, 1977); Gordon Schochet, *Patriarchalism in Political Thought: The Authoritarian Family and Political Speculation and Attitudes* (Oxford: Blackwell, 1975); Kathleen Davies, "The Sacred Condition of Equality—How Original Were Puritan Doctrines of Marriage?" *Social History*, no. 5 (May 1977): 563–78.

7. An early analysis of the economic effects of capitalism on women is Alice Clark, *Working Life of Women in the Seventeenth Century* (London: Routledge, 1919; rpt. 1982, with an introduction by Miranda Chaytor and Jane Lewis). See also Hans Medick, "The Proto-Industrial Family Economy: The Structural Function of Household and Family during the Transition from Peasant Society to Industrial Capitalism," *Social History*, no. 3 (October 1976), and Roberta Hamilton, *The Liberation of Women: A Study of Patriarchy and Capitalism* (London: Allen and Unwin, 1978.) Barnabe Rich's *My Ladies Looking Glasse* (London, 1616) is a typical denunciation of the "fantasies" of women's fashions and the women who follow them in order to imitate their betters. See Jardine, *Still Harping*, chap. 5, for an argument that criticism of women's inappropriate apparel displaced general anxiety about rising classes onto their female members.

8. On humanist educators, see Constance Jordan, "Feminism and the Humanists: The Case of Sir Thomas Elyot's *Defense of Good Women*," *Renaissance Quarterly* 36 (1983): 181–201, rpt. in *Rewriting the Renaissance*; Janice Butler Holm, "The Myth of a Feminist Humanism," *Soundings* 68 (Winter 1984): 443–52; Elaine Beilin, *Redeeming Eve: Women Writers of the English Renaissance* (Princeton: Princeton University Press, 1987), chap. 1. See also the studies in *Beyond Their Sex: Learned Women of the European Past*, ed. Patricia Labalme (New York: New York University Press, 1984), and Jardine, *Still Harping*, 51–58. For literary instances of the backlash against feminine erudition in England, see Rogers, *The Troublesome Helpmate*, 129–31.

9. *Les Enseignements d'Anne de France à sa fille Susanne de Bourbon*, ed. A. M. Chazard (Moulins: C. Des Rosiers, 1878), 8.

10. On male courtiers' training, see Daniel Javitch, *Poetry and Courtliness in Renaissance England* (Princeton: Princeton University Press, 1978); Stephen Greenblatt, *Renaissance Self-Fashioning: from More to Shakespeare* (Chicago: University of Chicago Press, 1980); Frank Whigham, "Interpretation at Court: Courtesy and the Performer-Audience Dialectic," *NLH* 14 (1983): 623–41, and his *Ambition and Privilege: The Social Tropes of Elizabethan Courtesy Theory* (Berkeley: University of California Press, 1984).

11. *Ragionamento del Sig. Annibal Guasco a D. Lavinia sua figliuola della maniera del governarsi ella in corte; andando per Dama* (Turin, 1586), sig. C3v.

12. Baldessar Castiglione, *Il Libro del Cortegiano* (Venice, 1523), trans. Thomas Hoby (London, 1561). The first page numbers in my text refer to Bruno Maier's edition of Castiglione, 2nd ed. (Turin: UTET, 1964), the second to J. H. Whitfield's edition of Hoby's translation (London: H. M. Dent, 1966; rpt. 1974). On the role Castiglione assigns to women at court, see J. R. Woodhouse, *Baldessar Castiglione: A Reassessment of 'The Courtier'* (Edinburgh: Edinburgh University Press, 1978); Frank Whigham, "Interpretation at Court," 623–39. Two excellent studies focused on women are José Guidi, "De l'amour courtois à l'amour sacré: la condition de la femme dans l'oeuvre de B. Castiglione," in *Images de la femme dans la littérature*

italienne de la Renaissance, ed. André Rochon (Paris: Centre de Recherche sur la Renaissance Italienne, Université de la Sorbonne Nouvelle) and Marina Zancan, "La donna e il cerchio nel *Cortegiano* di B. Castiglione: le funzioni del femminile nell'immagine di corte," in *Nel Cerchio della Luna: Figure di donna in alcuni testi del XVI secolo,* ed. Marina Zancan (Venice: Marsilio, 1983).

13. For discussions of the association made between articulateness and promiscuity in women, see Jardine, *Still Harping,* chap. 4, and Peter Stallybrass, "Patriarchal Territories: The Body Enclosed," in *Rewriting the Renaissance,* 123–42.

14. Arturo Graf cites an early use of the word "cortegiana" in a Roman census taken under Pope Leo X in "Una cortegiana fra mille: Veronica Franco," in *Attraverso il Cinquecento* (Turin: Chiantore, 1926), 182.

15. Pietro Aretino, *Sei Giornati,* ed. Giovanni Aquilecchia (Bari: Laterza, 1969), *Dialogo di Messer Pietro Aretino . . . ,* "Seconda giornata," 234. Trans. as *Aretino's Dialogues* by Raymond Rosenthal (New York: Stein and Day, 1971), 256.

16. *La civil conversatione del Signor Stefano Guazzo* (Venice, 1575), 1:324; 290. My quotations are from the translation by George Pettie (London, 1581; rpt. George Constable, 1925, ed. Edward Sullivan). Page numbers refer first to Pettie, then to the Italian text.

17. Foucault's argument is that beginning with the Counter-Reformation, speech on sexual matters was institutionally encouraged, in fact, coerced, as a form of social control. See *The History of Sexuality,* trans. R. Hurley (New York: Pantheon, 1978), 24 and passim.

18. Alessandro Piccolomini, *Dialogo, nel quale si ragiona della bella creanza delle donne* (Venice, 1539), trans. as *A Dialogue of the Fair Perfectioning of Ladies* by John Nevinson (Glasgow: MacLehose, 1968).

19. For *the Querelle des amies,* see Ferdinand Gohin's introduction to Antoine Héroët, *Oeuvres poétiques* (Paris: Cornély, 1909; rpt. Paris: Droz, 1943); Richmond Hawkins, *Maistre Charles Fontaine, Parisien* (Cambridge: Harvard University Press, 1916); Emile Telle, *L'Oeuvre de Marguerite d'Angoulême, Reine de Navarre, et la querelle des femmes* (Toulouse: Lion, 1937; rpt. Geneva: Slatkine, 1969); and Marie-Thérèse Cuyx-Barnes, "Etude de la 'Querelle des amies'" (Ph.D. diss., Florida State University, 1974). Cuyx-Barnes points out many parallels between La Borderie's Amie and Castiglione's *donna di palazzo,* but they do not convince me that La Borderie meant his portrait to be positive.

20. *The Complete Works of Ben Jonson,* ed. C. H. Herford Percy and Evelyn Simpson (Oxford: Clarendon Press, 1947), 8:222.

21. For an excellent discussion of the male courtier's displacement of his own self-disguises onto women, see Whigham, *Ambition and Privilege,* 116–17 and notes.

22. For a citation and comment, see Hawkins, *Maistre Charles Fontaine,* 88.

23. Leon Battista Alberti, *I Libri della famiglia,* ed. Ruggiero Romano and Alberto Tenenti (Turin: Einaudi, 1972). I quote from an English translation, *The Albertis of Florence: Leon Battista Alberti's "Della Famiglia",* ed. Guido Guarino (Lewisburg, Pa.: Bucknell University Press, 1971), 122–23. For an introduction to Alberti, see Renée Watkins, *The Family in Renaissance Florence* (Columbia, S.C.: University of South Carolina Press, 1969). For Florentine family history in general, see David Herlihy and Christiane Klapisch-Zuber, *Tuscans and their Families* (New Haven: Yale University Press, 1985).

24. Lionardo Bruni d'Arezzo, "Concerning the Study of Literature: A Letter Addressed to the Illustrious Lady, Baptista Malatesta," in *Vittorino da Feltre and Other Humanist Educators,* ed. William Harrison Woodward (New York: Columbia University Teachers College, 1963), 126.

25. Francesco Barbaro, *De re uxoria,* trans. in *The Earthly Republic: Italian Humanists on Government and Society,* ed. Benjamin Kohl et al. (Philadelphia: University of Pennsylvania Press, 1978), 204.

26. Gloria Kaufman, "Juan Luis Vives on the Education of Women," *Signs* 3 (Summer 1978), 891–97; Valerie Wayne, " 'Some Sad Sentence': Vives' *Instruction of a Christian Woman*," in *Silent But for the Word: Tudor Women as Patrons, Translators and Writers of Religious Works*, ed. Margaret Hannay (Kent, Ohio: Kent State University Press, 1985), 15–29; Jordan, "Feminism and the Humanists"; Beilin, *Redeeming Eve*.

27. Juan Luis Vives, *The First Book of the Instruction of a Christian Woman*, in *Vives and the Renascence Education of Women*, ed. Foster Watson (New York: Longmans, Green and Co., 1912), 90. Quotations from Vives, Hyrde, and More are from the texts in this compilation.

28. Giovanni Bruto, *La Institutione di una fanciulla nata nobilmente* (Anvers, 1555), trans. Thomas Salter, *The Mirrhor of Modestie* (London, 1579), sig. C5v. For a critical analysis of this text, see Holm, "Myth of Feminist Humanism."

29. Theodore Agrippa d'Aubigné, *Oeuvres complètes*, ed. Eugène Réaume and F. de Caussade (Paris: Alphonse Lemerre, 1873), 1:449–50.

30. Thomas Becon, preface to *The Christian State of Matrimony* (London, 1543), sig. B3v. The text was actually written by Heinrich Bullinger, as Suzanne Hull points out in *Chaste, Silent and Obedient: English Books for Women, 1475–1640* (San Marino, Calif.: Huntington Library, 1982), 155.

31. Edward Hake, *A Touchestone for this time present, expresly declaring such ruines, enormities, and abuses as trouble the Churche of God and our Christian common wealth at this daye* (London, 1574), facsimile ed. (Norwood, N.J.: Walter B. Johnson, 1974), D2r.

32. Thomas Powell, *The Art of Thriving, or the plaine path-way to preferment* (London, 1635), 114.

33. Brathwaite, *The English Gentlewoman*, 48–50.

34. William Perkins, *Christian Oeconomie*, trans. Thomas Pickering (London, 1609), sig. 3r–3v.

35. William Gouge, *Of Domesticall Duties: Eight Treatises* (London, 1622; 3rd ed., 1634), 138.

36. Robert Greene, *Penelope's Web* (London, 1587; rpt. 1601), C1r–v.

37. Orazio Lombardelli, *Dell'Uffizio della Donna Maritata: Capi Centottanta* (Florence, 1585; written 1574), 20.

38. Edmund Tilney, *A briefe and pleasant discourse of duties in Marriage, called the Flower of Friendshippe* (London, 1568), sig. E4v.

39. Robert Snawsel, *A Looking glasse for Married Folkes* (London, 1631), facsimile ed. (Norwood, N.J.: Walter Johnson, 1975), 55.

40. For the Echo episode, see Book 3 of the *Metamorphoses* (356–401); for Philomel, see Book 6 (424–674).

41. Robert Cleaver, *A godly forme of houshold government* (London, 1588), 94. Compare Alessandro Piccolomini's remark, in *Della institutione di tutta la vita dell'uomo nato nobile e in città libera* (Venice, 1552), that a wife should play Echo to her husband (H6).

42. Gaspara Stampa, *Rime* (Venice, 1554), in *Scrittori d'Italia*, vol. 52, ed. Abdelkader Salza (Bari: Laterza, 1913), Sonnet 152, 84. See the fuller analysis in chap. 4 and in my "New Songs for the Swallow: Ovid's Philomela in Tullia d'Aragona and Gaspara Stampa," in *Refiguring Woman: Gender Studies and the Italian Renaissance*, ed. Marilyn Migiel and Juliana Schiesari (Ithaca: Cornell University Press, 1990).

43. A number of family and devotional writings by Englishwomen are collected by Betty Travitsky in *The Paradise of Women: Writings by Englishwomen of the Renaissance* (Westport, Conn.: Greenwood Press, 1981).

44. For the limits confronted by women humanists, see Margaret L. King, "The Religious Retreat of Isotta Nogarola (1418–1486)," *Signs* 3 (1978): 807–22, and her "Book-lined Cells: Women and Humanism in the Early Italian Renaissance," in *Beyond Their Sex*, ed. Patricia Labalme, 66–90.

45. For the links between courtiership and love poetry, see Greenblatt, *Renaissance Self-Fashioning*; Arthur Marotti, " 'Love is not love:' Elizabethan Sonnet Sequences and the Social Order," *ELH* 49 (Summer 1982): 396–428 ; and Ann Rosalind Jones and Peter Stallybrass, "The Politics of *Astrophil and Stella*," *SEL* 24 (Winter 1984): 53–68.

46. Abdelkader Salza cites the epitaph in "Madonna Gasparina Stampa secondo nuove indagini," *GSLI* 62 (1913): 79. Maria Bellonci in her introduction to Stampa's *Rime* (Milan: Rizzoli, 1976) suggests Aretino as the author of this and other scurrilous poems about Stampa (20).

47. Cited by Josephine Roberts, *The Poems of Lady Mary Wroth* (Baton Rouge: Louisiana State University Press, 1983), 32, 34.

48. For defenses of women, see Marc Angenot, *Les Champions des femmes* (Montréal: Presses de l'Université de Québec, 1977), and Joan Kelly, "Early Feminist Theory and the *Querelle des femmes*, 1400–1789," *Signs* 8 (Fall 1982): 4–28.

49. Christine de Pisan, *Le Livre de la Cité des Dames* (Paris, 1405), trans. as *The Book of the City of Ladies* by Earl Jeffrey Richards (New York: Persea Books, 1982), 20.

50. Hélisenne de Crenne, *Epistres invectives* (1539), 3, quoted in *Le Grief des femmes*, ed. Maïté Albistur and Daniel Armogathe (Paris: Hier et Demain, 1978), I:37.

51. Louise Labé, "A M.C.D.B.L.," in *Oeuvres complètes*, ed. François Rigolot (Paris: Flammarion, 1986), 41.

52. Marie de Gournay, *L'Egalité des hommes et des femmes* (Paris, 1622), ed. Mario Schiff (Paris: Champion, 1910; rpt. Geneva: Slatkine, 1978), 65.

53. Marie de Gournay, *Le Grief des femmes* (1626), Schiff ed., 94.

54. François Billon, *Le Fort inexpugnable de l'honneur du sexe femenin* (Paris, 1555), 34–38.

55. Ludovico Ariosto, *Orlando furioso* (1532), ed. Lanfranco Caretti (Milan: Riccardo Ricciardi, 1954), XXXVII, vi, 8.

56. Richard Mulcaster, *Positions Concerning the Training Up of Children* (1581), cited by Beilin, *Redeeming Eve*, 11.

57. Ginevra Conti Odorisi, *Donne e società nel seicento* (Rome: Bulzoni, 1979), 35–46. See also Adriana Chemello, "La donna, il modello, l'immaginario: Moderata Fonte e Lucrezia Marinelli," in *Nel cerchio della luna*, 102–103.

58. Quoted by Chemello, "La donna," 109.

59. Marinelli's remark about Gambara is cited by Chemello, "La donna," 159.

60. Veronica Gambara, *Rime* (Venice, 1554), in *Rime di tre gentildonne del secolo XVI*, ed. Olindo Guerrini (Milan: Sonzogno, 1930), 345.

61. Vittoria Colonna, *Tutte le rime della Illustriss. et Eccellentissima Signora Vittoria Colonna, Marchesana di Pescara* (Venice, 1558), Sonnet 79, Guerrino, 51.

62. Veronica Gambara, *Rime* (1554), "Rime di vari autori a Veronica Gambara," in Guerrino, 373. Bertani was Bolognese, a Petrarchan poet who corresponded with Annibal Caro and exchanged verses with Luigi Battiferri.

2. WRITING TO LIVE

1. For writers' claims that their writing had been pirated, see Edwin Miller, *The Professional Writer in Elizabethan England* (Cambridge: Harvard University Press, 1959), 141–48.

2. For the "hopeless economic predicament" of Elizabethan professional writers, see Miller's chapter "Writers and Stationers," especially 137–40. An interesting analysis of the economic and ideological situation of Renaissance writers is Elizabeth Eisenstein, "The Rise of a New Class of 'Men of Letters,' " in *The Printing Revolution in Early Modern Europe* (Cambridge: Cambridge University Press, 1983), 97–104. For an analysis of popular writers in sixteenth-century France, see Natalie Zemon Davis,

"Printing and the People," in *Society and Culture in Early Modern France* (Stanford: Stanford University Press, 1975).

3. On the patronage of Mary Sidney, see Mary Ellen Lamb, "The Countess of Pembroke's Patronage," *ELR* 12 (Spring 1982). Lamb argues that many dedications written to Mary Sidney were actually attempts to reach her husband and her oldest son through her rather than appeals to her alone.

4. I intend this term, which comes from the verb *bricoler*, literally "to tinker, to improvise, to do it oneself," slightly differently from Claude Lévi-Strauss. In *Totemism* and *The Savage Mind*, he used it to refer to the spontaneous logic through which preliterate peoples translate natural phenomena into symbolic codes in order to make cultural sense of their surroundings. I use it to describe a literate kind of tinkering, the hybridization of disparate literary modes through which women produce new mixed genres. For a discussion of the term, see Terence Hawkes, *Structuralism and Semiotics* (Berkeley and Los Angeles: University of California Press, 1977), 51–54.

5. R. J. Fehrenbach studies Whitney's publisher in "Isabella Whitney and the Popular Miscellanies of Richard Jones," *Cahiers élisabéthains* 19 (1981): 85–87.

6. Isabella Whitney, *A Sweet Nosgay, Or Pleasant Posye: contayning a hundred and ten Phylosophicall Flowers* (London: Richard Jones, 1573), sig. A5r. A facsimile of both of Whitney's texts has been edited by Richard Panofsky in *The Floures of Philosophie (1572) by Sir Hugh Plat and A sweet Nosgay (1573) and The Copy of a Letter (1567) by Isabella Whitney* (Delmar, N.Y.: Scholars' Facsimiles and Reprints, 1982). For an introduction to Whitney's poems and excerpts from several, see Betty Travitsky, *The Paradise of Women: Writings by Englishwomen of the Renaissance* (Westport, Conn.: Greenwood Press, 1981), 117–27. R. J. Fehrenbach identifies Whitney's family and local connections in "Isabella Whitney, Sir Hugh Plat, Geoffrey Whitney, and 'Sister Eldershae,'" *ELN* 21 (1983): 7–11.

7. Miller, *Professional Writer*, 120.

8. For observations about the self-defenses implicit in Whitney's preface, I am indebted to Tina Krontiris's dissertation, "Oppositional Voices: Women's Secular Writings and Dominant Ideology in the English Renaissance" (University of Sussex, 1987), chap. 3. Vives's *Instruction of a Christian Woman* is one source for the view that women should not interpret Scripture on their own: he mentions the Gospels and the Epistles as useful texts but adds, "But as touching some, wise and learned men must be asked counsel of in them. Nor the woman ought not to follow her own judgment" (*Vives and the Renascence Education of Women*, ed. Foster Watson [New York: Longmans, 1912], 62). Vives also states that women's reading should expose them to ennobling models rather than historical villainy; hence his recommendation that moral philosophers rather than poets be emphasized in the curriculum for girls (59–60, 146–47).

9. Betty Travitsky, "'The Wyll and Testament' of Isabella Whitney," *ELR* 10 (1980): 77.

10. Krontiris points out Berrie's remark about Whitney's choice of genre in her chapter on Whitney. By "brute" he may mean Brutus, the Trojan hero represented as the founder of Britain by Tudor historians such as Polydore Virgil.

11. Panofsky, *Floures*, xii–xiii.

12. For an overview of Elizabethan uses of Ovid, see Elizabeth Story Donno's introduction to *Elizabethan Minor Epics* (New York: Columbia University Press, 1963; rpt. 1967). A useful study of the *Heroides*, stressing the inward-looking quality of the psychological portraits, is Howard Jacobson, *Ovid's "Heroides"* (Princeton: Princeton University Press, 1974), chap. 18, "The Role of Perspective." My point is that Whitney incorporates a much more public perspective into her use of Ovid's form and characters.

13. For these and other controversies about women, see Linda Woodbridge, *Women and the English Renaissance: Literature and the Nature of Womankind, 1540–1620* (Urbana: University of Illinois Press, 1984), chaps. 1–6.

14. An analysis of English conduct books that takes Greene's concerns as its title is Suzanne Hull's *Chaste, Silent and Obedient: English Books for Women, 1475–1640* (San Marino, Calif.: Huntington Library, 1982).

15. For a study of "The Admonition" as an example of early feminist protest, see Betty Travitsky, "The Lady Doth Protest: Protest in the Popular Writings of Renaissance Englishwomen," *ELR* 14 (1984): 255–63.

16. Travitsky makes this point in "The Lady Doth Protest," 262.

17. For biographical information about the Des Roches, see George Diller, *Les Dames des Roches: Etude sur la vie litteraire à Poitiers dans la deuxième moitié du XVIe siècle* (Paris: Droz, 1936), Part 1, chap. 1. I am indebted to Diller's groundbreaking study throughout my discussion of the Des Roches.

18. *Les Missives des Mes-dames Des Roches de Poitiers mère et fille* (Paris: Abel L'Angelier, 1586), "Epistre à ma fille," A2r.

19. *Missives*, 5r and 9r, cited by Diller, *Les Dames*, 22–23. For an excellent study of Madeleine as well as Catherine des Roches, see Anne R. Larsen, "The French Humanist Scholars: Les Dames des Roches," in *Women Writers of the Renaissance and Reformation*, ed. Katharina Wilson (Athens: University of Georgia Press, 1987).

20. Cited by Diller, *Les Dames*, 85.

21. *Les Missives des Mes-dames des Roches de Poitiers mère et fille* (Lyon: Nicholas Hamilton, 1604), 130. This final collection includes the first and second *Oeuvres* in addition to *La Puce*.

22. Diller discusses this manuscript, *Les Dames*, 163–67.

23. Quoted in Diller, *Les Dames*, 23.

24. For Scaliger's letter praising Madeleine des Roches, see Diller, *Les Dames*, 12–13; for Catherine's letter on the sonnet in which Ronsard praised her lover-hero, Sincero, 39–40; for Marie de Romieu, 22.

25. For a discussion of this salon, see Louis Clark Keating, *Studies on the Literary Salon in France, 1550–1615* (Cambridge: Harvard University Press, 1941).

26. Cited in Diller, *Les Dames*, 67. My translation.

27. For the sources for flea poems and an analysis of how Catherine as a woman poet transforms the poet-audience relationships in the tradition, see Cathy Yandell, "Of Lice and Women: Rhetoric and Gender in *La Puce de Madame des Roches*," forthcoming in *Romance Notes*.

28. For remarks on the fetishistic voyeurism of this much-republished collection, see Françoise Charpentier, Préface, *Louise Labé, Oeuvres poétiques; Pernette du Guillet, Rymes* (Paris: Gallimard, 1983), 13–16. For analysis of the sexual politics implicit in *blason* poetry in the Petrarchan mode, see Nancy Vickers, "Diana Described: Scattered Woman and Scattered Rhyme," *Critical Inquiry* 8 (1981): 265–79.

29. *La Puce de Madame Des-Roches, qui est un recueil de divers poèmes Grecs, Latins et François, Composez par plusieurs doctes personnages aux Grans Jours tenus à Poitiers l'an MDLXXIX* (Paris: Abel L'Angelier, 1583), 4.

30. Diller, *Les Dames*, 73.

31. I have conjecturally changed the verb in this line from "mommer" (to disguise) to "nommer" (to name). Although either reading makes sense, Catherine's play on names in the poem disposes me to think "nommer" was intended.

32. Baldessare Castiglione, *Il Cortegiano* (Venice, 1523), ed. Bruno Maier, 2nd ed. (Turin: UTET, 1964), 343.

33. Nifo's courtly manual includes many examples of *affabilità*, verbal maneuvers through which his ideal *donna di corte* makes her way through erotic repartee. See Ruth Kelso, *Doctrine for the Lady of the Renaissance* (Urbana: University of Illinois Press, 1956; rpt. 1978), 215–17, and my "Nets and Bridles: Early Modern Conduct Books and Sixteenth-century Women's Lyric," in *The Ideology of Conduct*, ed. Nancy Armstrong and Len Tennenhouse (New York: Methuen, 1987), 46–47.

34. Théodore de Bèze, "Les Vertus de la femme fidele et bonne mesnagere," in *Le Miroir des femmes*, ed. Luce Guillerm, Jean-Pierre Guillerm, Laurence Hordoir, and Marie-Françoise Piéjus (Lille: Presses Universitaires, 1983), 21.

35. *Les Oeuvres de Mes-dames des Roches de Poetiers, mère et fille* (Paris: Abel L'Angelier, 1578), 148.

36. I am grateful to Thalia Pandiri and E. Brown Kennedy for a stimulating discussion of this poem. Barbara Johnson, in a paper on Phillis Wheatley (MLA, 1987), identified "excessive compliance" as a strategy of mocking racial constraints; Catherine's maneuver is similar. For a pessimistic view of the poem's "fragmenting ambivalence," which I do not share, see Tilde Sankovitch, "Inventing Authority of Origin: The Difficult Enterprise," in *Women of the Middle Ages and Renaissance: Literary and Historical Perspectives*, ed. Mary Beth Rose (Syracuse: Syracuse University Press, 1986), 239–42.

37. Larsen, "French Humanist Scholars," 239.

38. *Les Secondes oeuvres de Mes-dames des Roches de Poictiers Mere et Fille* (Poitiers: Nicholas Courtoys, 1583), 35.

39. See Larsen, "French Humanist Scholars," for an explanation of Catherine's pseudonym, 241 n. 11.

40. Diller argues for Pellejay as Sincero, *Les Dames*, 35–51.

41. The sonnet (*Canzoniere*, 189) begins, "Passa la nave mia colma d'obblio" (My ship, loaded with forgetfulness, moves). Franceso Petrarca, *Il Canzoniere*, ed. Gianfranco Contini (Turin: Einaudi, 1972), 245.

42. Compare, for example, the opening of the last *dizain* of Maurice Scève's *Dèlie* (1544): "Flamme si saincte en son cler durera / Tousjours luysante en publique apparence, / Tant que ce Monde en soy demeurera, / Et qu'on aura Amour en reverence" (A flame so holy will last in its brilliance / Shining forever in public view, / As long as this World endures, / And Love is still revered), *"La Délie" de Maurice Scève*, ed. I. D. McFarlane (Cambridge: Cambridge University Press, 1966), 365.

43. Diller, *Les Dames*, 124–27.

44. *The Poems of Sir Philip Sidney*, ed. William Ringler, Jr. (Oxford: Clarendon Press, 1962), 236.

45. I am using "specular" here in the sense that Luce Irigaray gives it in her study of men's use of women as the other to construct masculinity-affirming images for themselves throughout Western philosophy (*Speculum de l'autre femme* [Paris: Minuit, 1974], trans. as *Speculum of the Other Woman* by Gillian Gill [Ithaca: Cornell University Press, 1985]). For a brilliant example of how the term can be used to analyze a specific text (Balzac's "Adieu"), see Shoshanna Felman, "Women and Madness: the Critical Phallacy," *Diacritics* 5, no. 4 (1975): 2–10.

46. I refer to Michel Foucault's historicization of the author as a changing cultural concept in "What Is an Author?" trans. Donald Bouchard and Sherry Simon, in *Language, Counter-memory, Practice: Selected Essays and Interviews of Michel Foucault*, ed. Donald Bouchard (Ithaca: Cornell University Press, 1977). Against Roland Barthes's call for a new kind of reading for the free play of modernist texts in "The Death of the Author," trans. Stephen Heath, in *Image, Music, Text* (New York: Hill and Wang, 1977), however, I am proposing a rehistoricizing reading, the replacement of women's lyric in its ideological contexts.

3. THE POETICS OF GROUP IDENTITY

1. Sperone Speroni, *Dialoghi d'amore* (Venice, 1542). For excerpts and a commentary on Scève's use of Speroni, see I. D. McFarlane, *The 'Délie' of Maurice Scève* (Cambridge: Cambridge University Press, 1966), appendix A, 482–90.

2. On Guazzo, see Frank Whigham, *Ambition and Privilege: The Social Tropes of Elizabethan Courtesy Theory* (Berkeley: University of California Press, 1984), especially 123–25. Whigham argues that Guazzo protects himself in his first and fourth books against accusations of treasonous thinking by attributing the criticism of princes to one character and having another one correct his views, and this double game is certainly one potential of dialogue form. In Book 2, however, Annibal's social sense clearly makes him the leader in the dialogue.

3. Mikhail Bakhtin, *Rabelais and his World*, trans. Helene Iswolsky (Bloomington: Indiana University Press, 1984); *Problems of Dostoevsky's Poetics*, trans. Caryl Emerson (Minneapolis: University of Minnesota Press, 1984); *The Dialogic Imagination: Four Essays by M. M. Bakhtin*, ed. Michael Holquist (Austin: University of Texas Press, 1981), especially "Discourse in the Novel."

4. David Marsh contrasts the open-ended Ciceronian dialogue, used to train rhetoricians in arguing both sides of a question, to the medieval dialogue, often closer to a catechism than to an investigation of possible truths, in *The Quattrocento Dialogue: Classical Tradition and Humanist Innovation* (Cambridge: Harvard University Press, 1980).

5. For a discussion of Ebreo's text, a model for Neoplatonic discourse throughout Europe, see T. Anthony Perry, "Dialogue and Doctrine in Leone Ebreo's *Dialoghi d'amore*," *PMLA* 88 (1973): 1173–79.

6. Jacqueline Risset, *L'Anagramme du desir: essai sur la "Délie" de Maurice Scève* (Rome: Bulzoni, 1971), chap. 1 .

7. Ibid., 20. Henri Weber makes the same point in his chapter "La Condition sociale des poètes et l'influence de la vie de cour," in *La Création poétique au XVIe siècle en France* (Paris: Nizet, 1956). On the economic and political circumstances promoting the cultural vitality of Lyon, see Lucien Romier, "Lyons and Cosmopolitanism at the Beginning of the French Renaissance," in *French Humanism, 1470–1600* , ed. Werner Gundersheimer (New York: Harper and Row, 1969) and Natalie Davis, "City Women and Religious Change," in *Society and Culture in Early Modern France* (Stanford: Stanford University Press, 1975).

8. For the Scève sisters, see Verdun Saulnier, "Etude sur Pernette du Guillet et ses *Rymes*," *Bibliothèque d'humanisme et Renaissance* 4 (1944): 26.

9. For studies stressing the relative informality of intellectual life in Lyon, see Saulnier's "Etude sur Pernette" and his *Maurice Scève* (Paris: Klincksieck, 1948); Enzo Giudici, *Louise Labé et l'"Ecole lyonnaise"* (Naples: Liguori, 1964); Ian McFarlane's introduction to *Délie*. François Rigolot emphasizes that the term "Ecole lyonnaise" is a later fiction, implying a more clearly defined group than actually existed in the 1550s; he relates Louise Labé's linguistic freedom to the "decentralized" situation of writers in Lyon in "Gender vs. Sex Difference in Louise Labé's Grammar of Love," in *Rewriting the Renaissance: The Discourses of Sexual Difference in Early Modern Europe*, ed. Margaret Ferguson, Maureen Quilligan, and Nancy Vickers (Chicago: University of Chicago Press, 1986).

10. Du Moulin remarks in his preface to *Les Rymes* that he is publishing Pernette's poems "pour satisfaire à ceulx, à qui privément en maintes bonnes compaignies elle les recitoit à propos" (*Les Rymes*, ed. Victor Graham [Geneva: Droz, 1966], 3). All further quotations from Pernette are from this edition.

11. For a discussion of this debate and the publication of poems by Pernette before *Les Rymes*, see Joachim Du Bellay, *Deffence et illustration de la langue françoyse*, ed. Henri Chamard (Paris: Didier, 1948; rpt. 1966), 114–16, and Saulnier's "Etude," 109–10.

12. Randle Cotgreve, in his 1611 *Dictionarie of the French and English Tongues*, offers five different categories of meaning for the word, none specifically linked to chastity: "Vertue: Vertue, goodnesse, honestie, sinceritie, integritie; worth, perfection, desert, merit; also, valour, prowesse, manhood; also, energie, efficacie, force, power, might; also, a good part or propertie, a commendable qualitie."

13. For the history of the epigram during this period, see Saulnier's "Etude" and Joyce Miller, "Convention and Form in the *Rymes* of Pernette du Guillet" (Ph.D. diss., University of Pennsylvania, 1977), chap. 2.

14. *Délie*, 119.

15. For "regraver," see Miller, "Convention and Form," 59.

16. For Ficino's summary of this interchange, see Sears Jayne, *Marsilio Ficino's Commentary on Plato's "Symposium"*, University of Missouri Studies, no. 1 (Columbia: University of Missouri Press, 1944), 144–45. For Ebreo's version in the form in which it was best known in Lyon, see the 1551 translation by Pontus de Tyard, *Léon Hebreu: Dialogues d'amour*, ed. T. Anthony Perry (Chapel Hill: University of North Carolina Press, 1974), 37–54.

17. *Ragionamento del Sig. Annibal Guasco a D. Lavinia sua figliuola della maniera del governarsi ella in corte* (Turin, 1586), C4v.

18. For an explanation of this term, see McFarlane, *Délie*, 448 n. 10.

19. Robert Griffin, "Pernette du Guillet's Response to Scève: A Case for Abstract Love," *L'Esprit créateur* 5 (1965): 116.

20. Robert Cottrell, in a more positive evaluation of Pernette, points out her use of the Neoplatonic code as a means of establishing a power balance between herself and Scève: "the Platonic myths . . . provided her with a pattern of behavior according to which she could regularize and determine her future contacts with the older poet. They determined in fact the form of her future relations with him by suggesting a code of manners" ("Pernette du Guillet's *Rymes*: An Adventure in Ideal Love," *Bibliothèque d'humanisme et renaissance* 31 [1969]: 555).

21. One citation of this image occurs in Orazio Lombardelli's *Dell'Uffizio della Donna Maritata* (Florence, 1585), 59.

22. Juan Vives, *Le Livre de l'institution de la femme chrestienne*, Book 2, chap. 3. Cited in *Le Miroir des femmes, 1: Moralistes et polémistes au XVIe siecle*, ed. Luce Guillerm et al. (Lille: Presses Universitaires, 1983), 76. My italics.

23. T. Anthony Perry, "Pernette du Guillet's Poetry of Love and Desire," *BHR* 35 (1973): 259–71. I took issue with his interpretation in my "Assimilation with a Difference: Renaissance Women Poets and Literary Influence," *Yale French Studies*, no. 62 (1981), but the rationalizing, self-correcting nervousness of Pernette's poem certainly indicates some kind of uneasiness.

24. Saulnier, *Maurice Scève*, 1:260; Risset, *L'Anagramme*, 59–61. The changeability of such judgments is amusingly demonstrated, however, in Saulnier's research on Pernette. Concentrating on her work four years earlier, he had argued that her poem was a rewriting of Scève's ("Etude," 27).

25. Graham points out that Marot also confused the two figures (*Rymes*, 56 n. 2). For a richly suggestive discussion of treatments of Danaë, see Leonard Barkan, *The Gods Made Flesh: Metamorphosis and the Pursuit of Paganism* (New Haven: Yale University Press, 1987), 189–98. Lynne Lawner argues that Italian paintings of Danaë were often modeled on courtesans in the Cinquecento, in *The Lives of the Courtesans* (New York: Rizzoli, 1987), 151–59.

26. For comments on La Borderie's "Amye de court," see my chap. 1 and Marie-Françoise Piéjus's preface to the text in *Le Miroir des femmes*, 199.

27. Cotgreve translates "equité" as follows: "Equitie, equalitie; evennesse; uprightnesse; mitigation of rigour; moderation of humour; mildnesse, clemencie, mercifulnesse." Constance Jordan suggests that the most accurate translation of Pernette's last two lines would be "Virtue, measured by the doctrine of fairness" in the application of the rule of male headship over women (private communication, March 7, 1988).

28. See, for example, in Pontus de Tyard's translation of Ebreo's *Dialoghi d'amore*, the distinction that Sophie makes at the end of the first dialogue: "Lovers certainly suffer many afflictions until they reach the point toward which their desire yearns; but after they have enjoyed it, all their tempests change into happy fortune; thus

their suffering obviously results from desire for the thing not yet possessed, rather than love of it" (Perry ed., 73).

29. A good early study of courtesans is Arturo Graf's "Veronica Franco: una cortigiana fra mille," in *Attraverso il Cinquecento* (Turin: Loescher, 1888); Graf lists various categories of courtesans and prostitutes, 188ff. Guido Biagi's biography of Tullia includes some history of courtesanship in Rome and Florence: *Tullia d'Aragona: una ètera romana* (Florence, 1887). See also Georgina Masson, *Courtesans of the Italian Renaissance* (New York: St. Martin's Press, 1976), chap. 5.

30. Masson, *Courtesans,* 91, 113, 101.

31. For a modern edition of Tullia's dialogue, see Giuseppe Zonta, *Trattati d'amore del Cinquecento* (Bari: Laterza, 1912).

32. Cited by S. Bongi, "Il velo giallo di Tullia d'Aragona," *Rivisita critica della letterature italiana* 3 (March 1886). See also Masson, *Courtesans,* 119–20.

33. Cited by Celani, *Rime,* xxxix.

34. Homosocial bonding is Eve Kosofsky Sedgwick's term and topic in *Between Men: English Literature and Male Homosocial Desire* (New York: Columbia University Press, 1985).

35. Page numbers and numbers of poems refer to the original edition of *Le Rime della Signora Tullia d'Aragona; et di diversi à lui* (Venice: Gabriel Giolito de Ferrari, 1547). I have used the 1547 edition rather than the 1891 edition by Enrico Celani, *Le Rime di Tullia d'Aragona, cortigiana del secolo XVI* (Bologna: Gaetano Romagnoli, 1891; rpt. 1968), because Celani rearranges the poems so as to erase the *proposte/risposte* sections. He also ends the first section of Tullia's sonnets with two elegiac poems that were either placed earlier in the 1547 edition ("Alma del vero bel chiara sembianza") or not included at all ("Lieto viss'io sotto un bianco lauro"). I have incorporated his modernization of "et" as "e" and his corrections of typographical errors, however.

36. For links between poets and courtly patrons in Italy, see José Guidi, "Baldessar Castiglione et le pouvoir politique: du gentilhomme de cour au nonce pontifical," in *Les Ecrivains et le pouvoir en Italie à l'epoque de la Renaissance,* ed. André Rochon (Paris: Sorbonne Nouvelle, 1975); for Ariosto, see Giorgio Padoan, "L'Orlando furioso e la crisi del Rinascimento," in *Ariosto 1974 in America,* ed. Aldo Scaglione (Ravenna: Longo, 1976) and Peter Marinelli, *Ariosto and Boiardo* (Columbia: University of Missouri Press, 1987), chap. 3, "Homage to the House."

37. Frank Whigham, "The Rhetoric of Elizabethan Suitors' Letters," *PMLA* 96 (1981): 864–82.

38. I am using "polylogue," the title of a collection of essays by Julia Kristeva (Paris: Tel Quel, 1977), in a slightly different sense from hers. She stresses the psychic multivalence and diversity of signifying modes in a single writer and text, while I use the term to describe the interactions within a group text.

39. I discuss Sannazaro and other Italian poets' use of the myth in "New Songs for the Swallow: Ovid's Philomela in Tullia d'Aragona and Gaspara Stampa," in *Refiguring Woman: Gender Studies and the Italian Renaissance,* ed. Marilyn Migiel and Juliana Schiesari (Ithaca: Cornell University Press, 1990).

40. *The Poems of Sir Philip Sidney,* ed. William Ringler (Oxford: Oxford University Press, 1962), 182.

4. FEMININE PASTORAL AS HEROIC MARTYRDOM

1. A long debate about whether or not Stampa was a courtesan is still unresolved. Abdelkader Salza argued that she was a courtesan in two articles in the *Giornale storico della letteratura italiana,* "Madonna Gasparina Stampa secondo nuove in-

dagini," 62 (1913): 1–101; "Madonna Gasparina Stampa e la società veneziana del suo tempo," 70 (1917): 1–60, 280–99. A long counterargument was published by Elisa Innocenzi Greggio, "In Difesa di Gaspara Stampa," *L'Ateneo veneto* 38, 1 (1915): 4–157. The issue was cooled down with a compromise suggested by Gioachino Brognoligo in a review of the debate (*GSLI* 76 [1920]: 134–45): as a *virtuosa*, Stampa led a life freer than any permitted to the noblewomen of Venice, but she was employed as a musical rather than a sexual performer (144–45). For a summary of her life and the debate, see Fiora Bassanese, *Gaspara Stampa* (Boston: Twayne, 1983), chap. 1.

2. For a study of academies that Stampa may have joined, including the Dubbiosi, see Greggio, "In Difesa," 29 and appendixes 1, 2, 4a.

3. For Wroth's biography, see Josephine Roberts's introduction to *The Poems of Lady Mary Wroth* (Baton Rouge: Louisiana State University Press, 1983) and a condensed account in Margaret Hannay's "Lady Wroth: Mary Sidney," in *Women Writers of the Renaissance and Reformation*, ed. Katharina Wilson (Athens: University of Georgia Press, 1987), 548–54.

4. Bassanese, *Gaspara Stampa*, 128, n. 16, citing Angelo Ventura, *Nobiltà e popolo nella società veneta del '400 e '500* (Bari: Laterza, 1964).

5. Maria Bellonci reproduces the double portrait and comments on it in her edition of *Le Rime* (Milan: Rizzoli, 1976), 64–65. Eugenio Donadoni offers the information that Collaltino's portrait is copied from a portrait by Titian, in *Gaspara Stampa: vita e opere* (Messina: Principato, 1919), 16.

6. Roberts, *Poems of Lady Mary Wroth*, 24.

7. For an extended discussion of the Denny/Wroth exchange, see Roberts, ibid., 31–35.

8. For an interpretation of Wroth's romance as both critique of and concession to Stuart constraints on women, see Carolyn Ruth Swift, "Feminine Identity in Lady Mary Wroth's Romance *Urania*," *ELR* 14 (Autumn 1984): 328–46. Elaine Beilin takes Pamphilia's constancy as the theme of the romance, which, she argues, Wroth contrasts to "the inconstancy and deviation from reason" of the male characters; see her chapter on Wroth in *Redeeming Eve: Women Writers of the English Renaissance* (Princeton: Princeton University Press, 1987), especially 217. See also Mary Ellen Lamb, *The Authorship of Women in the Sidney Circle* (forthcoming, University of Wisconsin Press), chaps. 4 and 5, and Maureen Quilligan, "The Anthropology of Intertextuality: Incest and Female Authority in Wroth's *Urania* Poems," in *Soliciting Interpretations: Essays on Seventeenth-Century Poetry*, ed. Elizabeth Harvey and Katherine Maus (Chicago: University of Chicago Press, 1990).

9. For a study of dedications and poetic exchanges that suggest how socially engaged Wroth remained even after she left the court, see May Nelson Paulissen, "The Love Sonnets of Lady Mary Wroth: A Critical Introduction" (Ph.D. diss., University of Houston, 1976), chap. 2.

10. All quotations from *Pamphilia to Amphilanthus* are from Roberts's edition of *The Poems*, including her numbering system.

11. Renato Poggioli, "The Oaten Flute," *Harvard Library Bulletin* 11 (1957): 158.

12. Giason Denores, *Apologia contra l'auttor del Verato*, cited by Bernard Weinberg in *A History of Literary Criticism in the Italian Renaissance* (Chicago: University of Chicago Press, 1961), 2:674–75.

13. Weinberg, *History of Literary Criticism*, 2: chap. 21.

14. *A Defence of Poetry*, in *Miscellaneous Prose of Sir Philip Sidney*, ed. Katherine Duncan-Jones and Jan Van Dorsten (Oxford: Clarendon, 1973), 95.

15. William Webbe, *A Discourse of English Poetrie*, in *Elizabethan Critical Essays*, ed. Gregory Smith (Oxford: Clarendon, 1904), 1:262.

16. Louis Adrian Montrose, " 'Eliza, Queene of Shepheardes,' and the Pastoral of Power," *ELR* 10 (Spring 1980): 155.

17. Kenneth Burke, *A Rhetoric of Motives* (New York: Prentice-Hall, 1950), 124.

18. For a study stressing, in part, the "archaeological" dimension of Sannazaro's project, see William J. Kennedy, *Jacopo Sannazaro and the Uses of Pastoral* (Hanover, N.H.: University Press of New England, 1983).

19. William Empson, "Proletarian Literature," in *Some Versions of Pastoral* (New York: New Directions, 1960), 23.

20. Louis Adrian Montrose, "Of Gentlemen and Shepherds: The Politics of Elizabethan Pastoral Form," *ELH* 50 (Fall 1983): 447–48.

21. On Wroth's masque, see Roberts, *Poems of Lady Mary Wroth*, 37–39. For Jonson's uses of pastoral in the country house poem, see Don Wayne, *Penshurst: The Semiotics of Place and the Poetics of History* (Madison: University of Wisconsin Press, 1984).

22. I cite Stampa's sonnet (267) from Bellonci's edition of *Le Rime*. Her edition is based on Abdelkader Salza's edition for *Scrittori d'Italia*, vol. 52: *Gaspara Stampa, Veronica Franco* (Bari: Laterza, 1913). Bellonci accepts Salza's reordering of the sequence, which suggests a religious conversion and suppresses the Neoplatonic turn with which it ends in the 1554 original. For readers' convenience, however, I, too, refer to his numbering of the sonnets.

23. Harry Berger, Jr., "Orpheus, Pan and the Poetics of Misogyny: Spenser's Critique of Pastoral Love and Art," *ELH* 50 (1983): 27–60. For an analysis of Cervantes's critique of masculine bias in pastoral, see Renato Poggioli, "The Pastoral of the Self," *Daedalus* 88 (1959): 686–99.

24. See Bellonci, *Le Rime*, 120 n. 1.

25. For a discussion of civic ritual and cultural modes celebrating the city, see Franco Gaeta, "Alcune considerazioni sul mito de Venezia," *Bibliothèque d'humanisme et Renaissance* 23 (1961): 58–75; Edwin Muir, *Civic Ritual in Renaissance Venice* (Princeton: Princeton University Press, 1980); Rona Goffen, *Patronage and Piety in Renaissance Venice* (New Haven: Yale University Press, 1986).

26. Kenneth Burke, *A Rhetoric of Motives*, 124. Cited in Montrose, "Of Gentlemen and Shepherds," 417.

27. For Stampa's reception, see Bassanese, *Gaspara Stampa*, chap. 2.

28. Francesco Petrarca, *Canzoniere*, ed. Gianfranco Contini (Turin: Einaudi, 1972), 125.

29. On differences between the Venetian patriciate and the nobles of the Terraferma, see Oliver Logan, *Culture and Society in Venice, 1470–1790* (New York: Scribner's, 1972), 33–34.

30. Croce describes the poem as "quella sorta d'inno da 'traviata,' " in *Conversazioni critiche* (Bari: Laterza, 1918), 2:230. His view is refuted by Bellonci, *Le Rime*, 181 n. 1, and Bassanese, *Gaspara Stampa*, 109.

31. Gustavo Ceriello, in a note to the poem in his edition of the *Rime* (Milan: Rizzoli, 1954), suggests Tibullus, *Elegies* I, 10, 5–15, as a source. For a discussion of Golden Age passages in Latin poets generally, see A. Bartlett Giamatti, *The Earthly Paradise and the Renaissance Epic* (Princeton: Princeton University Press, 1966), chap. 1.

32. Benedetto Croce, "La Lirica cinquecentesca," in *Poesia populare e poesia d'arte* (Bari: Laterza, 1933), 369.

33. Justin Vitiello, "Gaspara Stampa: The Ambiguities of Martyrdom," *Modern Language Notes* 90 (1975): 63–64.

34. Donata Chimenti Vassalli, "Emancipazione e schiavitù in Gaspara Stampa," *Osservatore Politico Letterario* 18, 9 (1972): 70–85. This ahistorical and peculiarly antifeminist summary of the poems treats them unquestioningly as autobiography and presents as fact many conjectures about Stampa's life.

35. The category of the marvelous, an adaptation of ancient attributions of that quality to the orator/poet, was central to Italian epic theory. Means for achieving it were discussed by Tasso in his *Discorso dell'arte poetica; et in particolare del poema*

heroico (1587); it was the single topic of Giovanni Talentoni's *Discorso sopra la maraviglia* (1597). See Weinberg, *History of Literary Criticism*, 1:238–39 and passim.

36. *Metamorphoses*, IX, 647–48. For a history of the Chimera in ancient and modern literature, see Ginevra Bompiani, "The Chimera Herself," in *Fragments for a History of the Human Body*, 1 (New York: Zone, 1989).

37. Frank Warnke, "Aphrodite's Priestess, Love's Martyr: Gaspara Stampa," in *Women Writers of the Renaissance and Reformation*, ed. Katharina Wilson (Athens: University of Georgia Press, 1987), 5–6.

38. Rainer Maria Rilke, *The Notebooks of Malte Laurids Brigge*, trans. Stephen Mitchell (New York: Vintage, 1985), 134, 235.

39. Donadoni, *Gaspara Stampa*, 58.

40. Jacopo Sannazaro, *Opere volgari*, ed. Alfredo Mauro (Bari: Laterza, 1961), 107, XIII, 46–54. See the comments of Ellen Lambert, *Placing Sorrow: A Study of the Pastoral Elegy Convention from Theocritus to Milton* (Chapel Hill: University of North Carolina Press, 1976), 92–93.

41. For analyses of love poetry as a discourse through which male courtiers dealt with political frustration, see the chapter on Thomas Wyatt in Stephen Greenblatt's *Renaissance Self-Fashioning: From More to Shakespeare* (Chicago: University of Chicago Press, 1980); Arthur Marotti, " 'Love is not Love': Elizabethan Sonnet Sequences and the Social Order," *ELH* 49 (1982): 396–428; and Ann Jones and Peter Stallybrass, "The Politics of *Astrophil and Stella*," *SEL* 24 (1984): 53–68.

42. Roberts, *Poems of Lady Mary Wroth*, 43–44.

43. Cited in ibid., 36.

44. For a parallel argument about a tree-carving sonnet written by Pamphilia in the *Urania*, see Maureen Quilligan, "The Anthropology of Intertextuality: Incest and Imitation in Wroth's *Urania*," n 5.

45. For details about the masques, see Roberts, *Poems of Lady Mary Wroth*, 12, 13 n. 28; D. J. Gordon, "The Imagery of Ben Jonson's Masques of Blacknesse and Beautie," in *The Renaissance Imagination: Essays and Lectures by D. J. Gordon*, ed. Stephen Orgel (Berkeley: University of California Press, 1975; rpt. 1980), 134–56; and Stephen Orgel and Roy Strong, *Inigo Jones: The Theatre of the Stuart Court* (Berkeley: Sotheby Parke Bernet and University of California Press, 1973), 1: "Colour Plates," figs. 1 and 88.

46. For these poems, see Paulissen, "Love Sonnets," 15.

47. For an analysis of Sidney's anticourtier poems, see Jones and Stallybrass, "Politics of *Astrophil and Stella*," 55–57.

48. Roy Strong analyzes melancholy as a visual and literary preoccupation during the period Wroth was composing her sonnets in "The Elizabethan Malady: Melancholy in Elizabethan and Jacobean Portraiture," *Apollo Magazine*, no. 79 (1964); rpt. in *The English Icon: Elizabethan and Jacobean Portraiture* (London: Routledge and Kegan Paul, 1969).

49. Len Tennenhouse argues that male dramatists' representations of women in physical torment reveal aristocratic clans' anxiety about the loss of control over women through misalliances, in *Power on Display: The Politics of Shakespeare's Genres* (Methuen, 1986), chap. 3: "The Theater of Punishment: Jacobean Tragedy and the Politics of Misogyny." His analysis has helped me to identify the conciliatory yet challenging strategy through which Wroth expiates her "sins" as a suitor for renewed favor. His focus on tragedy as a genre also helps to account for the theatrical imagery in Wroth's "torture" sonnets.

50. For a history of Wroth's difficulties in settling her debts, see Roberts, *Poems of Lady Mary Wroth*, 38–39.

51. Beilin, *Redeeming Eve*, 236–41.

52. See Elaine Beilin, " 'The Onely Perfect Virtue': Constancy in Mary Wroth's *Pamphilia to Amphilanthus*," *Spenser Studies* 2 (1985): 229–45, and *Redeeming Eve*; also Roberts, *Poems of Lady Mary Wroth*, 47–48. Paulissen points out the complication

introduced by the second appearance of the labyrinth line, however ("Love Sonnets," 136).

5. EROS EQUALIZED

1. Marie de Gournay, *L'Egalité des hommes et des femmes*, ed. Mario Schiff (Paris: Champion, 1910; rpt. Geneva: Slatkine, 1978), 65. Schiff cites her description of Italian women as "recluses en des cachots" from her treatise *De l'education des enfans de France*, 65 n. 1.

2. Lucien Bourgeois, *Quand la cour de France vivait à Lyon* (Paris: Fayard, 1980).

3. For publishing in Lyon, see Lucien Febvre and H.-J. Martin, *L'Apparition du livre* (Paris: Albin Michel, 1958), trans. as *The Coming of the Book* by David Gerard (Atlantic Highlands, N.J.: Humanities Press, 1976).

4. On Jean de Tournes, see A. Cartier, M. Audin, and E. Vial, *Bibliographie des éditions des De Tournes, imprimeurs lyonnais* (Paris: Bibliothèques nationales de la France, 1937), vol. 2.

5. Françoise Charpentier comments on the "porous" quality of social classes in Lyon in her preface to *Louise Labé, Oeuvres poétiques; Pernette du Guillet, Rymes* (Paris: Gallimard, 1983), 8.

6. The first research on Labé and her family was carried out by Charles Boy, in his edition of her *Oeuvres* (Paris: Lemerre, 1887), vol. 2. See also Jean Tricou, "Louise Labé et sa famille," *Bibliothèque d'humanisme et Renaissance* 5 (1944): 60–104.

7. Karine Berriot, *Louise Labé: La Belle Rebelle et le François nouveau* (Paris: Seuil, 1985), 167. See also Natalie Davis's estimate that over twenty women in Lyon at this period had reputations as writer/scholars, although she identifies most of them as the daughters of noblemen and professionals: "Printing and the People," in *Society and Culture in Early Modern France* (Stanford: Stanford University Press, 1975), 217.

8. For a study of this group, see Verdun Saulnier, *Maurice Scève* (Paris: Klincksieck, 1984), 1: chap. 6; also François Rigolot, "L'Hommage de 1555 à Louise Labé: les vers grecs, latins et italiens," in *Mélanges sur la littérature de la Renaissance à la mémoire de V.-L. Saulnier* (Geneva: Droz, 1984), 719–26.

9. Cited by Berriot, *La belle rebelle*, 187, following Fernand Zamaron, one of the first critical investigators of rumors relating to Labé in his *Louise Labé: dame de la franchise* (Paris: Nizet, 1968).

10. Cited in *Louise Labé: Oeuvres complètes*, ed. François Rigolot (Paris: Flammarion, 1986), 238–39. All quotations from Labé and from men writing about her come from this edition.

11. Natalie Zemon Davis, "City Women and Religious Change," in *Society and Culture*, 85–86.

12. For interpretations of attacks on Labé, see Zamaron, *Dame de la franchise*, 62–88; Berriot, *La belle rebelle*, chap. 10; Ann Rosalind Jones and Nancy J. Vickers, "Canon, Rule and the Restoration Renaissance," *Yale French Studies*, no. 75 (Fall 1988: *The Politics of Tradition: Placing Women in French Literature*).

13. Aubert recorded that she fought at the siege of 1542 in the ode he wrote in her honor (cited in Rigolot, *Louise Labé*, 183–84, stanzas 9–10). Charles Boy offered the plausible counterreading that Louise performed at a typically elaborate celebration staged by the Lyonnais for the Dauphin during his stay before the battle took place (*Oeuvres*, 2:38–42).

14. Cited in Boy, *Oeuvres*, 2:106.

15. Jean Calvin, *Gratulatio ad venerabilem dominum Gabrielum de Saconay* (1551), cited in Boy, *Oeuvres*, 2:101.

16. Cited in Boy, *Oeuvres*, 2:92.

17. "Des louenges de Dame Louïse Labé, Lionnoize," cited in Rigolot, *Louise Labé*, 193 (lines 441–48), 200 (line 651).

18. Jacques Peletier du Mans, *Opuscules* (Lyon: Jean de Tournes, 1555), cited in Rigolot, *Louise Labé*, 234.

19. Enzo Giudici, *Louise Labé: essai* (Paris: Nizet, 1981), 14.

20. Berriot, *La belle rebelle*, 163, and chap. 6 passim.

21. Giudici notes that the *L* disappeared from the second edition of 1555 but was replaced in 1556, when Jean de Tournes, consistently a promoter of the city, supervised the printing again (*Louise Labé: Oeuvres complètes* [Geneva: Droz, 1981], 17 n. 1).

22. Giudici, *Essai*, 59. For a discussion of sources for the preface, see 73–76; Berriot, *La belle rebelle*, 168–71. Anne R. Larsen relates the dedicatory epistle to "Louise Labé's *Débat de Folie et d'Amour*: Feminism and the Defense of Learning," *Tulsa Studies in Women's Literature* 2 (Spring 1983): 45–55.

23. Zamaron identifies Edouard Turquety and Prosper Blanchemain as the initiators of the Olivier de Magny and Henri II legends (*Dame de la franchise*, 32); Berriot points to Luc van Brabant as the source of the Marot and Henri II myths (*La belle rebelle*, 252 n. 3).

24. Olivier de Magny, *Odes amoureuses de 1559*, ed. Mark Whitney (Geneva: Droz, 1964), 132–36. For a "complete dossier" on Olivier de Magny, see the poems collected in Zamaron, *Dame de la franchise*, 149–77.

25. *Odes amoureuses*, Bk. 4, 11 (38–40).

26. For the two sonnets, see Rigolot, *Louise Labé*, 227–28. I analyze their relation briefly in "Assimilation with a Difference: Renaissance Women Poets and Literary Influence," *Yale French Studies*, no. 62 (1981): 148–50.

27. I discussed this elegy from a slightly different perspective in "City Women and their Audiences: Louise Labé and Veronica Franco," in *Rewriting the Renaissance*, ed. Margaret Ferguson, Maureen Quilligan, and Nancy Vickers (Chicago: University of Chicago Press, 1986), 299–316, and in "Surprising Fame: Renaissance Gender Ideologies and Women's Lyric," in *The Poetics of Gender*, ed. Nancy Miller (New York: Columbia University Press, 1986), 74–95.

28. Françoise Joukovsky links Labé's self-esteem in this exchange to the feminism she shared with her contemporaries in *La Gloire dans la poésie française et néolatine du XVIe siècle* (Geneva: Droz, 1969), 176–77.

29. Several critics remark on Labé's challenging posture: Gillian Jondorf, "Petrarchan Variations in Pernette du Guillet and Louise Labé," *MLR* 71 (1976): 773–74; M. W. Baker, "The Sonnets of Louise Labé: A Reappraisal," *Neophilologus* 60 (1976): 28; Charpentier, *Oeuvres poétiques*, 25, 29–30.

30. Charpentier, *Oeuvres poétiques*, 29; Rigolot, *Louise Labé*, 22–23.

31. Zamaron argues that Labé must have written the lines first (164–67), but both poets were probably circulating sonnets in manuscript during the year or so preceding their publication in 1555 and 1556.

32. One point of reference here is Julia Kristeva's notion of the semiotic, the pre-Oedipal desire for fusion with the mother, repressed but always present beneath the logical and gender rules of official language (the Symbolic order). See, for example, *La Révolution du langage poétique* (Paris: Seuil, 1974), trans. Margaret Waller (New York: Columbia University Press, 1984), chap. 1; and "D'une identité l'autre," *Tel Quel* 62 (Summer 1975), trans. as "From One Identity to Another" by Tom Gora and Alice Jardine in *Desire in Language* (New York: Columbia University Press, 1980), 124–47. Labé's desire for a permanent, gender-erasing fusion with the beloved man also needs to be explained historically, on the basis of her particular family, class, and cultural circumstances: the death of her mother before she was seven, the commuting careers of humanists such as Magny, and a society whose rigidly differentiated gender roles officially excluded women from poetic production.

33. François Rigolot, "Gender vs. Sex Difference in Louise Labé's Grammar of Love," in *Rewriting the Renaissance*, 287–98.

34. I. D. McFarlane, commenting on an emblem in his edition of Scève's *Délie*, cites a use of the tree-and-ivy image in Barthélemy Aneau's 1552 *Picta Poesis* to illustrate

the dangers of a woman's lust (201). It is possible that Labé was revising the connotation the image had been given by her male contemporary.

35. For an argument about these as Labé's "apprentice" poems and some very interesting comments on the implications of her name, see Anne Freadman, "Of Cats and Companions and the Name of George Sand," in *Grafts: Poststructuralism and Feminist Cultural Criticism*, ed. Susan Sheridan (London: Verso, 1989).

36. Robert Greene, *The Debate betweene Follie and Love, translated out of French by Robert Greene, Maister of Artes*, 4th ed. (London, 1608), T3r.

37. For an analysis of the male gaze at work in Petrarch's *blasons*, see Nancy J. Vickers, "Diana Described: Scattered Woman and Scattered Rhyme," *Critical Inquiry* 8 (Winter 1981): 265–79, and " 'The blazon of sweet beauty's best': Shakespeare's *Lucrece;*" in *Shakespeare and the Question of Theory*, ed. Geoffrey Hartman and Patricia Parker (New Haven: Yale University Press, 1985); also Patricia Parker, "Rhetorics of Property: Exploration, Inventory, Blazon," in *Literary Fat Ladies: Rhetoric, Gender, Property* (New York: Methuen, 1987).

38. Lance K. Donaldson-Evans objects to my earlier statement of this lack in "Assimilation with a Difference." In "The Taming of the Muse: The Female Poetic Voice in Pernette du Guillet's *Rymes*," in *Pre-Pléiade Poetry*, ed. Jerry Nash (Lexington, Ky.: French Forum Monographs, no. 57), he points out that traditions of representing male beauty have existed since Ovid (91). He is right; since ancient Greece, in fact. My point is that no *female*-composed standard of masculine beauty was current at the time Labé wrote her sonnet. The assumption that women poets would have found Ovidian or homoerotic *descriptio* directly suited to their needs seems dubious to me.

39. Parodic intent is also identified in this sonnet by Elisabeth Schultz-Witzenrath, *Die Originalität der Louise Labé: Studien zum Weiblichen Petrarkismus* (Munich: Fink, 1974), 115–20.

40. *Catulli carmina*, ed. C. J. Fordyce (Oxford: Clarendon Press, 1978), V, 7–13. For a useful reading of Labé's sonnet in relation to this and other possible sources, see François Rigolot, "Signature et signification: les baisers de Louise Labé," *Romanic Review* 75 (January 1984): 10–24.

41. Rigolot discusses male poets' mid-1500 uses of the genre in "Les Baisers," 11.

42. Rigolot identifies Ficino as the first author of this formula in his commentary on the *Symposium* ("Les Baisers," 12), but he also cites Edgar Wind on its frequent occurrence throughout Renaissance texts. Both Pernette du Guillet and Scève write versions of the same idea (*Rymes*: Epigram 14, *Chanson* 3; *Délie*: 376).

43. Peggy Kamuf, "A Double Life (Femmenism II)," in *Men in Feminism*, ed. Alice Jardine and Paul Smith (New York: Methuen, 1987), 93–94.

44. Maïté Albistur and Daniel Armogathe, *Le Grief des femmes: anthologie des textes féministes du moyen age à la seconde république* (Paris: Hier et Demain, 1978), 6.

45. On Cereta and Nogarola, see Margaret King, "Book-Lined Cells: Women and Humanism in the Early Italian Renaissance," in *Beyond Their Sex: Learned Women of the European Past*, ed. Patricia Labalme (New York: New York University Press, 1984), 66–90.

46. The source for most Renaissance treatments of Semiramis is chapter 2 of Boccaccio's *De claris mulieribus*, trans. Guido Guarini, *Concerning Famous Women* (New Brunswick, N.J.: Rutgers University Press, 1963).

47. Pierre de Ronsard, *Le second livre des sonets pour Helene*, in *Les Amours*, ed. Henri and Catherine Weber (Paris: Garnier, 1963), 431–32.

48. Cited in Rigolot, *Louise Labé*, 246–47. My translation.

49. Recent research on women of the patriciate modifies de Gournay's view somewhat. See, for example, Stanley Chojnacki, "Patrician Women in Early Renaissance Venice," *Studies in the Renaissance* 21 (1974): 176–203; and John Martin, "Out of the Shadow: Heretical and Catholic Women in Renaissance Venice," *Journal of Family History* (Spring 1985): 21–33.

50. For a summary of arguments about the number of Venetian prostitutes, see Paul Larivaille, *La Vie quotidienne des courtisanes en Italie (Rome et Venise, XV et XVIe siècles)* (Paris: Hachette, 1975), 39–40.

51. See, for example, Guido Ruggieri, *The Boundaries of Eros: Sex Crime and Sexuality in Renaissance Venice* (New York and Oxford: Oxford University Press, 1985), 152–53.

52. *Catalogo de tutte le principal et più honorate cortigiane di venetia,* reproduced by Rita Casagrande di Villaviera in *Le cortigiane veneziane nel Cinquecento* (Milan: Longanesi, 1968), 275–93.

53. Michel Eyquem de Montaigne, *Journal de voyage en Italie,* ed. Maurice Rat (Paris: Garnier, 1955), 73.

54. These categories are discussed in one of the earliest and still most interesting studies of courtesanship, Arturo Graf's "Veronica Franco: una cortigiana fra mille," in *Attraverso il Cinquecento* (Turin: Loescher, 1888), 226ff.

55. Senatorial edicts against prostitution mention the "dilapidation of personal fortunes" as a major motive. Guido Ruggieri suggests, however, that prostitution was a pragmatic way of socially "placing" young women unequipped with the dowries that would allow them to enter legitimate marriages (*Boundaries of Eros,* 153; 170 n. 4). He also suggests that toleration of prostitution was related to fears of male homosexuality.

56. For citations of Venetian laws against prostitutes, including sumptuary, residential, and ecclesiastic prohibitions, see Casagrande, *Le cortigiane,* 64ff., 79ff., 106ff.

57. Cited in ibid., 60–61.

58. For visitors' comments on the reclusiveness of Venetian noblewomen, see Patricia Labalme, "Venetian Women on Women: Three Early Modern Feminists," *Archivio veneto* 117 (1981): 104–105 n. 77.

59. Thomas Coryat, *Coryats Crudities,* 2 vols. (London, 1611; rpt. Glasgow: MacLehose, 1905), 1:405.

60. Fees went as high as thirty *scudi,* according to the *Catalogo.* Achillo Olivieri argues that the courtesan's role as specialist in the techniques of pleasure corresponded to increasing specialization throughout Venetian commerce in "Erotisme et groupes sociaux à Venise au XVIe siècle: la Courtisane," trans. Philippe Braunstein and Lucia Bergamasco, *Communications* 35 (1982): 85–91. Like Ruggiero, Olivieri suggests that the toleration of courtesanship in the city was a hedge against male homosexuality (87).

61. On Roman courtesans, see Georgina Masson, *Courtesans of the Italian Renaissance* (New York: St. Martin's Press, 1976), 17, 51. On Franco's wills, see Alvise Zorzi, *Cortigiana veneziana: Veronica Franco e i suoi poeti* (Milan: Camunia, 1986), chap. 2.

62. On the *cittadino,* see Brian Pullan, *Rich and Poor in Renaissance Venice* (Cambridge: Harvard University Press, 1971), 99–109.

63. For Franco's biography and the family coat of arms, see Zorzi, *Cortigiana veneziana,* chap. 1; 21. For a detailed English-language treatment, see Tita Rosenthal, "Veronica Franco: The Courtesan as Poet in Sixteenth-Century Venice" (Ph.D. diss., Yale University, 1985) and her "Veronica Franco: The Venetian Courtesan's Defense," *Renaissance Quarterly* 42 (Summer 1989).

64. For a recent study of the Accademia della Fama, stressing its autonomy from ducal or ecclesiastic control, see Lina Bolzoni, "L'Accademia veneziana: splendore e decadenza di una utopia enciclopedica," in *Università, accademie e società in Italia e Germania dal Cinquecento al Settecento,* ed. Laetitia Boehm and Ezio Raimondi (Bologna: Mulino, 1981), 117–167.

65. For bibliographical details, see Abdelkader Salza, "Note" to *Veronica Franco: Rime, Scrittori d'Italia,* 52 (Bari: Laterza, 1913), 381. All quotations from Franco are from this edition.

66. Lynne Lawner, *The Lives of the Courtesans* (New York: Rizzoli, 1987), 205–206 n. 12, figs. on 58 and 102.

67. Veronica Franco, *Lettere*, ed. Benedetto Croce (Naples: Ricciardi, 1949), 34.
68. See the citation from Marin Sanudo's diaries, Casagrande, *Le cortigiane*, 29.
69. Manlio Dazzi, *Il fiore della lirica veneziana: il libro chiuso di Maffio Venier* (Vincenza: Pozza, 1956), 1:9–57 and appendix. For a summary of his polemic with Franco, see Zorzi, *Cortigiana veneziana*, chap. 6.
70. Rosenthal, "Veronica Franco" (1985), 180–235.
71. Zorzi, *Cortigiana veneziana*, 18 and chap. 1 passim.
72. See Lynne Lawner, *"I Modi" nell'opera di Giulio Romano, Marcantonio Raimondi e Jean-Frédric Maximilien de Waldeck* (Milan: Longanesi, 1984), trans. by Lynne Lawner as *I Modi: The Sixteen Pleasures* (Evanston, Ill.: Northwestern University Press, 1988).
73. For this consensus in relation to English poetry, see Arthur Marotti, " 'Love is not love': Elizabethan sonnet sequences and the social order," *ELH* 49 (1982): 396–428; and Ann Jones and Peter Stallybrass, "The Politics of *Astrophil and Stella*," *SEL* 24 (1984): 53–68.
74. See Edward Muir, *Civic Ritual in Renaissance Venice* (Princeton: Princeton University Press, 1981) and Rona Goffen, *Piety and Patronage in Renaissance Venice* (New Haven: Yale University Press, 1986), chap. 5. For a citation from one of Petrarch's letters in praise of the city, see John Julius Norwich, *Venice: The Rise to Empire* (London: Penguin, 1977), 254.
75. Cited in Zorzi, *Cortigiana veneziana*, 97.
76. See Masson, *Courtesans*, for an early version of this illustration, in which the courtesan's skirt actually flips up to reveal her cross-sexed underwear (ills., 11).
77. Ruggiero, *Boundaries of Eros*, 119, 170 n. 4.
78. Lawner, *Lives of the Courtesans*, 20, citing Aretino's *Lettere* (Paris, 1609), 6:249.
79. See Labalme, "Venetian Women on Women." The texts of Marinelli, Fonte, and Arcangela Tarabotti are reproduced in Ginevra Conti Odorisi, *Donne e società nel seicento* (Rome: Bulzoni, 1979), Part II.
80. For Agrippa, see Henry Care's translation, *Female Pre-eminence* (London, 1670), in *The Feminist Controversy of the Renaissance*, ed. Diane Bornstein (Delmar, N.Y.: Scholars' Facsimiles and Reprints, 1980), and for Italy specifically, Conor Fahey, "Three Early Renaissance Treatises on Women," *Italian Studies* 11 (1956): 30–35.
81. Robert Finlay, *Politics in Renaissance Venice* (New Brunswick, N.J.: Rutgers University Press, 1980), 22.
82. See also Berriot's use of "franchise" to characterize Lyon and its poet, *La belle rebelle*, 162–63.

Bibliography

I. Contexts: History and Culture (Primary Texts)

Agrippa, Henricus Cornelius. *De nobilitate et praecellentia foeminei sexus*. Antwerp, 1529. Translated by Henry Care as *Female Pre-eminence*. London, 1670. Reprinted in *The Feminist Controversy of the Renaissance*, edited by Diane Bornstein. Delmar, N.Y.: Scholars' Facsimiles and Reprints, 1980.

Alberti, Leon Battista. *I Libri della famiglia*. Edited by Ruggiero Romano and Alberto Tenenti. Turin: Einaudi, 1972. Translated by Guido Guarino. In *The Albertis of Florence: Leon Battista Alberti's "Della Famiglia."* Lewisburg, Pa.: Bucknell University Press, 1971.

Aretino, Pietro. *Sei Giornati*. Edited by Giovanni Aquilecchia. Bari: Laterza, 1969. Translated as *Aretino's Dialogues* by Raymond Rosenthal. New York: Stein and Day, 1971.

Ariosto, Ludovico. *Orlando furioso*. Ferrara, 1532. Edited by Lanfranco Caretti. Milan: Riccardo Ricciardi, 1954.

Aubigné, Theodore Agrippa d'. *Oeuvres complètes*. Edited by Eugène Réaume and F. de Caussade. Paris: Alphonse Lemerre, 1873.

Barbaro, Francesco. *De re uxoria*. Florence, 1416; Italian translation 1548. Translated as *On Wifely Duties*. In *The Earthly Republic: Italian Humanists on Government and Society*, edited by Benjamin Kohl et al. Philadelphia: University of Pennsylvania Press, 1978.

Beaujeu, Anne de [Anne de France]. *Les Enseignements d'Anne de France à sa fille Susanne de Bourbon*. Edited by A. M. Chazard. Moulins: C. Des Rosiers, 1878.

Becon, Thomas [actual author Heinrich Bullinger]. *The Christian State of Matrimony*. London, 1543.

Bertani, Luciana. "Rime di vari autori a Veronica Gambara." Edited by Olindo Guerrini. In *Rime di tre gentildonne del secolo XVI*. Milan: Sonzogno, 1930.

Bèze, Théodore de. "Les Vertus de la femme fidele et bonne mesnagere." In *Le Miroir des femmes*, edited by Luce Guillerm et al. Lille: Presses Universitaires, 1983.

Billon, François. *Le Fort inexpugnable de l'honneur du sexe femenin*. Paris, 1555.

Boccaccio, Giovanni. *De claris mulieribus*. Translated by Guido Guarini as *Concerning Famous Women*. New Brunswick, N.J.: Rutgers University Press, 1963.

Brathwaite, Richard. *The English Gentlewoman*. London, 1631.

Bruni d'Arezzo, Lionardo. "Concerning the Study of Literature: A Letter Addressed to the Illustrious Lady, Baptista Malatesta." In *Vittorino da Feltre and Other Humanist Educators*, edited by William Harrison Woodward. New York: Columbia University Teachers College, 1963.

Bruto, Giovanni. *La Institutione di una fanciulla nata nobilmente*. Anvers, 1555. Translated by Thomas Salter as *The Mirrhor of Modestie*. London, 1579.

Castiglione, Baldessar. *Il Libro del Cortegiano*. Venice, 1523. Edited by Bruno Maier. 2nd ed. Turin: UTET, 1964.

———. *The Booke of the Courtier*. Translated by Thomas Hoby. London, 1561. Edited by J. H. Whitfield. London: H. M. Dent, 1966; rpt. 1974.

Catalogo de tutte le principal et più honorate cortigiane di venetia. In Rita Casagrande di Villaviera, *Le cortigiane veneziane nel Cinquecento*. Milan: Longanesi, 1968.

Catullus. *Catulli carmina*. Edited by C. J. Fordyce. Oxford: Clarendon Press, 1978.

Cleaver, Robert. *A godly forme of houshold government*. London, 1588.

Colonna, Vittoria. *Tutte le rime della Illustriss. et Eccellentissima Signora Vittoria Colonna, Marchesana di Pescara*. Venice, 1558. Edited by Olindo Guerrini. In *Rime di tre gentildonne del secolo XVI*. Milan: Sonzogno, 1930.

Coryat, Thomas. *Coryats Crudities*. London, 1611. Rpt. 2 vols. Glasgow: MacLehose, 1905.

Cotgreve, Randle. *Dictionarie of the French and English Tongues*. London, 1611.

Crenne, Hélisenne de. *Epistres invectives*. Paris, 1539. In *Le Grief des femmes*, 1, edited by Maïté Albistur and Daniel Armogathe. Paris: Hier et Demain, 1978.

Denores, Giason. *Apologia contra l'auttor del Verato*. In *A History of Literary Criticism in the Italian Renaissance*, edited by Bernard Weinberg, 2:674ff. Chicago: University of Chicago Press, 1961.

Du Bellay, Joachim. *Deffence et illustration de la langue francoyse*. Edited by Henri Chamard. Paris: Didier, 1948; rpt. 1966.

Ebreo, Leone. *Léon Hebreu: Dialogues d'amour*. Translated by Pontus de Tyard. Lyon, 1551. Edited by T. Anthony Perry. Chapel Hill: University of North Carolina Press, 1974.

Fonte, Moderata [Modesta de' Pozzi]. *Il Merito delle donne*. Padua, 1600.

Gambara, Veronica. *Rime*. Venice, 1554. In *Rime di tre gentildonne del secolo XVI*, edited by Olindo Guerrini. Milan: Sonzogno, 1930.

Gouge, William. *Of Domesticall Duties: Eight Treatises*. London, 1622; 3rd ed., 1634.

Gournay, Marie de. *L'Egalité des hommes et des femmes*. Paris, 1622. Edited by Mario Schiff. Paris: Champion, 1910. Rpt. Geneva: Slatkine, 1978.

Greene, Robert. *Penelope's Web*. London, 1587.

———. *The Debate betweene Follie and Love, translated out of French by Robert Greene, Maister of Artes*. 4th ed. London, 1608.

Guasco, Annibal. *Ragionamento . . . a D. Lavinia sua figliuola della maniera del governarsi ella in corte; andando per Dama*. Turin, 1586.

Guazzo, Stefano. *La civil conversatione del Signor Stefano Guazzo*. Venice, 1575. Translated by George Pettie. London, 1581. Edited by Edward Sullivan. 2 vols. London: George Constable, 1925.

Hake, Edward. *A Touchestone for this time present, expresly declaring such ruines, enormities, and abuses as trouble the Churche of God and our Christian common wealth at this daye*. London, 1574. Facsimile ed. Norwood, N.J.: Walter B. Johnson, 1974.

Héroët, Antoine. *Oeuvres poétiques*. Edited by Ferdinand Gohin. Paris: Cornély, 1909. Rpt. Paris: Droz, 1943.

Jonson, Ben. The Under-wood (1640). In *The Complete Works of Ben Jonson*, edited by C. H. Herford Percy and Evelyn Simpson. Vol. 8. Oxford: Clarendon Press, 1947.

Lombardelli, Orazio. *Dell'Uffizio della Donna Maritata: Capi Centottanta*. Florence, 1585.

Magny, Olivier de. *Odes amoureuses de 1559*. Edited by Mark Whitney. Geneva: Droz, 1964.

Marinelli, Lucrezia. *La Nobiltà e l'eccellenza delle donne*. Venice, 1600.

Middleton, Thomas. *A Chaste Maid in Cheapside*. London, 1630.

Montaigne, Michel Eyquem de. *Journal de voyage en Italie*. Edited by Maurice Rat. Paris: Garnier, 1955.

Mulcaster, Richard. *Positions Concerning the Training Up of Children*. London, 1581.

Nifo, Agostino. *De re aulica ad Phausinam libri duo*. Naples, 1534. Italian translation, *Il Cortigiano del Sesso*. Genoa, 1560.

Peletier du Mans, Jacques. *Opuscules*. Lyon: Jean de Tournes, 1555.

Perkins, William. *Christian Oeconomie*. Translated by Thomas Pickering. London, 1609.

Petrarca, Francesco. *Canzoniere*. Edited by Gianfranco Contini. Turin: Einaudi, 1964.

Piccolomini, Alessandro. *Dialogo, nel quale si ragiona della bella creanza delle donne*. Venice, 1539. Translated as *A Dialogue of the Fair Perfectioning of Ladies* by John Nevinson. Glasgow: MacLehose, 1968.

Pisan, Christine de. *Le Livre de la Cité des Dames*. Paris, 1405. Translated as *The Book of the City of Ladies* by Earl Jeffrey Richards. New York: Persea Books, 1982.

―――. *Le Livre des trois vertus*. Paris, 1405. Translated as *The Treasure of the City of Ladies, or The Book of the Three Virtues* by Sarah Lawson. Harmondsworth, England: Penguin Books, 1985.

Powell, Thomas. *The Art of Thriving, or the plaine path-way to preferment*. London, 1635.

Rich, Barnabe. *My Ladies Looking Glasse*. London, 1616.

Ronsard, Pierre de. *Le second livre des sonets pour Helene*. In *Les Amours*, edited by Henri and Catherine Weber. Paris: Garnier, 1963.

Sannazaro, Jacopo. *Opere volgari*. Edited by Alfredo Mauro. Bari: Laterza, 1961.

Scève, Maurice. *The 'Délie' of Maurice Scève*. Edited by I. D. McFarlane. Cambridge: Cambridge University Press, 1966.

Sidney, Sir Philip. *The Poems of Sir Philip Sidney*. Edited by William Ringler, Jr. Oxford: Clarendon Press, 1962.

―――. *A Defence of Poetry*. In *Miscellaneous Prose of Sir Philip Sidney*, edited by Katherine Duncan-Jones and Jan Van Dorsten. Oxford: Clarendon, 1973.

Snawsel, Robert. *A Looking glasse for Married Folkes*. London, 1631. Facsimile ed. Norwood, N.J.: Walter Johnson, 1975.

Sperone Speroni. *Dialoghi d'amore*. Venice, 1542.

Talentoni, Giovanni. *Discorso sopra la maraviglia* (1597). In *A History of Literary Criticism in the Italian Renaissance*, edited by Bernard Weinberg, vol. 1. Chicago: University of Chicago Press, 1961.

Tasso, Torquato. *Discorso dell'arte poetica; et in particolare del poema heroico* (1587). In Weinberg, *Literary Criticism*, vol. 1.

Tilney, Edmund. *A briefe and pleasant discourse of duties in Marriage, called the flower of friendshippe*. London, 1568.

Venier, Maffio. *Il fiore della lirica veneziana: il libro chiuso di Maffio Venier*. Edited by Manlio Dazzi. Vincenza: Pozza, 1956.

Vives, Juan Luis. *The First Book of the Instruction of a Christian Woman*. In *Vives and the Renascence Education of Women*, edited by Foster Watson. New York: Longmans, Green and Co., 1912.

―――. *Le Livre de l'institution de la femme chrestienne*. Book 2. Cited in *Le Miroir des femmes, I: Moralistes et polémistes au XVIe siécle*, edited by Luce Guillerm et al. Lille: Presses Universitaires, 1983.

Webbe, William. *A Discourse of English Poetrie*. In *Elizabethan Critical Essays*, edited by Gregory Smith. Vol. 1. Oxford: Clarendon, 1904.

II. Contexts: History and Criticism

Albistur, Maïté and Daniel Armogathe. *Le Grief des femmes: anthologie des textes féministes du moyen age à la seconde république*. Paris: Hier et Demain, 1978.

Amussen, Susan. *An Ordered Society: Family and Village in England 1560–1725*. Oxford: Basil Blackwell, 1988.

Angenot, Marc. *Les Champions des femmes*. Montréal: Presses de l'Université de Québec, 1977.

Barkan, Leonard. *The Gods Made Flesh: Metamorphosis and the Pursuit of Paganism*. New Haven: Yale University Press, 1987.

Bayne, Diane. "The Instruction of a Christian Woman: Richard Hyrde and the Thomas More Circle." *Moreana* 12 (February 1975): 5–15.

Beilin, Elaine. *Redeeming Eve: Women Writers of the English Renaissance*. Princeton: Princeton University Press, 1987.

Berger, Harry, Jr. "Orpheus, Pan and the Poetics of Misogyny: Spenser's Critique of Pastoral Love and Art." *ELH* 50 (1983).

Bolzoni, Lina. "L'Accademia veneziana: splendore e decadenza di una utopia enciclopedica." In *Università, accademie e società in Italia e Germania dal Cinque-*

cento al Settecento, edited by Laetitia Boehm and Ezio Raimondi. Bologna: Mulino, 1981.

Bompiani, Ginevra. "The Chimera Herself." In *Fragments for a History of the Human Body*. Vol. 1. New York: Zone, 1989.

Bourgeois, Lucien. *Quand la cour de France vivait à Lyon*. Paris: Fayard, 1980.

Cahn, Susan. *The Industry of Devotion: The Transformation of Women's Work in England, 1500–1660*. New York: Columbia University Press, 1987.

Cartier, A., M. Audin, and E. Vial. *Bibliographie des éditions des De Tournes, imprimeurs lyonnais*. Paris: Bibliothèques nationales de la France, 1937.

Chemello, Adriana. "La donna, il modello, l'immaginario: Moderata Fonte e Lucrezia Marinelli." In *Nel cerchio della luna*, edited by Marina Zancan. Venice: Marsilio, 1983.

Chojnacki, Stanley. "Patrician Women in Early Renaissance Venice." *Studies in the Renaissance* 21 (1974).

Clark, Alice. *Working Life of Women in the Seventeenth Century*. London: Routledge, 1919; rpt. 1982, edited by Miranda Chaytor and Jane Lewis.

Cuyx-Barnes, Marie-Thérèse. "Etude de la 'Querelle des amies.' " Ph.D. diss., Florida State University, 1974.

Davies, Kathleen. "The Sacred Condition of Equality: How Original Were Puritan Doctrines of Marriage?" *Social History* 5 (May 1977): 563–80.

Davis, Natalie Zemon. "City Women and Religious Change." In *Society and Culture in Early Modern France*. Stanford: Stanford University Press, 1975.

_____. "Printing and the People." In *Society and Culture*.

_____. "Women on Top." In *Society and Culture*.

Duby, Georges. *The Chivalrous Society*. Translated by Cynthia Postan. London: Edward Arnold, 1977.

Eisenstein, Elizabeth. "The Rise of a New Class of 'Men of Letters.' " In *The Printing Revolution in Early Modern Europe*. Cambridge: Cambridge University Press, 1983.

Empson, William. "Proletarian Literature." In *Some Versions of Pastoral*. New York: New Directions, 1960.

Fahey, Conor. "Three Early Renaissance Treatises on Women." *Italian Studies* 11 (1956).

Febvre, Lucien, and H.-J. Martin, *L'Apparition du livre*. Paris: Albin Michel, 1958. Translated as *The Coming of the Book* by David Gerard. Atlantic Highlands, N.J.: Humanities Press, 1976.

Ferguson, Margaret, Maureen Quilligan, and Nancy Vickers, eds. *Rewriting the Renaissance: The Discourses of Sexual Difference in Early Modern Europe*. Chicago: University of Chicago Press, 1986.

Finlay, Robert. *Politics in Renaissance Venice*. New Brunswick, N.J.: Rutgers University Press, 1980.

Fumerton, Patricia. " 'Secret Arts': Elizabethan Miniatures and Sonnets." *Representations* 15 (Summer 1986).

Gaeta, Franco. "Alcune considerazioni sul mito de Venezia." *Bibliothèque d'humanisme et Renaissance* 23 (1961).

Giamatti, A. Bartlett. *The Earthly Paradise and the Renaissance Epic*. Princeton: Princeton University Press, 1966.

Goffen, Rona. *Patronage and Piety in Renaissance Venice*. New Haven: Yale University Press, 1986.

Gordon, D. J. "The Imagery of Ben Jonson's Masques of Blacknesse and Beautie." In *The Renaissance Imagination: Essays and Lectures by D. J. Gordon*, edited by Stephen Orgel. Berkeley: University of California Press, 1975.

Greenblatt, Stephen. *Renaissance Self-Fashioning: From More to Shakespeare*. Chicago: University of Chicago Press, 1980.

———. *Shakespearean Negotiations: The Circulation of Social Energy in Renaissance England*. Berkeley: University of California Press, 1988.

Greene, Thomas. *The Light in Troy: Imitation and Discovery in Renaissance Poetry*. New Haven: Yale University Press, 1982.

Guidi, José. "Baldessar Castiglione et le pouvoir politique: du gentilhomme de cour au nonce pontifical." In *Les Ecrivains et le pouvoir en Italie à l'epoque de la Renaissance*, edited by André Rochon. Paris: Sorbonne Nouvelle, 1975.

———. "De l'amour courtois à l'amour sacré: la condition de la femme dans l'oeuvre de B. Castiglione." In *Images de la femme dans la littérature italienne de la Renaissance*, edited by André Rochon. Paris: Centre de Recherche sur la Renaissance Italienne, Université de la Sorbonne Nouvelle, 1980.

Guillerm, Luce, Jean-Pierre Guillerm, Laurence Hordoir, and Marie-Françoise Piéjus, eds. *Le Miroir des femmes, I: Moralistes et polémistes au XVIe siècle*. Lille: Presses Universitaires, 1983.

Hamilton, Roberta. *The Liberation of Women: A Study of Patriarchy and Capitalism*. London: Allen and Unwin, 1978.

Hanawalt, Barbara, ed. *Women and Work in Preindustrial Europe*. Bloomington: Indiana University Press, 1986.

Hawkins, Richmond. *Maistre Charles Fontaine, Parisien*. Cambridge: Harvard University Press, 1916.

Herlihy, David, and Christiane Klapisch-Zuber. *Tuscans and Their Families*. New Haven: Yale University Press, 1985.

Hill, Christopher. *Society and Puritanism in Pre-Revolutionary England*. Manchester: Panther, 1969.

Holm, Janice Butler. "The Myth of a Feminist Humanism." *Soundings* 68 (Winter 1984): 443–52.

Hull, Suzanne. *Chaste, Silent and Obedient: English Books for Women, 1475–1640*. San Marino, Ca.: Huntington Library, 1982.

Jardine, Lisa. *Still Harping on Women: Women and Drama in the Age of Shakespeare*. Totowa, N.J.: Barnes and Noble, 1983.

Javitch, Daniel. *Poetry and Courtliness in Renaissance England*. Princeton: Princeton University Press, 1978.

Jayne, Sears. *Marsilio Ficino's Commentary on Plato's "Symposium."* University of Missouri Studies, no. 1. Columbia: University of Missouri Press, 1944.

Jones, Ann Rosalind. "Assimilation with a Difference: Renaissance Women Poets and Literary Influence." *Yale French Studies*, no. 62 (1981).

———. "Surprising Fame: Renaissance Gender Ideologies and Women's Lyric." In *The Poetics of Gender*, edited by Nancy Miller. New York: Columbia University Press, 1986.

———. "Nets and Bridles: Early Modern Conduct Books and Sixteenth-Century Women's Lyric." In *The Ideology of Conduct*, edited by Nancy Armstrong and Len Tennenhouse. New York: Methuen, 1987.

Jones, Ann Rosalind, and Peter Stallybrass. "The Politics of *Astrophil and Stella*," *SEL* 24 (Winter 1984): 53–68.

Jones, Ann Rosalind, and Nancy Vickers. "Canon, Rule and the Restoration Renaissance." *Yale French Studies*, no. 75 (Fall 1988: *The Politics of Tradition: Placing Women in French Literature*).

Jordan, Constance. "Feminism and the Humanists: The Case of Sir Thomas Elyot's *Defense of Good Women*." *Renaissance Quarterly* 36 (1983): 181–201; rpt. in *Rewriting the Renaissance*.

Joukovsky, Françoise. *La Gloire dans la poésie française et néolatine du XVIe siècle*. Geneva: Droz, 1969.

Kaufman, Gloria. "Juan Luis Vives on the Education of Women." *Signs* 3 (Summer 1978): 891–97.

Keating, Clark. *Studies on the Literary Salon in France, 1550–1615.* Cambridge: Harvard University Press, 1941.

Kelly-Gadol, Joan. "Did Women Have a Renaissance?" In *Becoming Visible: Women in European History,* edited by Renate Bridenthal and Claudia Koonz. Boston: Houghton Mifflin, 1977.

_____. "Early Feminist Theory and the *Querelle des femmes,* 1400–1789." *Signs* 8 (Fall 1982): 4–28.

Kelso, Ruth. *Doctrine for the Lady of the Renaissance.* Urbana: University of Illinois Press, 1965; rpt. 1978.

Kennedy, William J. *Jacopo Sannazaro and the Uses of Pastoral.* Hanover, N.H.: University Press of New England, 1983.

King, Margaret. "Thwarted Ambitions: Six Learned Women of the Italian Renaissance." *Soundings* 59 (Fall 1976): 280–304.

_____. "The Religious Retreat of Isotta Nogarola (1418–1486)." *Signs* 3 (1978): 807–22.

_____. "Book-lined Cells: Women and Humanism in the Early Italian Renaissance." In *Beyond Their Sex,* edited by Patricia Labalme.

Klapisch-Zuber, Christiane. *Women, Family, and Ritual in Renaissance Italy.* Translated by Lydia Cochrane. Chicago: University of Chicago Press, 1985.

Labalme, Patricia. "Venetian Women on Women: Three Early Modern Feminists." *Archivio veneto* 117 (1981).

_____, ed. *Beyond Their Sex: Learned Women of the European Past.* New York: New York University Press, 1984.

Lamb, Mary Ellen. "The Countess of Pembroke's Patronage." *ELR* 12 (Spring 1982).

Lambert, Ellen. *Placing Sorrow: A Study of the Pastoral Elegy Convention from Theocritus to Milton.* Chapel Hill: University of North Carolina Press, 1976.

Larivaille, Paul. *La Vie quotidienne des courtisanes en Italie (Rome et Venise, XV et XVIe siècles).* Paris: Hachette, 1975.

Lawner, Lynne. *"I Modi" nell'opera di Giulio Romano, Marcantonio Raimondi e Jean-Frédric Maximilien de Waldeck.* Milan: Longanesi, 1984. Translated by Lynne Lawner as *I Modi: The Sixteen Pleasures, An Erotic Album of the Italian Renaissance.* Evanston, Ill.: Northwestern University Press, 1988.

_____. *The Lives of the Courtesans.* New York: Rizzoli, 1987.

Logan, Oliver. *Culture and Society in Venice, 1470–1790.* New York: Scribners, 1972.

Marinelli, Peter. *Ariosto and Boiardo.* Columbia: University of Missouri Press, 1987.

Marotti, Arthur. " 'Love is not love:' Elizabethan Sonnet Sequences and the Social Order." *ELH* 49 (Summer 1982): 396–428.

Marsh, David. *The Quattrocento Dialogue: Classical Tradition and Humanist Innovation.* Cambridge: Harvard University Press, 1980.

Martin, John. "Out of the Shadow: Heretical and Catholic Women in Renaissance Venice." *Journal of Family History* (Spring 1985).

Masson, Georgina. *Courtesans of the Italian Renaissance.* New York: St. Martin's Press, 1976.

Medick, Hans. "The Proto-Industrial Family Economy: The Structural Function of Household and Family during the Transition from Peasant Society to Industrial Capitalism." *Social History* 3 (October 1976): 291–315.

Miller, Edwin. *The Professional Writer in Elizabethan England.* Cambridge: Harvard University Press, 1959.

Montrose, Louis Adrian. "Celebration and Insinuation: Sir Philip Sidney and the Motives of Elizabethan Courtship." *Renaissance Drama,* n.s. 8 (1977).

_____. " 'Eliza, Queene of Shepheardes,' and the Pastoral of Power." *ELR* 10 (Spring 1980).

_____. "Of Gentlemen and Shepherds: The Politics of Elizabethan Pastoral Form." *ELH* 50 (Fall 1983).

Muir, Edwin. *Civic Ritual in Renaissance Venice*. Princeton: Princeton University Press, 1980.

Norwich, John Julius. *Venice: The Rise to Empire*. London: Penguin, 1977.

Odorisi, Ginevra Conti. *Donne e società nel seicento*. Rome: Bulzoni, 1979.

Olivieri, Achillo. "Erotisme et groupes sociaux à Venise au XVIe siècle: la Courtisane." Translated by Philippe Braunstein and Lucia Bergamasco. *Communications* 35 (1982).

Orgel, Stephen, and Roy Strong. *Inigo Jones: The Theatre of the Stuart Court*. Berkeley: Sotheby Parke Bernet and University of California Press, 1973.

Padoan, Giorgio. "*L'Orlando furioso* e la crisi del Rinascimento." In *Ariosto 1974 in America*, edited by Aldo Scaglione. Ravenna: Longo, 1976.

Parker, Patricia. "Rhetorics of Property: Exploration, Inventory, Blazon." In *Literary Fat Ladies: Rhetoric, Gender, Property*. New York: Methuen, 1987.

Perry, T. Anthony. "Dialogue and Doctrine in Leone Ebreo's *Dialoghi d'amore*." *PMLA* 88 (1973).

Poggioli, Renato. "The Oaten Flute." *Harvard Library Bulletin* 11 (1957).

———. "The Pastoral of the Self." *Daedalus* 88 (1959).

Pullan, Brian. *Rich and Poor in Renaissance Venice*. Cambridge: Harvard University Press, 1971.

Rilke, Rainer Maria. *The Notebooks of Malte Laurids Brigge*. Translated by Stephen Mitchell. New York: Vintage, 1985.

Risset, Jacqueline. *L'Anagramme du désir: essai sur la "Délie" de Maurice Scève*. Rome: Bulzoni, 1971.

Rogers, Katharine. *The Troublesome Helpmate: A History of Misogyny in Literature*. Seattle: University of Washington Press, 1966.

Romier, Lucien. "Lyons and Cosmopolitanism at the Beginning of the French Renaissance." In *French Humanism, 1470–1600*, edited by Werner Gundersheimer. New York: Harper and Row, 1969.

Ruggieri, Guido. *The Boundaries of Eros: Sex Crime and Sexuality in Renaissance Venice*. Oxford: Oxford University Press, 1985.

Sankovitch, Tilde. *French Women Writers and the Book: Myths of Access and Desire*. Syracuse: Syracuse University Press, 1988.

Saulnier, Verdun. *Maurice Scève*. 2 vols. Paris: Klincksieck, 1948.

Schochet, Gordon. *Patriarchalism in Political Thought: The Authoritarian Family and Political Speculation and Attitudes*. Oxford: Basil Blackwell, 1975.

Stallybrass, Peter. "Patriarchal Territories: The Body Enclosed." In *Rewriting the Renaissance*, edited by Margaret Ferguson et al.

———. " 'An enclosure of all the best people in the world': Nationalism and Imperialism in Late Sixteenth-Century England." In *Patriotism: Ideology and Myth in the Making of English National Identity*, edited by Raphael Samuel. London: Routledge and Kegan Paul, 1989.

Stone, Lawrence. *The Family, Sex and Marriage in England, 1500–1800*. New York: Harper and Row, 1977.

Strong, Roy. "The Elizabethan Malady: Melancholy in Elizabethan and Jacobean Portraiture." *Apollo Magazine*, no. 79 (1964). Rpt. in *The English Icon: Elizabethan and Jacobean Portraiture*. London: Routledge and Kegan Paul, 1969.

Telle, Emile. *L'Oeuvre de Marguerite d'Angoulême, Reine de Navarre, et la querelle des femmes*. Toulouse: Lion, 1937. Rpt. Geneva: Slatkine, 1969.

Tennenhouse, Len. *Power on Display: The Politics of Shakespeare's Genres*. Methuen, 1986.

Travitsky, Betty. *The Paradise of Women: Writings by Englishwomen of the Renaissance*. Westport, Ct.: Greenwood Press, 1981.

Ventura, Angelo. *Nobiltà e popolo nella società veneta del '400 e '500*. Bari: Laterza, 1964.

Vickers, Nancy J. "Diana Described: Scattered Woman and Scattered Rhyme." In *Writing and Sexual Difference*, edited by Elizabeth Abel. Chicago: University of Chicago Press, 1982.

――――. " 'The blazon of sweet beauty's best': Shakespeare's *Lucrece*." In *Shakespeare and the Question of Theory*, edited by Patricia Parker and Geoffrey Hartman. New York: Methuen, 1985.

Watkins, Renée. *The Family in Renaissance Florence*. Columbia, S.C.: University of South Carolina Press, 1969.

Wayne, Don. *Penshurst: The Semiotics of Place and the Poetics of History*. Madison: University of Wisconsin Press, 1984.

Wayne, Valerie. " 'Some Sad Sentence': Vives' *Instruction of a Christian Woman*." In *Silent But for the Word: Tudor Women as Patrons, Translators and Writers of Religious Works*, edited by Margaret Hannay. Kent, Ohio: Kent State University Press, 1985.

Weber, Henri. *La Création poétique au XVIe siècle en France*. Paris: Nizet, 1956.

Whigham, Frank. "The Rhetoric of Elizabethan Suitors' Letters," *PMLA* 96 (1981): 864–82.

――――. "Courtesy and the Performer-Audience Dialectic." *NLH* 14 (1983): 623–41.

――――. *Ambition and Privilege: The Social Tropes of Elizabethan Courtesy Theory*. Berkeley: University of California Press, 1984.

Woodbridge, Linda. [Linda Fitz]. " 'What Says the Married Woman?' Marriage Theory and Feminism in the English Renaissance." *Mosaic* 13 (Winter 1980): 1–22.

――――. *Women and the English Renaissance: Literature and the Nature of Womankind, 1540–1620*. Urbana: University of Illinois Press, 1984.

Woodhouse, J. R. *Baldessar Castiglione: A Reassessment of 'The Courtier.'* Edinburgh: Edinburgh University Press, 1978.

Zancan, Marina. "La donna e il cerchio nel *Cortegiano* di B. Castiglione: le funzioni del femminile nell'immagine di corte." In *Nel Cerchio della Luna: Figure di donna in alcuni testi del XVI secolo*, edited by Maria Zancan. Venice: Marsilio, 1983.

Zonta, Giuseppe. *Trattati d'amore del Cinquecento*. Bari: Laterza, 1912.

III. Cultural and Feminist Theory

Bakhtin, Mikhail. *Rabelais and his World*. Translated by Helene Iswolsky. Cambridge: MIT Press, 1968. Rpt. Bloomington: Indiana University Press, 1984.

――――. *The Dialogic Imagination: Four Essays by M. M. Bakhtin*. Edited by Michael Holquist. Austin: University of Texas Press, 1981.

――――. *Problems of Dostoevsky's Poetics*. Translated by Caryl Emerson. Minneapolis: University of Minnesota Press, 1984.

Barthes, Roland. "The Death of the Author." Translated by Stephen Heath. In *Image, Music, Text*. New York: Hill and Wang, 1977.

Burke, Kenneth. *A Rhetoric of Motives*. New York: Prentice-Hall, 1950.

Felman, Shoshanna. "Women and Madness: The Critical Phallacy." *Diacritics* 5 (1975): 2–10.

Foucault, Michel. "What Is an Author?" Translated by Donald Bouchard and Sherry Simon. In *Language, Counter-memory, Practice: Selected Essays and Interviews of Michel Foucault*, edited by Donald Bouchard. Ithaca: Cornell University Press, 1977.

――――. *The History of Sexuality*. Translated by R. Hurley. New York: Pantheon, 1978.

Gledhill, Christine. "Pleasurable Negotiations." In *Female Spectators: Looking at Film and Television*, edited by Deidre Pribram. London: Verso, 1988.

Gramsci, Antonio. *The Modern Prince and Other Writings*. Translated by Louis Marx. New York: International Publishers, 1957.

Hall, Stuart. "Encoding/Decoding." In *Culture, Media, Language,* edited by Stuart Hall et al. London: Hutchinson, 1980.

Hall, Stuart, and Tony Jefferson, eds. *Resistance through Rituals.* London: Hutchinson, 1976.

Hawkes, Terence. *Structuralism and Semiotics.* Berkeley and Los Angeles: University of California Press, 1977.

Hermann, Claudine. *Les Voleuses de langue.* Paris: des femmes, 1976.

Irigaray, Luce. *Speculum de l'autre femme.* Paris: Minuit, 1974. Translated as *Speculum of the Other Woman* by Gillian Gill. Ithaca: Cornell University Press, 1985.

Jehlen, Myra. "Archimedes and the Paradox of Feminist Criticism." In *The Signs Reader,* edited by Elizabeth Abel and Emily K. Abel. Chicago: University of Chicago Press, 1983.

Kristeva, Julia. *La Révolution du langage poétique.* Paris: Seuil, 1974. Translated as *Revolution in Poetic Language* by Margaret Waller. New York: Columbia University Press, 1984.

———. "D'une identité l'autre," *Tel Quel* 62 (Summer 1975). Translated as "From One Identity to Another" by Tom Gora and Alice Jardine. In *Desire in Language.* New York: Columbia University Press, 1980.

———. *Polylogue.* Paris: Tel Quel, 1977.

Lévi-Strauss, Claude. *The Savage Mind.* London: Weidenfeld and Nicholson, 1966.

———. *Totemism.* Translated by Rodney Needham. Harmondsworth: Penguin, 1969.

Newton, Judith. "Making—and Remaking—History: Another Look at 'Patriarchy.'" In *Feminist Issues in Literary Scholarship,* edited by Shari Benstock. Bloomington: Indiana University Press, 1987.

Sedgwick, Eve Kosofsky. *Between Men: English Literature and Male Homosocial Desire.* New York: Columbia University Press, 1985.

Showalter, Elaine. "Toward a Feminist Poetics." In *Women's Writing and Writing about Women,* edited by Mary Jacobus. London: Croom Helm, 1979.

———. "Feminist Criticism in the Wilderness." *Critical Inquiry* 8 (Winter 1981).

Woolf, Virginia. *A Room of One's Own.* New York: Harcourt, Brace and Co., 1929.

IV. Editions and Literary Criticism, by Poet

Tullia d'Aragona

Aragona, Tullia d'. *Le Rime della Signora Tullia d'Aragona; et di diversi à lui.* Venice: Gabriel Giolito de Ferrari, 1547.

———. *Le Rime di Tullia d'Aragona, cortigiana del secolo XVI.* Edited by Enrico Celani. Bologna: Gaetano Romagnoli, 1891; rpt. 1968.

Biagi, Guido. *Tullia d'Aragona: una ètera romana.* Florence, 1887.

Bongi, S. "Il velo giallo di Tullia d'Aragona." *Rivista critica della litteratura italiana* 3 (March 1886).

Jones, Ann Rosalind. "New Songs for the Swallow: Ovid's Philomela in Tullia d'Aragona and Gaspara Stampa." In *Refiguring Woman: Gender Studies and the Italian Renaissance,* edited by Marilyn Migiel and Juliana Schiesari. Ithaca: Cornell University Press, 1990.

Veronica Franco

Franco, Veronica. *Rime.* Edited by Abdelkader Salza. In *Scrittori d'Italia,* 52. Bari: Laterza, 1913.

———. *Lettere.* Edited by Benedetto Croce. Naples: Ricciardi, 1949.

Graf, Arturo. "Una cortigiana fra mille: Veronica Franco." In *Attraverso il Cinquecento.* Turin: Loescher, 1888.

Rosenthal, Tita. "Veronica Franco: the Courtesan as Poet in Sixteenth-Century Venice." Ph.D. diss., Yale University, 1985.

_____. "Veronica Franco: The Venetian Courtesan's Defense." *Renaissance Quarterly* 42 (Summer 1989).

Zorzi, Alvise. *Cortigiana veneziana: Veronica Franco e i suoi poeti.* Milan: Camunia, 1986.

Pernette du Guillet

Guillet, Pernette du. *Les Rymes.* Edited by Victor Graham. Geneva: Droz, 1968.

Cottrell, Robert. "Pernette du Guillet's *Rymes*: An Adventure in Ideal Love." *Bibliothèque d'humanisme et renaissance* 31 (1969).

Donaldson-Evans, Lance K. "The Taming of the Muse: The Female Poetic Voice in Pernette du Guillet's *Rymes.*" In *Pre-Pléiade Poetry*, edited by Jerry Nash. Lexington, Ky.: French Forum Monographs, no. 57, 1984.

Griffin, Robert. "Pernette du Guillet's Response to Scève: A Case for Abstract Love." *L'Esprit créateur* 5 (1965).

Jondorf, Gillian. "Petrarchan Variations in Pernette du Guillet and Louise Labé." *MLR* 71 (1976).

Miller, Joyce. "Convention and Form in the *Rymes* of Pernette du Guillet." Ph.D. diss., University of Pennsylvania, 1977.

Perry, T. Anthony. "Pernette du Guillet's Poetry of Love and Desire." *BHR* 35 (1973): 259–71.

Saulnier, Verdun. "Etude sur Pernette du Guillet et ses *Rymes.*" *Bibliothèque d'humanisme et Renaissance* 4 (1944).

Louise Labé

Louise Labé. *Oeuvres.* Edited by Charles Boy. Paris: Lemerre, 1887. 2 vols.

_____. *Ouevres complètes.* Edited by Enzo Giudici. Geneva: Droz, 1981.

_____. *Oeuvres complètes.* Edited by François Rigolot. Paris: Flammarion, 1986.

Baker, M. W. "The Sonnets of Louise Labé: A Reappraisal." *Neophilologus* 60 (1976).

Berriot, Karine. *Louise Labé: La Belle Rebelle et le François nouveau.* Paris: Seuil, 1985.

Charpentier, Françoise. "Préface." In *Louise Labé, Oeuvres poétiques; Pernette du Guillet, Rymes.* Paris: Gallimard, 1983.

Freadman, Anne. "Of Cats, and Companions, and the name of George Sand." In *Grafts: Feminist Cultural Criticism*, edited by Susan Sheridan. London: Verso, 1988.

Giudici, Enzo. *Louise Labé et l' "Ecole lyonnaise."* Naples: Liguori, 1964.

_____. *Louise Labé: essai.* Paris: Nizet, 1981.

Jondorf, Gillian. "Petrarchan Variations in Louise Labé and Pernette du Guillet." *MLR* 71 (1976).

Jones, Ann Rosalind. "City Women and their Audiences: Louise Labé and Veronica Franco." In *Rewriting the Renaissance*, edited by Margaret Ferguson et al. Chicago: University of Chicago Press, 1986.

Kamuf, Peggy. "A Double Life (Femmenism II)." In *Men in Feminism*, edited by Alice Jardine and Paul Smith. New York: Methuen, 1987.

Larson, Anne M. "Louise Labé's *Débat de Folie et d'Amour*: Feminism and the Defense of Learning." *Tulsa Studies in Women's Literature* 2 (Spring 1983): 45–55.

Rigolot, François. "L'Hommage de 1555 à Louise Labé: les vers grecs, latins et italiens." In *Mélanges sur la littérature de la Renaissance à la mémoire de V.-L. Saulnier.* Geneva: Droz, 1984.

_____. "Signature et signification: les baisers de Louise Labé." *Romanic Review* 75 (January 1984).

_____. "Gender vs. Sex Difference in Louise Labé's Grammar of Love." In *Rewriting the Renaissance*, edited by Margaret Ferguson et al. Chicago: University of Chicago Press, 1986.

Schultz-Witzenrath, Elisabeth. *Die Originalität der Louise Labé: Studien zum Weiblichen Petrarkismus*. Munich: Fink, 1974.

Tricou, Jean. "Louise Labé et sa famille." *Bibliothèque d'humanisme et Renaissance* 5 (1944).

Zamaron, Fernand. *Louise Labé: dame de la franchise*. Paris: Nizet, 1968.

Catherine des Roches

des Roches, Madeleine and Catherine. *Les Oeuvres de Mes-dames des Roches de Poetiers, mère et fille*. Paris: Abel L'Angelier, 1578.

————. *Les Secondes oeuvres de Mes-dames des Roches de Poictiers Mere et Fille*. Poitiers: Nicholas Courtoys, 1583.

————. *Les Missives de Mes-dames des Roches de Poitiers mère et fille*. Paris: Abel L'Angelier, 1586.

————. *Les Missives de Mes-dames des Roches de Poitiers mère et fille*. Lyon: Nicholas Hamilton, 1604. (Contains poems from the first and second *Oeuvres* and from *La Puce*).

Diller, George. *Les Dames des Roches: Etude sur la vie litteraire à Poitiers dans la deuxième moitié du XVIe siècle*. Paris: Droz, 1936.

Larsen, Anne R. "The French Humanist Scholars: Les Dames des Roches." In *Women Writers of the Renaissance and Reformation*, edited by Katharina Wilson (Athens: University of Georgia Press, 1987).

Pasquier, Etienne, ed. *La Puce de Madame Des-Roches, qui est un recueil de divers poèmes Grecs, Latins et François, Composez par plusieurs doctes personnages aux Grans Jours tenus à Poitiers l'an MDLXXIX*. Paris: Abel L'Angelier, 1583.

Sankovitch, Tilde. "Inventing Authority of Origin: The Difficult Enterprise." In *Women of the Middle Ages and Renaissance: Literary and Historical Perspectives*, edited by Mary Beth Rose. Syracuse: Syracuse University Press, 1986.

————. *French Women Writers and the Book: Myths of Access and Desire*. Syracuse: Syracuse University Press, 1988.

Yandell, Cathy. "Of Lice and Women: Rhetoric and Gender in *La Puce de Madame des Roches*." Forthcoming, *Romance Notes*.

Gaspara Stampa

Stampa, Gaspara. *Rime*. Venice: Plinio Pietrasanta, 1554.

————. *Rime*. Edited by Maria Bellonci. Milan: Rizzoli, 1976.

————. *Rime*. Edited by Gustavo Ceriello. Milan: Rizzoli, 1954.

————. *Rime*. Edited by Abdelkader Salza. In *Scrittori d'Italia*, 52. Bari: Laterza, 1913.

Bassanese, Fiora. *Gaspara Stampa*. Boston: Twayne, 1983.

Brognoligo, Gioachino. "Gaspara Stampa." *Giornale storico della letteratura italiana* 76 (1920): 134–45.

Croce, Benedetto. *Conversazioni critiche*, 2:230ff. Bari: Laterza, 1918.

————. "La Lirica cinquecentesca." In *Poesia populare e poesia d'arte*. Bari: Laterza, 1933.

Donadoni, Eugenio. *Gaspara Stampa*. Messina: Principato, 1919.

Innocenzi Greggio, Elisa. "In Difesa di Gaspara Stampa." *L'Ateneo veneto* 38, 1 (1915): 1–158.

Salza, Abdelkader. "Madonna Gasparina Stampa secondo nuove indagini." *Giornale storico della letteratura italiana* 62 (1913): 1–101.

———— "Madonna Gasparina Stampa e la società veneziana del suo tempo," *GSLI* 70 (1917): 1–60, 280–99.

Vassalli, Donata Chimenti. "Emancipazione e schiavitù in Gaspara Stampa." *Osservatore Politico Letterario* 18, 9 (1972).

Vitiello, Justin. "Gaspara Stampa: The Ambiguities of Martyrdom." *Modern Language Notes* 90 (1975).

Warnke, Frank. "Aphrodite's Priestess, Love's Martyr: Gaspara Stampa." In *Women Writers of the Renaissance and Reformation*, edited by Katharina Wilson. Athens: University of Georgia Press, 1987.

Isabella Whitney

Whitney, Isabella. *The Copy of a letter lately written in meeter by a yonge Gentilwoman: to her unconstant lover.* London: Richard Jones, 1567.

_____. *A Sweet Nosgay, Or Pleasant Posye: contayning a hundred and ten Phylosophicall Flowers.* London: Richard Jones, 1573.

_____. *The Floures of Philosophie (1572) by Sir Hugh Plat and A sweet Nosgay (1573) and The Copy of a Letter (1567) by Isabella Whitney.* Edited by Richard Panofsky. Delmar, N.Y.: Scholars' Facsimiles and Reprints, 1982.

Fehrenbach, R. J. "Isabella Whitney and the Popular Miscellanies of Richard Jones." *Cahiers élisabéthains* 19 (1981).

_____. "Isabella Whitney, Sir Hugh Plat, Geoffrey Whitney, and 'Sister Eldershae.'" *ELN* 21 (1983): 7–11.

Krontiris, Tina. "Oppositional Voices: Women's Secular Writings and Dominant Ideology in the English Renaissance" (chap. 3). Ph.D. diss., University of Sussex, 1987.

Travitsky, Betty. "The Lady Doth Protest: Protest in the Popular Writings of Englishwomen." *ELR* 14 (Autumn 1984).

_____. "'The Wyll and Testament' of Isabella Whitney." *ELR* 10 (1980).

Mary Wroth

Wroth, Mary. *The Poems of Lady Mary Wroth.* Edited by Josephine Roberts. Baton Rouge: Louisiana State University Press, 1983.

Beilin, Elaine. "'The Onely Perfect Virtue': Constancy in Mary Wroth's Pamphilia to Amphilanthus." *Spenser Studies* 2 (1985).

_____. *Redeeming Eve: Women Writers of the English Renaissance.* Princeton: Princeton University Press, 1987.

Hannay, Margaret. "Lady Wroth: Mary Sidney." In *Women Writers of the Renaissance and Reformation*, edited by Katharina Wilson. Athens: University of Georgia Press, 1987.

Lamb, Mary Ellen. *The Authorship of Women in the Sidney Circle*, chaps. 4 and 5. Forthcoming, University of Wisconsin Press.

Paulissen, May Nelson. "The Love Sonnets of Lady Mary Wroth: A Critical Introduction." Ph.D. diss., University of Houston, 1976.

Quilligan, Maureen. "The Anthropology of Intertextuality: Incest and Imitation in Wroth's *Urania* Poems." In *Soliciting Interpretations: Essays on Seventeenth-Century Poetry*, edited by Elizabeth Harvey and Katherine Maus. Chicago: University of Chicago Press, 1990.

Swift, Carolyn Ruth. "Feminine Identity in Lady Mary Wroth's Romance *Urania*." *ELR* 14 (Autumn 1984): 328–46.

Index

Numbers in italics indicate an illustration.

ANN ROSALIND JONES is Associate Professor of Comparative Literature at Smith College.